Francis W. Pixley

The Profession of a Chartered Accountant and Other Lectures,

delivered to the Institute of chartered accountants in England and Wales, the Institute of Secretaries, &c., &c

Francis W. Pixley

The Profession of a Chartered Accountant and Other Lectures,
delivered to the Institute of chartered accountants in England and Wales, the Institute of Secretaries, &c., &c

ISBN/EAN: 9783337322489

Printed in Europe, USA, Canada, Australia, Japan

Cover: Foto ©Thomas Meinert / pixelio.de

More available books at **www.hansebooks.com**

THE PROFESSION
OF A
CHARTERED ACCOUNTANT
AND OTHER LECTURES,

Delivered to the Institute of Chartered Accountants in England and Wales, the Institute of Secretaries, &c., &c.

BY

FRANCIS W. PIXLEY,

OF THE MIDDLE TEMPLE, BARRISTER-AT-LAW, A FELLOW AND MEMBER OF THE COUNCIL OF THE INSTITUTE OF CHARTERED ACCOUNTANTS IN ENGLAND AND WALES,

AUTHOR OF "AUDITORS, THEIR DUTIES AND RESPONSIBILITIES," &c., &c.

London:
HENRY GOOD & SON, 12, MOORGATE STREET E.C.

1897.

PREFACE.

The following Papers have been read before the various Societies mentioned under the headings of each Chapter between the years 1883 and the present date.

It occurred to the Author that their publication in one volume would be appreciated by the younger members of the various Institutes of Chartered Accountants in the United Kingdom, and more especially by those preparing for the Intermediate and Final examinations of the Institute of Chartered Accountants in England and Wales, and for the examinations of the Scottish and Irish Institutes.

Having this object in view, the Lectures are not in the exact words as delivered, but have been thoroughly revised.

F. W. P.

LONDON, 1*st May*, 1897.

CONTENTS.

LECTURE I.

THE PROFESSION OF A CHARTERED ACCOUNTANT.

Read before the Chartered Accountants' Students' Society of London 29th September, 1885.

Lecture I.

Profession of a Chartered Accountant in England.

The profession of a Chartered Accountant cannot boast of greater antiquity in England than the 11th May, 1880, on which day a Royal Charter, incorporating the Institute of Chartered Accountants in England and Wales, was granted by the Privy Council.

For nearly fifty years previous to that date the duties now devolving upon the members of the newly-created profession were performed by their predecessors, who, for want of a better title, were designated Public Accountants, and from whose ranks the first Chartered Accountants were recruited.

In Scotland.

Such also was the origin of the profession in Scotland; but in that country a Charter was granted to the practising Accountants more than a quarter of a century earlier. The Society of Accountants in Edinburgh was incorporated by Royal Charter on the 23rd October,

Lecture I. 1854; while the Institute of Accountants and Actuaries in Glasgow was similarly incorporated on the 15th March, 1855, and the Society of Accountants of Aberdeen in 1867.

In Ireland. The leading members of the profession in Ireland were incorporated by Royal Charter on the 14th May, 1888, under the style of the Institute of Chartered Accountants in Ireland.

Previous to the grant of the Charter in England, no qualification was required for the practice of a professional Accountant. Any person who chose was entitled to so practise without being required to show that he possessed any qualifications for the duties he thereby undertook to transact, and, as many adopted this profession, destitute alike of moral principles as of business capabilities, practising Accountants, as a body, fell into a certain amount of disrepute. The obtainment of the Charter was therefore welcomed, not only by the respectable practitioners, but also by the commercial world, who felt the great advantage of there being a recognised institution, from the members of which they might choose their professional advisers in matters of account, and to whom they might refer any question of difference.

The Charter.

Bye-Laws. Since the recognised practising Accountants have been known as Chartered Accountants, admission to their ranks has been regulated by the Charter and Bye-Laws of the Institute, and candidates are required to serve an apprenticeship on conditions similar to those which have prevailed for many years in the Solicitors' branch of the legal profession, by entering into Articles with a member of the Institute for five years, with the exception that to graduates of an University two years of service are dispensed with.

Articled Clerks. As a consequence of the obtainment of the Charter, many have turned their attention to this new profession, and have entered into Articles of Clerkship with a member of the Institute; but it should be borne in mind by those who think of following in their footsteps that the duties devolving on a Chartered Accountant are of a nature not suitable to all intellects. Although exceedingly varied, they all require a knowledge of accounts and an aptitude for figures which is only enjoyed by a proportion, and they are most likely to succeed in the profession who at school or college select mathematics for their principal study in preference to classics. It is not only extremely possible, but most probable, that the men who take high honours in the latter would be very unlikely to take an interest in the work of a professional Accountant. Lecture I.

Another point worthy of consideration is the probability of success in the profession after the expiration of the articles and the admission to membership of the Institute.

It frequently happens that instructions are received from family connections and private friends, in their capacity as Executors and Trustees, Directors of Public Companies or owners of property; but, as a rule, by far the greater number of the matters transacted in a Chartered Accountant's chambers are introduced by Solicitors. It is, therefore, evident that success depends upon obtaining the confidence and support of members of this profession. Clients.

The *clientèle* of a Chartered Accountant is, therefore, practically the same as of a barrister, the latter being sought by a Solicitor, either as an advocate or as an expert in law, the former as an expert in accounts.

It is not, however, only for those who intend to practise professionally that the Institute, through its Members, offers advantages. The possession of the certificate of having passed the final examination of the Institute has been proved to be of the highest value

Lecture I. in competition for many appointments, such as that of secretary, accountant, or book-keeper of companies, banks, or firms, or as agent of a landed proprietor, it being known to those making the selection that any holding this certificate must possess a special knowledge, which may possibly also be enjoyed by other candidates, but of which they can show no proof beyond testimonials, which, as a rule, are more or less flattering to the owners.

For those who have resolved upon being articled, three examinations are prescribed.

Preliminary Examination.

The first, or preliminary examination, is entirely an educational one, and is conducted wholly in writing, in the following subjects :—

(1) Writing from Dictation.
(2) Writing a short English Composition.
(3) Arithmetic.
(4) Algebra, to quadratic equations (inclusive).
(5) Euclid (the first four books).
(6) Geography.
(7) History of England.
(8) Latin (elementary).
(9) Any two of the following subjects, one of which, at least, must be a language, to be selected by the candidate :—

(1) Latin; (2) Greek (ancient); (3) French; (4) German; (5) Italian; (6) Spanish; (7) Higher Mathematics; (8) Physics; (9) Chemistry; (10) Animal Physiology; (11) Zoology; (12) Botany; (13) Electricity, Magnetism, Light and Heat; (14) Geology; (15) Stenography.

Should, however, the candidate be a graduate of an University, or have passed certain public examinations prescribed by the bye-laws, this preliminary examination is dispensed with, and in their case, and for those

Articles of

Clerkship.

who have passed this preliminary examination, articles must be entered into with a member of the Institute. A form of articles can be obtained at the Institute.

At the time of entering into these articles a premium is usually paid, which varies according to the professional standing of the member of the Institute to whom the clerk is articled; the solicitor's costs of the preparation of the articles are also paid by the articled clerk.

Intermediate Examination.

The intermediate examination must be passed after the expiration of half the term of service, and the final may be passed any time after two years after passing the intermediate examination, except that graduates of Universities, articled for three years only, may present themselves after one year of passing the intermediate examination.

The intermediate examination is conducted in writing in the following subjects :—

(1) Book-keeping and Accounts (including Partnership and Executorship Accounts).

(2) Auditing.

(3) The Rights and Duties of Liquidators, Trustees, and Receivers.

Final Examination.

The final examination is conducted in writing in the same three subjects, and, in addition :—

(4) The Principles of the Law of Bankruptcy.

(5) The Principles of the Law relating to Joint Stock Companies.

(6) The Principles of Mercantile Law.

(7) The Principles of the Law of Arbitrations and Awards.

Chartered Accountants Experts in Accounts.

It can be seen from the above subjects that the duties of a Chartered Accountant are varied, and they may be divided into two heads :—

(1) Those appertaining to their practice as Experts in Accounts.

Lecture I.

(2) The Administration of Trusts and the Distribution of Assets.

Under the first heading are included the designing and opening the books of firms and individuals, of executors and trustees, of companies and other public bodies, including corporations.

The keeping of these Accounts, the auditing of Accounts, the examination of Accounts after frauds have been committed, and the preparation for and giving evidence as a qualified witness in trials, arbitrations, and compensation cases, also acting as Arbitrators and Umpires when the matters referred involve questions of account.

As Administrators of Trusts.

Under the second heading are comprehended the acting as Trustee under schemes of arrangement or in bankruptcy, also as Special Manager under the Bankruptcy Act, 1883, acting as the Liquidator of a company (either under the Companies (Winding-up) Act, 1890, or in a voluntary liquidation under the Companies Act, 1862), acting as Receiver in Chancery, or as a Judicial Trustee under the Judicial Trustees Act, 1896.

Opening Books of Account.

To design and open a set of Books of Account not only requires a knowledge of the general principles of book-keeping, but also a special acquaintance with official work which is only gained by experience. Technical knowledge cannot of itself enable its possessor to design a set of books which shall contain a complete record of the transactions of a business with as little clerical labour as possible.

It therefore follows that it is extremely advisable for everyone commencing business to secure the services of a Chartered Accountant in designing his Books of Account. It is a duty every trader owes, not only to himself, but to all with whom he transacts business, to keep a proper record of all his transactions. Lord Esher, the Master of the Rolls, in giving a decision, made the following remarks: "I say distinctly that the proper "keeping of books is a matter of primary importance. "A person is most reckless who does not keep proper "books. It shows that the trader is utterly regardless of "anyone but himself. It is quite certain that a trader who "does not keep books will sooner or later be bankrupt." Lecture I.

In many offices more clerks are engaged on the books than are really required, in consequence of their being kept upon a bad system, and the cost of employing a Chartered Accountant to re-model the system will frequently be repaid in the first year by the saving effected in dispensing with the services of these unnecessary clerks.

It must be evident that experience only will enable anyone to undertake duties of this nature, and such experience can only be gained by a training in a Chartered Accountant's office, where investigations and audits of the books of companies and businesses of various descriptions are conducted.

The auditing of the Accounts of individuals, firms, and public companies, also of executors and trustees, and corporations, forms the foundation of the practice of Professional Accountants. Auditing.

The advantages of their being employed in this capacity, although not yet fully appreciated, is becoming more and more recognised, and it may be safely predicted that the time is not far distant when every person engaged in a profession or trade will have their books periodically audited.

At present many consider that the fee for this service is a useless expense, but experience has proved otherwise, and there can be no doubt many frauds are prevented through a knowledge that the books of an employer are subjected to a periodical scrutiny by experts, the probability of detection being considered too great to be risked.

Lecture I.

In my work on "Auditors: their Duties and Responsibilities," I have discussed very fully the nature and principles of an audit, and although this book was written more particularly for Auditors of public companies, still the principles are the same, no matter what class of audit be undertaken.

Varieties of Audits.

There are many varieties of audits, differing according to the instructions received from the client, the most effectual being the one where the only instructions given to the Auditor are to do all that is necessary in the interests of the principals. Where these instructions are given great responsibility rests upon the Auditor. He has to guard, as much as possible, against errors of every description, require a proper sum to be charged against the profit and loss account in respect of depreciation of leases, plant, machinery, &c., and satisfy himself that the Accounts he presents to his clients are, to the best of his ability, accurate in every respect.

Previous to commencing an audit of this description, the Auditor should call for the legal documents by which those whose Accounts he is auditing are bound together. In the case of a Company this would be the special Act of Parliament incorporating it, or the Articles of Association when it is registered under the Companies Act, 1862; in the case of a firm, the Deed of Partnership must be perused; while if he has to audit the Accounts of executors or trustees, he should ask for the Will of the Testator. All these documents are, of course, subject to the Public Acts, with the sections of which, and with the most important decisions of Judges in matters affecting Accounts, a Chartered Accountant is supposed to be familiar.

Private Audits.

In some cases the parties interested give express instructions as to the extent of the audit they require; for example, in a firm the partners may agree that the full amount expended on plant and machinery, or on a lease, may be taken as an asset, without any allowance for depreciation being charged against the profit and loss account. The parties interested, therefore, being unanimous, the Auditor has no responsibility for any inaccuracy in this respect, but, in order to protect himself, he will, of course, in signing the Accounts, refer to the instructions received.

Audit of Accounts of Executors.

The desirability of having a periodical investigation by a Professional Accountant of the Accounts of public Companies and firms has long been recognised, but for some unexplained reason executors, trustees, and their solicitors have not yet fully appreciated the advantages of an audit of their Accounts, which, as a rule, are kept in a most slovenly fashion. An idea prevails that anyone can keep a set of books of account of this nature, and, no matter who the executors or trustees may be, they, as a rule, consider they are quite capable of keeping a proper record of their transactions. Where they do not do this themselves, they very frequently hand over the books to the book-keeper of a merchant or tradesman, who, naturally, records the transactions on the system to which he is most accustomed.

The books are closed periodically, and the transactions are, as a rule, recorded; but when a person interested in the trust asks for information, wishes to know the financial position of the estate, what was the position of the testator at the time of his death, and how the *corpus* and income has been disposed of, it is, as a rule, impossible to answer him. When it is absolutely necessary to prepare a statement an immense amount of time is occupied, and, most probably, the result when furnished is incorrect.

The Accounts of executors and trustees should be kept on a system totally different to that of traders, and

Lecture I

it is surprising how executors and trustees care to take upon themselves an unnecessary personal responsibility, or to pay incompetent persons, when they are entitled to employ a Professional Accountant, and instruct him to open and keep their books properly.

The practice, however, of doing so is becoming gradually, although slowly, recognised, and many solicitors hand over to a Professional Accountant the duty of preparing the Accounts for probate, the residuary Accounts, the opening of the books of executors and trustees, with instructions either to keep them or, if they are kept by an agent, to audit them periodically, and report the result of the investigation.

Many trustees now, after the Accounts have been prepared, adopt the plan of having them signed by those interested in the income, as it reduces to a minimum the chance of any dispute arising hereafter.

Of Land-owners.

The owners of landed estates are also beginning to appreciate an independent audit of the Accounts of their agents, and, although a little jealousy or feeling of resentment on the part of the agent has frequently to be removed, yet experience has shown that, ultimately, they themselves are as much in favour of their transactions being examined and reported on as their employers. The fact of an agent being asked to lay open his books to a Chartered Accountant does not imply his employer has any suspicion of his integrity, or expects to be informed his agent has been dishonest, or even neglectful of his interests, and when this is recognised the audit is welcomed by both. The employer has the satisfaction of receiving statements showing clearly and concisely his income and expenditure, duly certified by an independent expert; while the agent obtains a recognition of his services having been properly performed during the period, which he would not receive in any other way. The mere acceptance of statements showing the sums received for rents of farms, houses, sales of stock and crops, &c., and how the same have been expended, cannot be so satisfactory to either landlord or agent as the knowledge the rent-rolls have been gone through, the payments vouched, and other items of receipts and expenditure verified by an independent examiner.

Chartered Accountants and Public Companies.

In connection with public companies, the practice of a Chartered Accountant is exceedingly varied. In addition to the office of Director, which is undertaken by men of every position, social and mercantile, Chartered Accountants are employed professionally in the formation, the administration, and the windings up of public companies of every description.

The promoters and proposed directors of a public company cannot do better than at once retain the services of a professional Accountant to assist them in the initial work, by affording temporary office accommodation, with the use of one of his clerks as secretary to the promoters. They will thus ensure proper minutes being kept of their proceedings, together with much valuable assistance in the various stages from the inception of the scheme to the issue of the prospectus, and in conjunction with the solicitor to the proposed company a Chartered Accountant will prevent them from falling into many pitfalls.

His services will also be equally valuable to the Board of Directors after the prospectus has been issued. The minute book of the directors will be properly kept; the applications for shares and the letters of allotment registered, and many instances are on record where innumerable complications have arisen from the fact of an application for shares and allotment book not having been properly kept.

The company having been successfully floated, it is then very desirable that the books should be properly

Lecture I.

opened, and, whatever may be the nature of the business the company intends to transact, and no matter how experienced a book-keeper may be engaged to keep the books of account, the directors will find the expense very trifling and will appreciate the comfort hereafter of having them opened by a Chartered Accountant.

Books of a Public Company.

The books of a public company may be divided into two heads: (1) Registry, or Statistical; (2) Financial, or Account; the former of which are prescribed by Act of Parliament and by general practice and custom. The directors of a company are liable to penalties if the former are not kept in a proper manner and entered up to date; and may also be caused an immense amount of trouble, and even anxiety, if they neglect to keep other books usually found in the offices of well-managed companies.

The form of the Financial or Account Books vary according to the nature of the business transacted, and a set of books opened by an incompetent person may involve a pecuniary loss to the company, by reason of their being so arranged as to not allow a sufficient check being kept, and also by being so cumbersome as to require a larger staff being maintained than is necessary.

Supervision by a Chartered Accountant desirable.

The books, having been opened and started on a good system, may then be handed over to the book-keeper appointed by the directors; but even then it is desirable for a Chartered Accountant to occasionally supervise them and report to the directors. There can be no objection to the Auditor being employed for this purpose, in which case he would, of course, act quite independently of his position as Auditor, and not relax any of his vigilance when, later on, he is auditing the Accounts because many of the entries may have been previously made under his instructions. As a professional Accountant he receives his instructions from the directors; as Auditor he is the agent of the shareholders, and it is quite possible he may, from fresh information acquired during his audit, refuse, as an Auditor, to certify accounts he has prepared or supervised as a professional Accountant.

Secretarial work.

Many Chartered Accountants also conduct entirely in their offices the secretarial and office work of companies, receiving from them a fee which covers the rent and salaries of secretary and clerks. In many cases this is highly advantageous to the company, and the directors have the satisfaction of feeling they are in the hands of a responsible person, who has a higher interest in conducting the business properly than an ordinary secretary.

The usual official position, however, of Chartered Accountants in connection with public companies is in their capacity as Auditors and Liquidators. The duties of Auditors of companies has been the subject of a separate work by me, while those of Liquidators will be referred to later on.

Investigation of Accounts on behalf of incoming Partner.

Chartered Accountants are almost universally instructed to examine the books of a firm on behalf of a proposed partner. Incoming partners have usually to introduce money into the firm as a contribution towards the working capital of the business, while sometimes they have to pay a premium for the privilege of being admitted into an established firm.

It would be exceedingly rash to take for granted the correctness of a statement that a certain share will yield on the average a certain income, and few would begrudge the fee paid for a proper investigation. It may be contended that, as a man may have to inquire into several businesses before he eventually joins one, he may have many fees to pay; but this is really an argument in favour of investigation, as the number of fees paid before finally deciding on a business is a proof

Lecture I.

of an equal number of dangers escaped. It is very simple, however, to avoid these fees, and it is customary to request the firm to submit their accounts, on the face of which they offer to take in a partner and receive his money, and then, if they appear satisfactory, to accept the partnership subject to their correctness being certified by a Chartered Accountant chosen by the proposed incoming partner, the fee to be paid by the firm should the statements put forward by them be proved to be incorrect.

Audit of Partnership Accounts.

When the partnership is eventually agreed upon, it is now very customary for a clause to be inserted in the deed of partnership that the Accounts shall be audited yearly or half-yearly by a Chartered Accountant named in the deed; and if the incoming partner is providing a large portion of the capital, he would, in most cases, be able to make a condition that a Chartered Accountant nominated by him should perform this duty.

In many cases capital is introduced into a business by a sleeping partner, who does not take any part in the management; it is then more than ever necessary, in his interests, that a Chartered Accountant selected by him should periodically audit the books and render statements to him showing the financial results of the management, together with a report thereon.

Of Hospitals

The audit of the Accounts of public institutions, such as hospitals, charitable and other societies, where the funds are derived from donations and periodical subscriptions, forms another department of a Chartered Accountant's practice, and since the governing bodies of the Hospital Sunday and Hospital Saturday Fund have refused to make any contributions to Hospitals or Dispensaries whose Accounts are not certified by a professional Accountant, the custom is becoming more general of issuing the Accounts to the subscribers with the certificate of a Chartered Accountant appended.

Lecture I.

Auditing as a Protection against Fraud

Although it is very often impossible for a Chartered Accountant to detect the committal of frauds in auditing Accounts, in the same way as it is impossible for a solicitor to protect his clients against losses by forgeries when advancing money on securities, still there can be no doubt that many frauds would be prevented were auditing more universal, but very much on the principle of "locking the stable door when the steed has gone," Chartered Accountants are too often called in when a fraud has been discovered, instead of having been employed to prevent it, and the analysis of books containing false entries form a very interesting part of his duties, and one frequently requiring his utmost skill.

The devices of absconding cashiers and book-keepers are too numerous to describe; but the clever-ness and astuteness often displayed to ward off the discovery of the peculation of a few hundred pounds would have often yielded the originator a more substantial reward had he turned his skill to better purposes.

Qualified Witnesses in Prosecutions.

This leads me up to another department of a Chartered Accountant's profession, namely, that of acting as a qualified witness.

Where a defaulter of the nature just described is apprehended and prosecuted, the most important evidence against him will probably be that of the Chartered Accountant who has examined the manipulated books, and, having regard to the fact that he will probably have to undergo a very severe cross-examination by the prisoner's counsel, he should fully qualify himself to give his evidence in a straightforward manner, and have his figures and facts carefully brought together, with references from his papers to the entries which will be produced as evidence.

Chartered Accountants are also frequently called as qualified witnesses in other trials and arbitrations, as,

Lecture I.

for example, where a purchaser of a business brings an action against the vendor on the grounds that the profits made have not been in accordance with the statements on which he was induced to purchase. In cases of this nature a Chartered Accountant may be either retained by the plaintiff or defendant or selected as arbitrator.

In Compensation Cases.

It is now the practice, where premises are taken compulsorily under Public Acts, by railways, corporations, school boards, &c., and part of the claim is for loss of business, for a Chartered Accountant to be employed by a plaintiff to investigate his books, to enable him to make his trade claim ; and also by a defendant to resist it. In these cases, unless the claim be settled before the hearing, the Chartered Accountant on either side will give evidence as a qualified witness.

Arbitrations.

A Chartered Accountant is very frequently appointed as an arbitrator or umpire where matters of account are in dispute, and in this capacity can hear the parties either in person or represented by counsel or solicitors. In his capacity as arbitrator he can administer an oath to all such witnesses as are legally called before him, and, unless an objection has been made by one of the parties to a legal assessor, he will generally be allowed one to sit with him, and in any case may obtain the assistance of counsel in framing his award.

It must be evident that, not only with reference to arbitrations, but in all the other official positions referred to by me, a Chartered Accountant should have a fair knowledge of mercantile law, and a glance at the papers of the intermediate and final examinations of the Institute will show the importance attached to this branch of a student's studies.

The following duties devolve upon Chartered Accountants in connection with that branch I have designated as Administration of Assets :—

Special Manager and Trustee in Bankruptcy.

Under the Bankruptcy Act of 1883, creditors can apply for the appointment of a Special Manager of the debtor's business pending the appointment of a Trustee, and also have the power at the first meeting to appoint their own Trustee.

Both these offices are now almost universally conferred upon Chartered Accountants, which is easily accounted for, as nearly every question occurring, with reference to the duties of a special manager, or trustee, are connected with matters involving a knowledge of accounts.

In order to undertake duties of this nature successfully, considerable experience in mercantile law and practice must have been gained, for it is quite possible that in either of these capacities a Chartered Accountant may at the same time act as a banker, East India merchant, warehouseman, wharfinger, or a wholesale and retail trader. Experience qualifying anyone to undertake these varied duties can only be gained in the training and practice of a Chartered Accountant's office, where the audit of books and Accounts of traders of every description have laid open the secrets of the various businesses thus examined.

Their Duties.

A Special Manager and Trustee in Bankruptcy are, during the tenure of their appointment, accountable to the Board of Trade. They have to give security, and have to pay all money received into the Bank of England; their Accounts are audited periodically by the Board of Trade, and they are accordingly in constant communication with the two departments of the Official Receiver and the Inspector-General in Bankruptcy. Whatever complaint may be made against the Act of 1883, the institution of the latter department was certainly to the advantage of the most respectable Chartered Accountants, and those who have worked under the two Acts greatly prefer the one now in force.

Lecture I. The creation of the Official Receiver's department has been proved to have been quite unnecessary, and has already fallen into public disfavour.

At the first meeting of creditors a Trustee can be appointed, either under a scheme of arrangement or in bankruptcy, the creditors in the latter case passing a resolution to adjudicate the debtor a bankrupt.

The duties of a Trustee under the scheme of arrangement are prescribed by the scheme itself. The Trustee under a bankruptcy has to realise the estate, and distribute it among the creditors as quickly as possible. In both cases he has to submit his accounts for audit to the Board of Trade.

Liquidator.

The liquidation of public companies is now almost entirely entrusted to Chartered Accountants. A public company may be wound up, either voluntarily, with or without the supervision of the Court, or compulsorily, and windings-up in the latter case are attached to the Chancery Division of the High Court of Justice.

In voluntary Winding-up.

A company is wound up voluntarily when the shareholders themselves at an extraordinary general meeting pass either an extraordinary or special resolution to that effect; and they can appoint a Liquidator, with or without security, to realise the assets and distribute them. In this case the Liquidator has to call a meeting of the shareholders annually until the liquidation is closed, and lay his Accounts before them. During the progress of the voluntary liquidation it is open to a creditor, or any person interested, to apply to the Court for the liquidation to be continued under the supervision of the Court, or for a compulsory winding-up. In the former case there is liberty to apply to the Court when thought desirable, and a Liquidator frequently takes advantage of this power to avoid responsibility.

In compulsory Winding-up.

When a company is wound up by Order of the

Lecture I.

Court, two meetings are held, both presided over by the Official Receiver, who has been acting as Provisional Liquidator. One is a meeting of the creditors of the company, the other of the contributories or shareholders, and, should both meetings decide on the same person to act as Liquidator, he receives the appointment. Should, however, each appoint a different person, the Official Receiver applies to the Court, who decides as to which of the nominees of the two meetings shall be selected, or it may select a third person to act as Liquidator. The Order to wind up is almost invariably made on the petition of a creditor who cannot obtain payment of his debt, although the Court has power to order a company to be wound up compulsorily for other reasons.

Reason for appointing Chartered Accountant.

As a rule a Chartered Accountant is appointed Liquidator, and it is easy to account for this. The first duty of a Liquidator, after taking possession of the Company's property, is to prepare a list of contributories or persons liable to contribute to the assets of a Company in a winding-up. This can only be done by examining the books containing the entries of the capital accounts of the shareholders, and ascertaining, not only the amounts unpaid on the shares, but also whether the amounts stated as having been paid have been properly credited.

The Liquidator's next duty is to investigate the claims sent to him in response to an advertisement stating the last day on which they can be received. Frequently before this can be done the books of the company have to be written up, being in arrear at the commencement of the winding-up; but in any case the claims have to be compared with the books before admitted, and when a difference exists, and the Liquidator is of opinion the claim is incorrect, he must be prepared to prove it so in Chambers or in Court. This requires a knowledge of Accounts seldom possessed by

Lecture I

any but a professional Accountant, and in order to avoid the double expense of appointing a person as Liquidator who has to employ others to do his work, it has gradually become the practice to confer the appointment upon Chartered Accountants.

Receiver in Chancery.

For the same reason Chartered Accountants are very frequently appointed Receivers in Chancery actions, where property claimed by two or more parties has to be protected until a decision has been given to whom it belongs, and a similar appointment is also made in what is known as a Debenture-holder's action, where a Receiver is appointed on behalf of the Debenture-holders of a company when their interest is in arrear, or the principal is not paid off when due and demanded.

Responsibilities of Chartered Accountants.

It is evident, therefore, that although the duties and responsibilities of Chartered Accountants are exceedingly varied, having regard to the nature of the appointments undertaken by them, yet they are nearly all conferred upon them as being experts in Accounts. The foundation, therefore, of the professional training is a knowledge of book-keeping, but the mastery of this subject leaves the student only on the threshold. A first-class book-keeper may not possess the qualifications to enable him to undertake the position of a second-class clerk in a professional Accountant's office, but a perfect knowledge of book-keeping is requisite for the analysis of the books of account in the simplest investigation entrusted to a Chartered Accountant.

Practical Training necessary.

This knowledge can be partly acquired by reading, but it must be supplemented by the experience gained during the period under articles; and the same remark applies to the legal portions of the training, by the experience acquired in attending at the Courts, the Chambers of the Judges, and the Official Receiver's department of the Board of Trade.

Theoretical knowledge is not sufficient. A student who takes every opportunity of becoming acquainted with the details of as many individual matters as he can, will find his zeal well repaid in his future career. The initial work may be monotonous, but no duties fall to the lot of members of any profession which can be more varied or interesting than those of a Chartered Accountant.

LECTURE II.

THE PREPARATION OF THE ACCOUNTS OF COMPANIES FOR THE PURPOSES OF AUDIT.

Read before the Institute of Secretaries 21st December, 1892.

Lecture II.

Importance of subject to Directors, &c.

The preparation of the accounts of a public Company for submission to the Auditors, which is practically required by the Articles of Association of every Company registered under the Companies Act of 1862, has not, so far as I am aware, ever received any practical attention at the hands of either directors or secretaries, although of the utmost importance to both class of officials.

Companies with Articles of Association.

I refer to the Articles of Association of Companies as requiring Accounts to be periodically prepared and laid before their shareholders after audit as it is a most singular omission from the sections of the Companies Act, 1862, which is practically the Act under which limited liability companies are registered, that with the exception of those companies which are not of sufficient importance to have Articles of Association of their own there is not only no provision whatever for the audit of Accounts, but, moreover, there is no provision for the publication of Accounts, or any direction that the shareholders are to be informed in any way as to the results of the transactions of their company.

Companies

For those Companies registered without Articles of

Association a schedule to the Act of 1862, generally known as Table "A," contains clauses requiring the directors to present Accounts to the shareholders annually, and for them to be audited. It also contains clauses as to the election of Auditors, including the most extraordinary one, that he may be a Member of the company. As I think there can be no doubt whatever that, inasmuch as the Auditor ought to be perfectly impartial, and not be influenced in any way as to the extent of the profit or the amount of the dividend to be declared, the holding of a single share in a company ought to disqualify any person for the appointment of Auditor.

Lecture I.

without Articles.

One later Act has laid down certain provisions for special audits, viz., the Companies Act, 1879, which requires that the Accounts of every banking company registered after the passing of the Act as a limited company shall be examined by an Auditor or Auditors, and regulations are laid down as to the nature of the audit, but it is certainly to be regretted that the opportunity was not taken advantage of for clauses to have been inserted making it compulsory for every company to have its Accounts audited. The omission has, however, been practically supplied by the insertion of clauses referring to the audit of Accounts which are to be found almost invariably in every Articles of Association, and which in these respects are based on the sections of Table "A." In spite of numbers of decisions of the Courts on matters relating to Accounts, improper payment of dividends, and other relevant questions, the drafting of suitable clauses seems to have been utterly neglected by companies' Solicitors and Counsel, whose special experience lies in preparing Articles of Association and other company legal work.

Accounts of Banking Companies.

The Articles of Association nearly always contain a clause which is practically paid very little attention to

Duty of Di[rec]tors to subm[it]

by secretaries, viz., that the Accounts have to be prepared by the officials of the companies themselves, and are to be assumed as absolutely and finally settled when submitted to the Auditors, whose strict duty is confined to either passing them as they stand, or condemning them, either entirely or partially, by means of a certificate, which is, of course, also intended to be irrevocable and to be issued to the shareholders as it leaves the Auditors' hands. Although the correct interpretation of this clause has been persistently ignored, it is still inserted in the Articles, and I think it worthy of the attention of secretaries that they should realise the responsibility thrown upon them by this common clause, as well as other clauses relating to the Accounts and Audit, in the Articles, and that they should endeavour to conform to them.

A practice has arisen of calling in the Auditors at a stage earlier than that contemplated by the Articles of Association, and varies according to the efficiency of the secretary or the official of the company in charge of the Accounts.

In many companies the books of account have been kept badly, or, perhaps, if well kept up to a certain point, the officials are, from want of experience, unable to balance the books and prepare the necessary statements. The Auditors are then expected to perform these duties themselves, and therefore when the Accounts are ultimately settled they are really the creation of the Auditors, who have subsequently to audit Accounts of their own compilation.

Fortunately for the directors and the officials of the company, the Auditors are now nearly always Chartered Accountants, who realise the responsibility of the duties thus imposed upon them; but it must be borne in mind that the Accounts as presented, no matter how prepared, are not the Auditors' Accounts, but the Accounts of the directors, and of the secretary or other official whose duty it is to prepare them. Lecture I

Auditor's dı to criticise, not prepare, Accounts.

In the event of any inaccuracy being discovered later on, the directors and the officials of the company are first of all responsible to the shareholders, the only responsibility attached to the Auditors being their omission to detect any inaccuracy. It is no answer for the directors or secretary to state that the Accounts were prepared by the Auditors, as the book-keeping itself is not in the hands of the Auditors, and there is no privity between the directors and the officials of the company and the Auditors, the latter are the agents of the shareholders and are accountable to them alone.

This remark, of course, does not apply where the directors have employed the Auditors, not as Auditors but as Chartered Accountants, to prepare the Accounts on their behalf, and have paid them a fee as professional Accountants for so doing. There is then the usual liability attaching to them as professional men acting for the directors and officials, who would, of course, have their remedy if necessary. This, however, does not alter the fact that the directors and officials are the persons first of all responsible to the shareholders.

Importance of good syst of Book-keeping.

One of the most constant sources of difficulty in connection with the preparation of the Accounts of a company at the close of its first financial year arises from the incomplete manner in which the books of the company have been opened, or through the adoption of a system of book-keeping not really adapted for the special requirements of the particular company. The reason for this is in many instances a very natural and to a certain extent a commendable one. The secretary of a new company is of course desirous of proving to the directors—who have just conferred on him the appointment, very often selecting him out of a large number of candidates—his efficiency for the duties entrusted to him. He has probably, in applying for the appointment, laid some stress on his experience including a knowledge of book-keeping, and it is extraordinary how many, whose sole experience lies in having kept one or a few books of a mercantile office, honestly believe themselves to be practical book-keepers, and do not realise the fact that, although the theory of book-keeping is comprised in a few rules, yet in actual practice there can hardly be found two offices of the many thousands in London whose set of books agree in every detail.

The books of a company, moreover, are distinctly of a class that may be called special, as distinct from ordinary mercantile books of account. In the first place, the capital account of the partners of a firm are contained in half a dozen accounts. The capital accounts of the partners of a public company have to be recorded in very many special ways, with a considerable amount of repetition, and frequently, through proper care not being taken of the letters of application, and want of detail in the bankers' pass book, an Auditor, in auditing the first Accounts of a company, finds the share books in a state of great confusion, and that it is exceedingly difficult to reconcile the total amount standing at the credit of the shareholders' individual accounts with the amounts standing at the credit of the capital account in the ledger.

It also often happens that the business undertaken by the company is of a totally different character to that with which the secretary is familiar, and after he has opened the books, taking as his model the Accounts he has been accustomed to, he may find, after a few weeks, that he is unable to grapple with the difficulties that arise. These are disposed of temporarily by a number of suspense accounts, but the day comes when they have to be reckoned with, and when the Auditor requires the natural explanation of entries which he cannot understand there is sometimes absolutely no proper one forthcoming.

Lecture

Books of Companie should be opened by Chartered Accounta

The remedy for this state of affairs is one which I have some delicacy in putting forward, but I have considerably less than I should have had half-a-dozen years ago, as the practice of employing Chartered Accountants to open the books of a new company is becoming more universal. It is practically a trifling expense, and the proposal, if properly represented by the secretary to the directors, would in very few instances meet with any opposition. The secretary, even of the smallest company, has usually enough to do in its early stages without having to inaugurate a system of book-keeping, and it is practically no reflection upon his capacity, or shows in any way a want of ability for carrying out his duties, should he have the books opened for him in a proper manner, so that he can subsequently keep them up efficiently.

For those secretaries, however, who are not inclined to follow my advice I can only say that there are one or two points to be carefully considered. It does not, of course, come within the scope of this address to go into details in connection with the Books of Account of a company. I will simply content myself with stating that before commencing to make entries in any of the books, the class of business the company has been formed to undertake should be considered. Let the secretary compare that with the class of business to which he has been accustomed, take note of points of difference, and endeavour to ascertain, before making any entries, what part of the old system had better be discarded, and what new system should take its place.

Share Bo

The share books also require some consideration, and secretaries should avoid the ready-made books of stationers, unless they have satisfied themselves that the forms submitted are really suitable for their require-

ecture II.

ments. The share books which comprise what is wanted for recording the entries relating to one company would be for others most incomplete in design and encumbered with unnecessary columns, and this specially applies to a company where there are different classes of shares.

When the prospectus of a new company has been issued, the pass book, together with the application forms, should be obtained from the bankers every day. The application forms should be arranged in the order in which the amounts paid on application are found on the credit side of the pass book, and should then be immediately fastened into a guard book and numbered; if there be any error between the amount in the pass book and the letter of application, the attention of the bankers should be immediately called to it and it should be at once rectified, mistakes of this nature being frequent in the bankers' pass book in connection with the issue of shares.

The draft cash book should be immediately opened, the entries also being made in the order of the credits in the bankers' pass book. The application for shares and allotment book should also be written up, the order still being the same; and when the list has been closed the book will be ready to be placed before the directors for considering the allotment, and, everything being in order, there will be no difficulty in the future; whereas, if this caution be neglected until the audit, it is frequently very troublesome to reconcile the amounts, as the bankers have perhaps to look up papers which have been filed for a long time and which it is perhaps difficult to get at.

oks of count should written up date.

After the books have been opened, the next duty of the officials in charge of them is to keep them up regularly, so that at any time queries which have to be ascertained from the books can be answered. The books should be written up systematically, and all kept as much as possible to an even date. A mistake which is too frequently committed in many offices is to keep, say, the cash book written up to date, and let the other books fall into arrears, such as having the ledger only posted spasmodically from time to time. When possible the correctness of the books should be tested periodically by taking out a trial balance, say, every three months; if there be any inaccuracy, it is always naturally more easy to find it than to wait until the close of the financial year, when the accounts are being prepared for the Auditors. The desire naturally exists in most offices to submit these accounts to the shareholders as soon as possible, and there is, of course, a very much larger field to search for the errors than when it is known that they must be found within the record of the transactions of a period of three months.

Date on w Books sho be closed.

Before deciding on the date on which to close the financial books of a company and to present its first Accounts to the shareholders, the Articles of Association of the Company should be consulted, as the date of closing the Accounts and the month in which the annual meeting must be held are frequently fixed by these Articles. When this is the case the date should be scrupulously adhered to, although, so far as I am aware, there is no penalty for not doing so, provided the section of the Act which requires the annual meeting to be held in every year be complied with.

I have already stated that the Act of 1862 does not contain any regulations as to audit, but the schedule known as Table "A," which applies to those companies not registered with Articles of Association, requires the directors to lay before the company in general meeting a statement of its income and expenditure for the past year made up to a date not more than three months before such meeting, and at the same meeting a balance

Lecture II. sheet should also be laid before them. It is evident, therefore, that a company working under this schedule must hold a meeting before the 31st December in any year, and that if that date be decided upon for the meeting the Accounts must be made up to a date not anterior to the 30th September.

Date of holding Annual Meetings.

It may not be out of place here to remark on the importance of selecting a suitable day for the annual meeting, which is frequently overlooked by officials of companies, or rather it is overlooked by directors and officials of sound undertakings, who have nothing to fear from meeting their shareholders, while it is most carefully considered by those who have not conducted the business of their company successfully, and still more in those cases where they have acted dishonestly and wish to avoid being called to account.

Observant shareholders are apt to look with suspicion when they receive notices of meetings to be held on Saturdays or Stock Exchange settling days, on days close to Easter or Christmas Day, or meetings fixed between the middle of August and the middle of October, the usual vacation of professional and business men, and especially the last fortnight of the year, when the Accounts are presented only up to a period not later than the end of September.

Having decided upon the date on which the first financial period shall end, preparation should be made anterior to that date for balancing the books, and for this purpose they should all be written up to date, and, where possible, if there should be any fear of the books not balancing at the first attempt, any spare time the clerks may have should be devoted to the calling over of the postings, checking the additions, &c. On the evening of the day the cash book should be ruled off and balanced, and a reconciliation should be at once prepared with the bankers' pass book, showing the cheques drawn on the company's account but not presented at the bankers, and the cheques paid in but not cleared. It is desirable, of course, to draw as few cheques as possible on the last two days of the period. Lecture —

Vouchers. The vouchers, if it has not been the custom to have them periodically arranged, should now be sorted, and either arranged in neat bundles in the order of the cash book entries, or else pasted in a guard book in the same order.

It must be remembered that simple acknowledgements of money received are not what Auditors understand as vouchers. Many companies, especially large ones, have their own printed form of receipt, which they require all persons to whom they make payments to sign. These receipts by themselves are practically of very little use to the Auditors. The object of vouching is for the Auditor to not only be satisfied that a payment has been actually made, but to see at the same time that the amount has been posted to the proper account, and it is necessary, therefore, that the actual invoices be affixed to the receipts.

Stock. Where stock has to be taken, the necessary arrangements should be made a few days previous to the close of the period, and most minute instructions given to those in charge of this important matter, so as to ensure correct measure, or correct weight, being taken, according to the nature of the stock; the prices should, of course, be taken from the invoices. Remarks as to depreciation, caused either through any portion of the stock being damaged, or becoming less fashionable, or for any other reason, should be noted opposite each item. In the case of a large business with heads of departments, each head should be made responsible for his stocktaking, and he should sign each sheet of the stock, certifying that it has been taken under his supervision, and that, in his opinion, it is correct in

Lecture II.

every detail; he should also state what, in his opinion, should be allowed for depreciation. It is very important for the secretary, or other head official, to make those under him in connection with the stocktaking give certificates of this nature, as in the event of it being subsequently discovered that there has been an error in the stocktaking he can place the blame on the right shoulders. It is, of course, understood that it is his duty to check, as far as possible, the work of his subordinates.

Auditor's duty with regard to Stock.

The Auditor is, of course, not responsible for the value of the stock being correct; but he will probably require, by testing selected items, to ascertain whether the correct value has been placed upon it, when he will, of course, consider the notes made as to depreciation. If evidence be not produced to him that proper care has been exercised in taking and valuing the stock, he will probably consider it necessary to put a special clause in his certificate that the responsibility rests with the directors and officials; but it is not usual to put this where the Auditor is satisfied that proper care has been taken.

Examination of Securities.

When a company has investments, it is desirable that the Auditor be requested to examine the securities representing the investments before they are changed, and the same remark applies more especially in the case of securities held against loans. It is usual in those cases where the Auditors are Chartered Accountants for them to attend immediately after the closing of the books, count the cash, verify the bank balance, examine the securities, and then withdraw until they are informed that the statements are prepared and the books ready for audit. It is always more troublesome for the Auditor to vouch for the correctness of the securities after they have been changed, as he frequently has to work back through various cash transactions in order to satisfy himself.

For the purposes of the examination by the Auditor a list of the securities should be prepared, to which should be affixed the cost price, the price proposed to be taken credit for in the balance sheet, and the market price, so that the Secretary or officials can first of all place the correct value upon the securities, and can subsequently justify this valuation to the Auditors. Lecture II.

Valuation of Securities.

It is not customary to revalue the securities at each period of closing the books, and the following is the usual method of arriving at the proper result, viz.: if the securities have not depreciated since they were purchased or are of greater value, the cost price is usually taken as the value for the balance sheet, but if there has been a depreciation from the cost price, taking the investments as a whole, a reserve should be made and charged against revenue account to cover such depreciation.

Provided the stock has been taken on the day up to which the books are closed, the cash in hand examined on that day or the following morning, and the securities examined before they are changed, the rest of the audit can be done more leisurely, and for many reasons it is not advisable it should take place in any hurried way after the date in question.

Depreciation.

Before finally settling the revenue account, the question of allowances for depreciation has to be considered, and this is a most important matter, and fraught with great responsibility and liabilities on the part of the directors, secretary, and officials. Certain assets, such as leasehold property, concessions, patents, plant, and machinery, stock-in-trade, tools, fittings, furniture, &c., gradually lose their value, more or less, according to the manner in which they are used. For this reason no company can be said to have made a fair profit until, in addition to the expenses of its business, there has been charged against the revenue a proper

Lecture II.

amount for depreciation in respect of this class of assets.

Usually a percentage on Cost.

The usual method adopted for arriving at this amount is to take a percentage on the original cost price, and it is evident that this can only be properly done by dividing these assets into various groups, the items in each approximating as near as possible to the number of years they will respectively last. In the case of long leaseholds and heavy plant and machinery, the depreciation will of course be very small, as compared with that of tools, driving bands, and other small articles in every-day use.

Unsound method of arriving at Depreciation.

A frequent method of arriving at the total amount to be written off for depreciation is one which is perhaps as thoroughly unsound as could be devised, viz., first ascertaining the profit without depreciation, then considering the amount of dividend which the directors desire to pay, and leaving any balance available as the proper amount for depreciation. A more mischievous and unsound system could not be acted upon, or from the directors' and officials' point of view a more foolish one. The object of directors and secretaries ought not to be to pay as high a dividend as possible, but to do exactly the reverse. A percentage on the capital paid away in dividend can never be recalled, while one retained in hand is always available. I go so far as to say that a director who consents to pay a quarter per cent. more dividend than he is absolutely compelled is exceedingly foolish, and that a secretary who assists him to do it is still more foolish. I have no hesitation in asserting that thousands of companies registered since the Act of 1862 came into existence have been wound up, and their secretaries have been thrown out of employment, through this insane craze of paying high dividends.

No injustice to

I have heard it argued that the Directors have

Lecture II.

existing Shareholders in charging too much for Depreciation.

no right, by writing off too much for depreciation in any one year, to minimise the profit of that year, and thus deprive those who may happen to be shareholders at the time when the dividend is declared, but who may sell their shares afterwards, of that to which they are legitimately entitled. In my opinion this theory is an entirely false one; it is not incumbent upon the directors to consider individual shareholders or a special group of shareholders in any way, and certainly not those who keep buying and selling shares and holding them for short periods. It is their duty to keep the capital of their company intact, and do their best to make it a permanent institution. For this purpose secretaries should endeavour to eliminate the fictitious assets from their balance sheets as soon as possible, and to replace them by investments which in bad times will be available to pay, say, a five per cent. dividend for several years. I have frequently come across companies which, after paying dividends of 15 and 20 per cent. for years, have gone into liquidation within twelve months of their last high dividend through their having nothing in hand to meet a temporary depression in their particular line of business.

In my opinion, therefore, the Directors and officials, in simply looking at the matter from their own point of view, and doing their best to preserve their fees and their situations for years to come, are acting in the true interests of the shareholders as well as of themselves. In further support of this, it is undoubtedly a fact that the shares of a company that has paid fair dividends, and has a large reserve, are more saleable and command higher prices than those of one that has paid large dividends and has practically nothing in its accounts to show that it has anything to fall back upon in case of emergency.

In settling, therefore, the amount of depreciation,

Lecture II. do not be influenced in the matter by its result upon the dividend; ascertain the very fullest amount that ought to be chargeable, even if the result shows a loss, while a little difference would show a profit; place the Accounts with the loss before the Directors, and do all in your power to influence them to keep it there.

Allowance for loss on realisation of Debts.

The same remarks apply as to the amount to be charged against the revenue account for losses likely to arise on the realisation of the book debts; the question should be carefully considered without any reference whatever to what will be the effect on the profit or loss. The amount of the debts which, in the opinion of the Secretary, are not likely to be collected, should be entirely charged against the revenue account, and then a careful estimate should be prepared of the loss likely to arise on what is known as "doubtful debts." There is, of course, no fixed rule for adoption, every class of business has its own experience, but a very common method is to charge a percentage on the total amount of the debts. There can be no objection whatever to this plan if adopted, provided the percentage be sufficiently high; it is far better to create too large a reserve than too small a one.

Spreading Expenditure over series of Years.

The Articles of Association of some companies contain a clause allowing the Directors to spread any special expenditure over several years, leaving the balance of the amount not charged against revenue on the credit side of the balance sheet. The greatest care must be exercised in taking advantage of this clause, as there can be no doubt the only justifiable way of thus treating expenditure is when it is fully expected that this expenditure will benefit the revenue of future years against which the balance will be charged. It is extraordinary how fond many boards of Directors and Secretaries are of treating any special expenditure as what is erroneously called an asset; one would think their great anxiety would be to get rid of items of this nature in the balance sheet.

Invoices.

The invoices connected with expenditure of this description should, of course, be particularly preserved, as the Auditor will naturally not allow any expenditure to remain on the credit side of the Balance Sheet without comment, unless it is proved to his satisfaction that the expenditure comes within that allowed by the Articles of Association to be so treated.

Importance of including all Liabilities in Balance Sheet

It is exceedingly important for the directors and other officials of the company that there should be no omission from the liabilities in the balance sheet, and in order to avoid this many companies now adopt the plan of sending out a printed notice to their creditors asking for a statement of their Account, to be sent in for the purpose of verification for the audit, or to state the amount for which the company believes them to be indebted to them, with a request that if incorrect a notice should be immediately sent of any difference that may exist. If many debts have been collected before the accounts are finally settled, it is easier to calculate the allowances for discounts, and for loss on realisation of the debts.

At the same time there should be no unnecessary delay between the date of the balance sheet and the meeting of the shareholders at which the Accounts are submitted, and in many companies the Articles of Association prescribe that not more than three months shall elapse between these two occurrences.

Apportionments.

Before finally closing the books a list should be prepared of all matters in which apportionments may have to be made, having regard to the date on which the books are closed. In the case of periodical payments, such as rent, rates, insurance, or, on the other hand, revenue, such as interest or dividends on investments, the necessary calculations must be made of all

Lecture II.

the liabilities and income which have accrued due to the date of closing the books. Where payments have been made in advance the company may take credit for the proportion of the payment applicable to the period after the date on which the books are closed until its expiration. The company may also take credit for interest accrued on investments where the rate of interest is fixed and it is confidently expected it will be paid when due, such as that on debentures, mortgages, &c. Where the dividends are on shares it may in some cases be allowable to take an estimated amount, basing it on the experience of the past, but this must of course be done cautiously.

Directors' Fees.

The amount due for directors' fees should also be agreed, and should for any reason or other the directors determine to forego any part of these fees, a minute should be made to that effect. Having settled these matters, the proper journal entries should be made, incorporating the results in the books of the company.

Trial Balance.

The books having been completed, their correctness should be tested by taking out what is known as the trial balance, and until this is perfectly correct the Auditor should not be called in. If it be found impossible from any cause whatever for the company's officials to balance the books, the directors would be quite justified to call in the Auditors, but in their capacity as professional Accountants, to balance the books, or they may, if they prefer it, employ another firm of Chartered Accountants for that purpose. The fee for this duty would, of course, be an extra one, and be included in the revenue account amongst the salaries or professional charges, as it must be distinctly understood that the fee voted at the meeting of shareholders to the Auditors is for the audit alone, and does not throw upon the Auditors any duties whatever in assisting the officials to balance the books or prepare the Accounts for audit.

When the trial balance comes out the same amount on both sides it is usually accepted as correct, but inasmuch as it has been frequently found that a small error may, on its being looked for, result in the discovery of very many larger ones, there is the slight chance that the trial balance may be wrong to the extent of errors of equal amount existing on both the credit and debit sides.

Revenue Account.

The trial balance having been agreed, the revenue account and the balance sheet can be prepared therefrom. As regards the revenue account, this can be divided into two or three sections—for example, as a trading account and profit and loss account, and sometimes this is prescribed by the Articles of Association. Where it is left to the discretion of the directors, it is sometimes a question as to whether it is advisable in the interest of the company to set out a trading account, having regard to the fact that the accounts may fall into the hands of competitors in trade; but where there is no objection it is advisable to set out fully the transactions of the company, as the more detail that is afforded to the shareholders in the accounts, the less responsibility is attached to the officials. Wherever a trading account is not published, the revenue account, will, of course, merely commence with the balance from the trading account; this is the gross profit, and here again the advisability of condensing the items of expenditure into as few headings as possible, or setting them forth fully, has for the same reasons to be considered.

Mortgaged Property.

The question as to how to deal in the Accounts with items representing property encumbered by mortgages and the personal accounts of the mortgagees is frequently a subject of argument. There can be no doubt that the strictly proper way in stating these items in a balance sheet is to place the amount standing at the credit of the mortgagees in short on the liability side of the balance sheet, stating there, also in short,

Lecture II.

the value of the property, and bringing in on the credit side the estimated surplus value of the property after paying off the debts. It is wrong to place the values of any encumbered property among the free assets, without a distinct reference, either immediately after them or in a footnote, that they are hypothecated. This practice is not, however, so objectionable when there is a reserve or reserve fund exceeding in amount the secured loans.

Accounts must be passed by Directors.

The revenue account and balance sheet, having been finally settled, should be placed by the secretary before a board meeting of the directors, a reference being made in the agenda book, and also in the notice convening the meeting, that part of the business is to consider these statements. Should any of the directors, either on their own initiation or prompted by any other official of the company, object to these statements as being, perhaps, too severely drawn, the secretary should use all his influence to prevent any alterations, and if finally the directors alter them to an extent with which he may not be satisfied, he should place in writing a record of his objections, so as to relieve himself of any responsibility in the future.

Then handed to Auditors.

The Accounts, having been approved by the board, should then be signed by them, and countersigned by the secretary, and then handed formally to the Auditors. There is, of course, no objection, and indeed it is preferable, for the secretary to see the Auditors on the proposed Accounts, and take their advice on any points before finally settling them for the directors. This will save, perhaps, considerable trouble afterwards.

Duty of Officials to assist Auditors.

It is the duty of the secretary and the other officials of a company to assist the Auditors in every way during the conduct of their audit; they should, also, unless absolutely impossible, arrange for the Auditors to have a room to themselves, as it is exceedingly inconvenient to Auditors to have to work where other clerks are engaged. It is also troublesome for Auditors to be interfered with in the course of the audit. Many secretaries, in their desire to be attentive, are frequently very troublesome in continually pressing their explanations and offers of assistance on the Auditors, who do their work best when left alone, and when they only come in contact with the officials in reply to a special request for information or assistance. On receiving the Accounts back from the Auditors with their certificate, the same should be immediately printed and dealt with according to the Articles of Association. If the Auditors make a report to the shareholders it should, of course, be printed and circulated to the shareholders with the Accounts and certificate, but should it be addressed to the directors, it may be either for their private information or else intended to be read to the shareholders at the meeting, in accordance with whatever request the Auditors may make when the report is forwarded.

The Accounts are always formally submitted to the general meeting of shareholders, and in order to be able to answer any questions which may be put by shareholders the secretary should have sufficient details by his side and some of the principal books of account. On the adoption of the Accounts his responsibility is at an end, although there can be little doubt that before long every company will be required to file a copy of their Accounts with the Registrar of Joint Stock Companies. At present, however, there is not any obligation on the Secretary to do so.

LECTURE III.

AUDITING.

Read before the Chartered Accountants' Students' Society of London 8th May, 1883.

Lecture III.

Auditing the principal professional work of a Chartered Accountant.

In every profession varied duties are undertaken by its members, but on examination it will be found they are all offshoots of one which forms the mainstay of the professional work.

The members of the profession among whom you aspire to enroll your names are called upon to undertake positions of great public responsibility and trust, and the true reason for their selection for these offices is their knowledge of auditing, as the investigation of Books of Account is now styled, the particular branch of our professional work upon which I have the honour of addressing you this evening. In addition to our acting as the Auditors of the Accounts of private individuals, of firms, and of public companies, we are now naturally selected for the offices of Arbitrators, Receivers, and Liquidators in the Chancery Division of the High Court of Justice, and Trustees in bankruptcy, and the only reason there can be for selecting us for these responsible positions is that our experience as Auditors renders us familiar with the intricacies of Accounts, with which those who hold the above offices are in nearly every instance called upon to deal.

Amateur Auditors.

Until within the last few years the only qualification

for an Auditor of the Accounts of a joint stock company was the holding of shares in the undertaking, and he was usually a friend of one of the directors, who recommended him as being willing to subscribe for one or more shares on condition of his receiving the appointment. Having been thus chosen by the board, the Auditor was almost certain to retain his appointment, as the shareholders seldom took the trouble to question his fitness for the office, his duties being looked upon as merely nominal. Lecture III.

The result.

A rude awakening, however, came upon both directors and shareholders. Companies, whose financial position was looked upon as beyond the slightest suspicion, fell with a crash which startled both the commercial and the social world, and on examination it was found that the revenue accounts which had been periodically presented, authorising large dividends, and balance sheets showing ample assets to meet the liabilities, together with reserve funds, rested on no proper foundation, and were merely prepared to look well before the shareholders and the public. It is true these Accounts had been audited, but who could blame an Auditor who never pretended to have any special qualifications for the duties entrusted to him beyond what were supposed to be possessed by every other shareholder, many of whom would have been willing to have accepted the appointment should a vacancy have occurred.

Companies Act, 1862.

The Companies Act of 1862, under which by far the greater number of companies now existing have been registered, does not require the Accounts of companies to be audited unless they are registered without Articles of Association, when certain clauses in the first schedule, usually known as Table "A," which provide that the Accounts shall be audited, come into force. This seems a curious omission, as this Act was passed seventeen years after the Companies Clauses Act, 1845, which

Lecture III.

governs all companies incorporated by a special Act of Parliament, and contains many clauses relating to the appointment of Auditors and the audit of Accounts; but the great blot as regards the subject on which I am now treating is that it compels the shareholders to select the Auditor from among their own body. There are many objections to this: First, unless a professional Accountant either happens to be a member, or is willing to qualify himself by taking at least one share, the shareholders may be compelled to appoint a thoroughly incompetent person; and, in the second place, I think you will all agree with me that no interested person should be appointed to any position which demands the strictest impartiality. Where an Auditor is interested in a company as a shareholder it may often be to his personal disadvantage to act in accordance with what he knows is his duty as the representative of his brother members. If he considers the accounts are too favourably presented, and he has a large holding, he knows that, in the event of his objecting to the Accounts and having them altered to suit his own views, his own property may be seriously depreciated. On the other hand, he may be tempted to pass without comment a too favourable revenue account and balance sheet, in order that his property may be materially increased, or, at any rate, not decreased, in value.

Objections to Auditor being a Shareholder.

Under the Regulation of Railways Act, 1868, it is specially enacted the Auditors of Railway Companies need not be shareholders, notwithstanding the fact that they are subject to the Companies Clauses Act, 1845, and, as a consequence, the Shareholder-Auditor of Railway Companies has been gradually replaced by the Chartered Accountant.

Auditors of Railway Companies need not be Shareholders.

This was a step in the right direction. No man ought to be placed in any judicial position when he is an interested party, and it is to be hoped that in any future

Lecture III.

Act that may be passed relating to companies of every description a clause may be inserted that no person who is a shareholder shall be eligible for the appointment of Auditor. It is, of course, proper that the directors should hold shares, as the larger their holding the more interested they will be in looking after their own interests, which are identical with those of the shareholders, by giving careful attention to the management.

Knowledge of Book-keeping essential.

I will not deal with the training of an Auditor, as the Institute of Chartered Accountants has prescribed the nature of the examinations which you will have to pass before obtaining your certificates; but of the many subjects you have to study the theory and practice of Book-keeping is above all others the most important, and the one you should thoroughly comprehend and master in every detail. A knowledge, however, of book-keeping is not the only qualification an Auditor should possess. It is merely the foundation on which his training is based, as it does not by any means follow that a most accomplished book-keeper, and one able to keep the Accounts of a large banking and mercantile firm, is capable of effectually auditing the books of a small retail business. The duties of a book-keeper are confined to recording the financial transactions, and his skill can go no higher than performing these operations in a manner which combines the highest accuracy with the simplest method, the least possible labour, and the least possible consumption of time.

An Auditor, on the other hand, is a critic of the book-keeper's work, and in some cases also a check upon his employers, for it is not only the Auditor's duty to verify the Accounts of the book-keeper, but also to endeavour to satisfy himself that the book-keeper has received full and proper information of the transactions of the business, and that they are duly entered in the books.

Lecture III.

Preliminary duties.

Previous to commencing an audit, the Auditor should thoroughly comprehend the nature of his responsibilities with regard to that particular audit. Where he is acting for one or a few persons, who tell him to take certain things for granted, and merely make a partial investigation, such as putting into proper shape the Accounts presented to him, or ascertaining that the statements as prepared by the Accountant or book-keeper are correct, his responsibilities are very light as compared with those he is under when he is called upon to audit Accounts on behalf of a number of persons who do not give him any particular instructions, but leave entirely in his hands the decision as to what may be necessary he should inquire into on their behalf. Audits of the Accounts of private individuals or firms come principally under the first class of audits, while those of the Accounts of public companies, where the Auditor acts for the general body of shareholders, as also where he is investigating Accounts on behalf of Executors or Trustees for the parties interested under a will, come under the latter.

Appointment of Auditor.

In the case of firms, the Auditor usually receives his instructions at an interview with one or more of the partners.

In the case of companies, his appointment rests in the first place with the directors, but subsequently with the shareholders, who elect him at their annual general meetings. When a new company is formed, it is now the practice for the directors to insert the names of Auditors in the prospectus, and their appointment is usually confirmed by the shareholders; but no matter from whom the Auditor receives his appointment, he must always remember that he is acting on behalf of the general body of shareholders, who are, therefore, his clients. An Auditor, by allowing his name to be placed upon the prospectus of a new company, does not, of course, render himself liable for any statement there may be in the prospectus unless such refer to him personally. The promoters, the directors, and the solicitors are, of course, responsible for the statements, but the Auditor's name on the prospectus merely notifies the fact that he is the person selected by the directors to audit the Accounts when they are placed before him for that purpose.

Responsibility in connection with new Companies.

As to whether an Auditor should allow his name to be placed on the prospectus of a company where he has reason to believe it is not promoted with *bonâ fide* intentions is a matter fairly open to discussion. By some it will undoubtedly be argued that a Chartered Accountant ought not to allow his name to be connected with any company until he is perfectly satisfied that everybody connected with it is thoroughly respectable, and that the expectations of those who invest their money have at least a fair chance of being realised, as his name may induce clients and others who have confidence in him to invest in the company's shares. Others may contend that, as Auditors, by allowing their names to be placed on the prospectus, do not in any way make themselves responsible for anything beyond the fact that they intend to investigate the Accounts when called upon to do so, it is their duty to allow their names to be placed indiscriminately on any prospectus that may be placed before them, so that should there be anything wrong in the Accounts as submitted to the members they may be able to expose the fraud. I am myself strongly of opinion Chartered Accountants should not have their names associated at all with unsound schemes, and I recommend you in your future careers to be very jealous of your professional reputation, and to be exceedingly careful not to allow your name to be made use of in connection with any enterprise until you are satisfied that it is launched *bonâ fide*.

Lecture III.

Legal knowledge required by Auditor.

Before commencing the actual examination of any Accounts in which more than one person is interested, the Auditor should make himself familiar with the legal position of his clients towards each other in the business the Accounts of which he is to investigate. In the case of a private partnership, he should peruse the articles of partnership; before investigating the Accounts of executors or trustees, he will be guided by the will, together with any codicils attached thereto; while in the case of a public company, the public Acts of Parliament relating to companies, taken in conjunction with either the private Acts of Parliament of the company, or, in the case of a limited company, the Memorandum and Articles of Association, or the first schedule of the Companies Act, 1862, already referred to as Table "A," will be his guide.

Articles of Association of Companies.

The Memorandum and Articles of Association of a company show an Auditor the nature and amount of the capital authorised and the classes of shares into which it is divided, also the powers of the directors as to its issue, the extent of the loans, mortgages, and debentures, and the regulations controlling the directors in respect of them, also the business authorised to be carried on by the directors, and the remuneration they are authorised to draw from the funds of the company for their services. There are also, as a rule, special clauses relating to Accounts and audit which require the special attention of an Auditor.

Public Acts of Parliament.

Chartered Accountants are, of course, supposed to be acquainted with the public Acts of Parliament bearing upon any of their professional duties, especially with the clauses relating to the Books of Account and the duties of Auditors, and before commencing his duties as an Auditor the Chartered Accountant should also peruse the articles of partnership, the will, the private Act of Parliament, or the Articles of Association

Lecture III.

of the company, as the case may be, and he should take notes of any clauses affecting the preparation of the Accounts, the manner in which they are to be presented, and any special duties laid upon the Auditor. Where he finds anything unusual he should take a careful note. And here it will not be out of place to strongly impress upon you the desirability of making careful notes of anything that may come under your observation during an audit which is not perfectly clear or satisfactory. Notes taken during an audit should be recorded systematically, and in such a manner that both the queries raised and the answers given can be referred to at a later period, in case an explanation be required as to any matter relating to the audit.

Auditor should make careful Notes.

Private Audits.

It is impossible to prescribe any fixed rules as to the manner in which an audit should be proceeded with, because in nearly every case they vary according to circumstances. Demands made by an Auditor which to one of his clients would be particularly pleasing, might in another instance be looked upon as an unwarrantable assumption of authority and an unnecessary interference. The general principle of an audit, when conducted on behalf of private individuals or partners, is that the Auditor investigates Accounts on behalf of the proprietor or proprietors of the business who have neither the time, the inclination, nor the ability to do so for themselves; he should understand his instructions clearly, and should inform his client what will be the result of their being carried out. If, in the Auditor's opinion, they are not sufficient, he should make that clear to his client, and point out what risks he may be under through not having the work done more completely. It is desirable in both interests that this should be clearly understood at the commencement of the audit, so that there may be afterwards no ground for complaint by the client that a sufficiently searching

Lecture III. investigation has not been made, or, on the other hand, that more has been done than the client intended, and consequently a heavier expense incurred than he is willing to pay.

Public Audits.

Where an Auditor is acting on behalf of partners who, on appointing him, do not give him any instructions—such as, for example, in the case of the appointment of the Auditor of a public company, as also in the case of executors or trustees—then his responsibilities are very great, as he is, of course, relied upon for the accuracy of the Accounts in every particular, his clients looking to him to protect their interests in every possible way. An Auditor of a company, however, although entrusted with the fullest powers, must always remember that he is in no sense responsible for the acts of the directors, managers, or *employés* of the company. The directors of a company are solely answerable to the shareholders for the management, and it is the duty of the Auditor merely to see that the results of the transactions as carried on under the superintendence of the directors are properly placed before the shareholders in the Accounts submitted to them. It is, however, quite within his province if, in his opinion, a certain class of transactions are not likely to conduce to the prosperity of the company, to point this out to the directors, and also to call their attention to any faulty system in the book-keeping, and to suggest improvements.

Auditor of assistance to Directors.

An Auditor has it thus very often in his power to prove of great assistance to the directors, by bringing to their notice matters of this sort which might otherwise escape their attention, and in this way he also benefits his clients. He must, however, remember that he has no power to enforce his views on the directors, nor interfere in any way with the management, except by making these suggestions in a friendly spirit.

Details of an Audit.

Having perused the private Acts of Parliament,

the Articles of Association, the articles of partnership, or the testator's will, as the case may be, the Auditor should then make himself familiar with the method to which the general principles of book-keeping are adapted for recording the particular transactions, the Accounts relating to which he is investigating, and he then proceeds with the practical part of his duties. As most of you are aware, the details of an audit are in the offices of Chartered Accountants performed by clerks, under superintendence, the principals devoting themselves more particularly to seeing that the statements which result from the book-keeping are properly drawn and represent all that they profess to do. It need scarcely be said that the greatest attention must be paid to performing every detail of an audit, and the most mechanical operation, namely, the checking, which is usually performed by one clerk calling over to another, requires the greatest care, as the slightest inaccuracy may often make it necessary for the whole of the checking to be done over again.

Errors in checking Books.

One of the most common sources of error in this respect is when an entry which ought to be posted to the debit has been posted to the credit, or *vice versâ*. A clerk who is only paying attention to the figures, and is not careful to see that every item called out to him is posted to the right side of the account, frequently passes a mistake of this nature and ticks it as correct. Every item thus passed creates an error of double the amount. Where the audit fee is fixed, it makes it far less profitable if the calling over has to be done twice, or possibly more times, and where the work is paid for by time it unduly swells the bill, and is as unsatisfactory to the client as it is to an honest Auditor.

Should the Auditor, in checking postings from one account to another, or from one book to another, notice any figures altered, crossed out, or written over an

Lecture III. erasure, he should endeavour to verify the correctness from some independent source, such as an invoice, a cheque, or counterfoil of a receipt book, and regard it with suspicion until he is satisfied of its correctness.

Audit of Cash Book.

In his examination of the cash book, the income side must be checked from the most independent source the Auditor can find available, for example, the counterfoils of receipt books, the pass books of a bank, although, of course, in this instance he can only attempt a few test cases, or a rough cash book; while the items on the credit or payment side can be checked with vouchers, and although this is a mere mechanical process, still it ought to be performed very carefully, and in many cases the vouchers form the only clue as to whether an item in the cash book has been posted to the correct account in the ledger.

Arrangement of Vouchers.

The Auditor, has, of course, a right to require that the vouchers should be handed to him in a proper manner, such as in a guard book, or so filed that they may come to his hand in the order in which they are entered in the cash book. They should consist of actual receipts, and, with the exception of those made by bills payable, the payments to merchants or tradesmen should be vouched by proper receipted accounts. In some cases endorsements on cheques may be accepted, especially where crossed "not negotiable," as then there can be no doubt that they have been paid to the persons represented on the face of the cheques.

Vouching.

In vouching purchases the Auditor may find it necessary to call for the original invoices where not attached to the receipts; for bills payable paid, the cancelled bills should be produced to him. When payments have been made to builders or others on account of a contract, the certificate of the architect or engineer authorising the payment should be asked for. In manufacturing accounts, where wages form a heavy item in the expenditure, the wages sheets should be signed by the clerk who makes up the sheet, the clerk who checks it, the official who pays the wages, and the manager or other official who is responsible for the payments. I mention these as examples, experience alone can decide an Auditor as to what proof he may require when vouching.

Lecture III.

Reconciliation of Cash Book balances with Banker's Ledger.

The balance as it appears in the cash book should be reconciled with the balance as shown in the banker's pass book. It is seldom they are identical, as cheques drawn on or before the day on which the books are closed may not have been presented for payment; neither will the bankers, unless a special arrangement has been made with them, have given credit for country cheques not cleared on that day. A reconciliation statement should, therefore, be prepared, and either entered in the cash book or given to the Auditor in a proper form to place amongst his own papers.

Trial Balance.

An Auditor must use his own discretion, guided by his experience, as to how far it may be necessary to check the details found in the subsidiary books. He should, however, make as much use as possible of documents obtained from independent sources, to guard against omissions. The checking being completed, and the cash book vouched, the balances of the ledgers are then checked into what is technically called the "Trial balance," from which the revenue account and balance sheet are prepared. At this point the duties of Auditors vary. In some cases, such as that of a company, the trial balance is given them, also the revenue account and balance sheet. In other cases they take out and agree the figures of the trial balance, and prepare the statement referred to, either for the partners, the executors, or the private client, as the case may be. It is far preferable for the Auditor to prepare his own statements, if his clients are willing he should do so, as

Lecture III. he can then draft them in any form he pleases, whereas where the accounts are submitted to him already prepared he may have to certify them, when, perhaps, he may not approve of the form, but as there may be nothing actually wrong in them he cannot object to append his certificate.

Special Statements.

When acting for a firm an Auditor usually prepares, in addition to a revenue account and balance sheet, the capital accounts of each of the partners, while in the preparation or audit of executorship accounts he usually prepares a statement showing the position of the testator at the date of his death and statements showing the position of the separate trusts created by the will. Occasionally the revenue or profit and loss account and balance sheet of a company are accompanied by a cash account, while sometimes, but now in rare instances, the cash account is substituted for the revenue account. When a cash account alone accompanies a balance sheet, shareholders are very apt to suppose it is a revenue account, and the Auditor should be careful to prevent their falling into such a mistake.

Difference between Revenue and Cash Accounts.

The difference between a revenue and a cash account is that the former shows the results of the transactions for the period, and beyond making due provision for bad and doubtful debts does not take into consideration whether contracts have been settled or not; while on the other hand the cash account is merely an abstract of the cash book, and it is, therefore, very easy for an account of this nature to be made as favourable as possible by not paying accounts due by the company until after the close of the period under audit, and on the other hand by collecting as much money as possible, and for this purpose even allowing extraordinary and improper discounts, so as to obtain payments before the date on which the books are closed.

Auditors and Dividends.

An Auditor should, of course, be careful not to sanction the payment of a dividend declared on the strength of a favourable balance of a cash account, but should in all cases require a revenue or profit and loss account to be prepared before the declaration of a dividend, although such statement may not be issued to the shareholders. It is nothing, however, to the Auditor of a company whether dividends are properly or improperly declared, provided he discharges his own duty to the shareholders. His business is to determine and state the true financial position of the company at the date to which the accounts are made up, and whether the balance of profit shown has been, in his opinion, fairly earned.

Profit and Loss Account of Trading Companies.

In the case of a trading company the best form of profit and loss account is one divided into three parts, the first showing the gross profit on the difference between buying and selling, the second part showing how this gross profit, after charging it with the profit and loss items, has resulted in a net profit or a net loss, while in the third part should be put the balance brought from the previous profit and loss account, the balance of the second part of the statement, and the dividend or bonus declared, if any, while the balance of this third part will then be carried into the balance sheet.

In the case of a non-trading company the first and second part of the revenue account will be included in one. By means of a revenue account prepared in the above manner shareholders are enabled to see in what the trading or business of the period has actually resulted, and whether, in the event of a dividend being declared, it has been earned out of the profits of the period, or taken partly or wholly out of the balance of the undivided profit brought forward from the previous accounts.

In examining a revenue or profit and loss account the Auditor should ascertain whether it is properly

Lecture III. charged with all the expenses incidental to earning the income taken credit for. When the client has not been successful during the period embraced by the audit, the revenue account is often prepared on too favourable a basis, and items which ought to be properly included on the debtor or charge side of the account are frequently carried to a suspense account, and thus included amongst the items on the credit side of the balance sheet.

Auditor's Report.

In the case of a firm the Auditor should draw the attention of the partners to any items which he thinks ought to be charged against revenue, and suggest their being thus treated. If this proposal be not carried out, he should protect himself in a report on the Accounts, and clearly point out that the partners have not sufficiently charged the revenue account, in consequence of which it would be unwise for them to divide as profits the amount assumed to be such in the statements so prepared.

In the case of a company the Auditor should be specially firm, as the correctness of the revenue account, including the sufficiency of the amounts to be written off for depreciation, is most certainly a question affecting him and his duty, it not being solely one of management, and he can very justly be blamed by the shareholders if he passes without comment accounts in which the revenue is not properly charged with all the outgoings incidental to the period embraced by the audit.

Allowance for loss on realisation of Debts.

For example, an Auditor should be satisfied that a proper provision is made for probable loss on the realisation of what may be considered bad and doubtful debts. For this purpose he should go through the schedule of the debtors, and where any of them are beyond a certain age he should inquire the reason why they have not been paid, and, if the answer be not satisfactory, he should include such items in an amount to be entirely or partly charged against the revenue account, the balance left, which would appear on the credit side of the balance sheet, being in his opinion the amount which will be ultimately realised. Unless due provision be made periodically for bad and doubtful debts, there will appear on the credit side of successive balance sheets an increasing amount due from debtors to the company, which will ultimately provoke comment, and on the true value of this outstanding amount ascertained, it may be found on writing this asset down to its real value that the difference absorbs a part or the whole of the net profits, which should properly be taken credit for in the period under audit, and that consequently a dividend cannot be declared.

Leasehold Investments.

The Auditor should also be satisfied that a proper amount has been written off any leases his client may hold, and charged against the revenue account, so that the balance standing in the ledger to the credit of the leases Account or Accounts may represent their proper value at the date of the balance sheet. This remark applies whether the leasehold premises are those on which a business is carried on, or whether they are held as an investment. In the latter case the rents received should be included amongst the income in the revenue account after the deduction of the incidental expenses connected therewith. When leasehold premises belong to a company for the purpose of carrying on in them its own business, the proportion written off and charged against revenue is equivalent, of course, to a rent paid, and should be treated accordingly.

Repairs and Renewals.

All amounts expended for renewals and repairs should be charged against the revenue or profit and loss account. There are, however, two ways at least of treating items of expenditure of this description. In some cases all amounts expended on renewals and repairs to plant, premises, &c., are added to the capital

Lecture III

accounts in the ledgers, and a percentage is periodically written off the balance and charged against the income. In other cases no addition is made to these ledger accounts except for actual purchases, and the whole expenditure incurred in maintenance or keeping it in a state of efficiency is charged against the revenue account. In my opinion the latter plan is the preferable.

Stock-in-Trade.

In all trading concerns the value of the stock in hand at the commencement and end of the period under audit is brought into the trading or revenue account. An Auditor is not, of course, responsible for the accuracy of this item, but he should inquire into the method on which the stock has been taken and priced, and require a certificate of its accuracy from one or more responsible officials, and by testing some of the prices where possible with original invoices, or in some other way, satisfy himself that the amount taken credit for at the end of the period is correct. The stock at the beginning of the period is of course inserted in a trading account at the same value as it was taken credit for in the previous balance sheet, and should it have been discovered in the interval that it was then incorrectly stated the difference should be either added to or deducted from that Account on the face of the following accounts, so that the figures can be checked on comparing the two revenue accounts. It is, of course, impossible in a lecture of this nature to discuss in detail the various items of expenditure which can be brought under the notice of Auditors in their investigations of profit and loss or revenue accounts. I will simply repeat that this statement should show the actual profit or loss of the period embraced by the accounts, and this it will not do unless every item of expenditure be properly charged against the revenue taken credit for.

Balance Sheet.

The balance sheet, frequently erroneously referred

to as the statement of assets and liabilities, contains, in the case of a company, amongst its liabilities its shareholders' capital, and in the case of a firm the capital of the partners, and there is no doubt the more correct form of preparing this statement is to divide it into two parts, the first part showing the assets and the amounts due to every description of creditors, while the balance, showing what is the value of the assets after providing for these outstanding liabilities, should be brought into the second part.

The second part will then consist solely of the shareholders' or partners' capital on the liabilities side, with the balance of the assets, after paying the outstanding liabilities and the other debtor balances of the ledgers, on the other side. The shareholders or partners would then distinctly see whether they were solvent or otherwise, and in the latter case how much in the pound they were worth. This method of preparing a balance sheet is, however, contrary to the usual practice, and is merely suggested as my own idea as to the best form. You must, of course, understand that any particular form for a revenue account or balance sheet can only be suggested by an Auditor, as he has no power to require Accounts to be presented as he may wish, except in those cases where the forms are prescribed by Act of Parliament, or by some authority in accordance with the provisions of an Act.

Forms of Accounts prescribed by Act of Parliament.

In the case of railway, gas, water, and life assurance companies the forms of Accounts are prescribed, as are also those for societies registered under the Friendly Societies Acts and the Building Societies Acts; but in the majority of companies, namely, those registered under the Companies Act, 1862, the directors are allowed to present Accounts in any form they may please, except in the case of companies to which Table "A" applies, for which a special form of balance sheet is prescribed, and

Lecture III.

in the case of a few companies where special directions are given in the Articles of Association.

Debts due from Directors and Officials.

The only special point calling for notice in the balance sheet prescribed by Table "A" is that any debt due from the directors or other officials of the company is to be separately stated on the credit side. With the exception of the companies just referred to, the Auditor is obliged to accept the accounts in any form the directors may think proper to place before him; but, on the other hand, any suggestions he may make are likely to receive attention, for the directors are aware that although the Auditor has no authority to prescribe the form of Accounts, except as already stated, still he has a power which can keep in check a board of directors, however unwilling they may be to fall in with his views, namely that of making a special report to the shareholders. In strict accordance with Table "A" already referred to, and with the clauses usually contained in Articles of Association, directors of a company are required to furnish the Auditor with the balance sheets and accounts as they propose to present them to the shareholders, and he can return them with a certificate thereon refusing to vouch their correctness, and make any remarks he may think proper, and the directors are bound to place the accounts before the shareholders with this certificate.

Duty of Directors of Companies to furnish Accounts to Auditors.

Not the universal practice.

Such a course, however, is not in accordance with practice and would be most unusual; in fact, I have never yet heard of the letter of the Act being so strictly adhered to. It is the recognised practice amongst Chartered Accountants, that where an Auditor disapproves of the Accounts submitted to him, he either sees the chairman or manager, or addresses a letter to them on the subject of the accounts, suggesting alterations which he thinks it advisable to make. These suggestions are usually carefully considered, and if not at once acquiesced in are discussed in a businesslike manner with the Auditor. It frequently happens that after a conference of this nature the Auditor is satisfied with the reasons or explanations offered by the directors, in which case he would withdraw his objections. But should he, after hearing the explanations, consider they are not satisfactory, and the directors absolutely refuse to agree with the Auditor's request, the latter is very often in a position of great difficulty, for the shareholders are his clients, and anything that may damage the reputation of the company must necessarily be injurious to their interests.

Disagreement between Directors and Auditors.

It is impossible, however, to lay down rules as to what course should be taken in the event of a disagreement between an Auditor and the board. It is only experience that can teach this, but the Auditor should remember he has a two-fold duty, that towards the shareholders, and that towards himself. He must protect the shareholders as much as possible, and at the same time he must have regard to his own character and reputation.

Auditor does not guarantee accuracy.

An Auditor of a company, however, is not bound to do more than exercise reasonable care and skill in making inquiries and investigations. He is not an insurer, he does not guarantee that the books do correctly show the true position of the company's affairs, he does not even guarantee that his balance sheet is accurate according to the books of the company. If he did, he would be responsible for error on his part, even if he were himself deceived, without any want of reasonable care on his part, say, by the fraudulent concealment of a book from him. His obligation is not so onerous as this. He must be honest, that is, he must not certify what he does not believe to be true, and he must take reasonable care and skill before he believes that what he certifies is true.

Lecture III.

Company holding its own Shares.

Should a company, whether its shares are fully paid-up or not, hold any of its own shares as an investment, it should be clearly shown in the balance sheet, as in the latter case the shareholders would not be fully aware of the extent of their liability in the event of the company going into liquidation. Should this happen, the shareholders would be liable in proportion to their holding to pay the amount which would otherwise be raised by payments on these shares were they in the hands of private owners, in addition to having to meet the calls on their own shares, and, moreover, it is illegal in any case for a company to hold its own shares.

Auditors should not accept Pass Books as proof of balances.

It is now not the practice for Auditors of a company to be satisfied with reconciling the balance as shown in the cash book with that of the banker's pass book, and in order to guard against any fraud he either calls on the bankers of the company, informing them of his position, and requesting them to show him their ledger account with the company, or else he addresses a letter to the bankers to the same effect. In either case the bankers usually require an authority from a director or the manager. Instances have been known of cashiers having kept duplicate pass books, and this, of course, can only be found out by application to the bankers.

Items in Balance Sheets representing expenditure.

In the balance sheets of nearly all companies are to be found, included on the credit side amongst the assets, balances of expenditure accounts which cannot be said to be represented by realisable assets. Such, for example, are the amounts paid for the goodwill of a business, preliminary or formation expenses of a company, establishment of agencies, &c. In the event of the company going into liquidation it is evident that these items in the balance sheet will not turn out to be realisable assets, and it is therefore desirable, at any rate in some instances, to extinguish these Accounts, either gradually or by charging

Preliminary Expenses.

the whole amount against the revenue of the first year. In the case of preliminary expenses, a certain amount should be charged against the revenue account say, for the first three, or five, or ten years at the most, until this balance disappears. Where plant, machinery, or property of any description is purchased under a hiring agreement, that is an agreement in which it is provided that after the lessee has paid a rent for the use of the article for a certain number of years, it shall become his absolute property on payment of a nominal sum at the expiration of the period, a company is entitled to take credit in its balance sheet for a proportionate part, after charging the revenue account with a fair and reasonable amount for wear and tear during the period under audit.

Inspection of Securities.

Having finally settled the form of balance sheet of a company, society, or public institution, the securities should be inspected by the Auditor, previous to which he should be supplied with a proper schedule dividing them into their various classes. When freehold or leasehold property forms part of the assets, the deeds should be produced, and also receipts for the last premiums on policies of insurance of perishable property.

Where a company holds stock, shares, or debentures, they should be counted; and, in the case of bonds to bearer, the Auditor should see that the coupons next due and those up to the date of repayment of the bond are attached, also any that may be overdue but which have not been paid.

Investments.

The investments of a company or public institution should stand in the names of the trustees, where there are properly appointed trustee; should there be none, then in the name of two or more of the directors or council, but investments should not stand in the names of a manager or secretary alone.

Should the securities be in the custody of the

Lecture III. bankers, and it is not stated in the Accounts that they are held as security for a loan, the Auditor should be careful to ascertain that this is the fact.

In the case of private Audits an Auditor only inspects securities representing investments when instructed to do so by his client, but when auditing the Accounts of executors he should inspect the securities or else report that he has not done so.

Audit of a Company having Branches.

Where a company has branches it is impossible, of course, for the Auditor to make such a thorough investigation as where all the records of the business are kept in one office. The returns must be examined, and the Auditor must ascertain that they are properly amalgamated with the books kept at the head office. In giving his certificate he should be careful to certify the correctness of the Accounts, subject to the returns from the branches representing accurately the transactions of their particular business.

Auditor's Report.

Having completed his investigation, the Auditor, in the case of a private client, addresses a letter or report explaining the Accounts. In the case of a company, society, or institution he has to append his certificate to the Accounts. If he make a report to the directors on any matter on which he considers the shareholders should be informed, he should be careful to intimate in his certificate that such report exists, so that the shareholders may ask for it at the meeting, should the directors not print a copy of it and forward it to the shareholders with the Accounts.

Concluding Remarks.

It has been my endeavour in the foregoing remarks to give an outline of the general principles of an audit and the duties of an Auditor, more especially of those of an Auditor of a company, without going into those details which can only be acquired by experience; but I trust I have made it evident that auditing is accompanied with many responsibilities, and that before anyone undertakes the duties he should be carefully trained.

The Chartered Accountants' Students' Society of London has been formed for the express purpose of assisting those who are desirous of acquiring, amongst other technical accomplishments, a knowledge of these duties; and, in conclusion, I hope that the few words I have addressed to you this evening may contribute in a small way towards the furtherance of the Society's aim.

LECTURE IV.

AUDITING.

Read before the Chartered Accountants' Students' Society of London 25th October, 1887.

Lecture IV.

Reference to the preceding Lecture.

Having already lectured to this Society on the subject of auditing, I naturally referred to my last paper in order to avoid repetition; but it is, of course, quite impossible to give a fresh address on auditing without going over the same ground to a certain extent. It is also impossible in a lecture to give more than a general idea of an audit and the principles which should guide an Auditor in his duties, as of course every business varies from other businesses, both in the manner of conduct and in the manner of recording the result of the transactions. My remarks, however, in the course of this lecture will apply to any audit, and it is only experience which can show how the various books of account should be checked, and the statements of accounts arrived at, which it is the duty of the Auditors to examine.

Knowledge of Auditing essential for many duties.

Auditing forms the main portion of the duties of Chartered Accountants, for although various matters are transacted in their offices which do not bear this name, still they nevertheless come under this branch of the profession. For example: investigation of accounts of every description; the majority of the work connected with the office of liquidators of companies, trusteeships in bankruptcy; reporting upon the accounts of executors and trustees of the estates of deceased persons; giving evidence as expert or qualified witnesses, or acting generally in compensation cases, and in many other matters before the Courts, all require a knowledge of auditing. It may, therefore, be said that it is the mainstay of a Chartered Accountant's practice.

Until within the last few years, the only qualifications for the appointment of Auditor to a joint stock company was the holding of a certain number of shares—at least one—in the undertaking. Appointments were made without reference to any other qualification, and therefore, if he desired to act as Auditor when a vacancy occurred, one of the largest shareholders would be appointed; but the revelations which have been made in the Courts of the results of this kind of auditing has so startled the financial world that the amateur Auditor is fast dying out.

It is not necessary for me to discuss the training which is required for an Auditor, this being prescribed by the Institute of Chartered Accountants, and you have all of you no doubt in your possession the list of subjects which are required for the various examinations.

Book-keeping.

The only one of these subjects with which I am at all concerned in this lecture is that one with which I presume you are all thoroughly acquainted, the principle and practice of book-keeping, for without this knowledge it would of course be absurd to attempt auditing, which is the object of ascertaining whether the accounts kept by others are or are not correct.

Audits divided into two classes.

Audits may be divided into two classes: the first, where the Auditor performs the work at the request of a client who gives certain directions as to the nature of the audit required, which the Auditor carries out, his responsibility being limited to ascertaining that the accounts are in accordance with the instructions of his

Lecture IV. client, and prepared in the form required by him. Such, for example, are the accounts of individuals, either of their trade or their private accounts, or of firms engaged in business. The second class includes those audits where the duties are defined, either by Act of Parliament or by general custom; such, for example, as of public companies, of executors or trustees of deceased persons' estates, and of all matters generally where capital is invested not under the entire control of the parties interested.

Private Audits. In the first case, the responsibility of the Auditor is limited by his instructions—if his clients say they only require a partial audit and wish him to take certain entries for granted, he is of course at liberty to undertake an audit of this sort, and his responsibility is limited. In the other case, his acceptance of the appointment involves the highest responsibility, and he must not allow himself to be influenced in any way by the wishes of the parties giving him instructions, for he has to perform his duties strictly and impartially, having regard to the interest of all the parties concerned.

Before commencing an audit of the first class, the Auditor has merely to request his clients to state distinctly the nature of the audit they require, and then his duty consists merely in verifying the books of account, and either certifying the statement of affairs already prepared in the form approved of by his clients, or else in preparing the accounts himself in the required form.

Public Audits. In audits of the second class, the Auditor must make himself thoroughly acquainted with the legal documents forming the basis upon which the accounts are prepared. For example, in the case of a firm where no special instructions are given to the Auditor, but he is required to make a complete investigation, he must peruse the deed of partnership, making extracts therefrom of all sections referring to the accounts, and his responsibility is the greater in every respect should there be a sleeping partner in the concern, to whom information is only conveyed through the Auditor's report and accounts. In the audit of accounts of executors and trustees the Auditor should peruse the will and codicils (if any), and he should also be acquainted with the general law relating to executors and trustees, more particularly the Apportionment Act of 1870. In the case of accounts of public companies he must be acquainted with the various Companies Acts, and if the company be incorporated under special Act of Parliament he must also be provided with a copy of the special Act. In the case of companies incorporated under the Act of 1862 he must see the Articles of Association, or, if there be none, he is supposed to be acquainted with the first schedule of the Companies Act, 1862, usually known as Table "A," which are the regulations applying to every company registered under that Act not provided with Articles of Association.

Acts of Parliament relating to Auditors.

It is, perhaps, as well to give the various Acts of Parliament relating to the books, accounts, and Auditors of Joint Stock Companies, including those of Building Societies, Friendly Societies, and Industrial and Provident Societies. They are as follows:—

The Companies Act, 1862.
The Companies Act, 1867.
The Companies Act, 1879.
The Companies Act, 1880.
The Companies (Colonial Registers) Act, 1883.

The above Acts refer entirely to what are known as Limited Liability Companies. The Companies (Colonial Registers) Act, of course, as its name implies, refers to those companies who transact business in the Colonies, and gives them power to keep a colonial register or branch register of members resident in the Colonies.

Companies.

The Companies Clauses Consolidation Act, 1845.

Lecture IV.

The Companies Clauses Act, 1863.

The Companies Clauses Act, 1869.

These three Acts refer to companies incorporated by special Act of Parliament, except where their provisions are expressly repealed or varied by either public or private Acts.

Railway Companies.

The Railway Construction Facilities Act, 1864.

The Railway Companies' Securities Act, 1866.

The Railway Companies Act, 1867.

The Railway Companies (Scotland) Act, 1867.

The Regulation of Railways Act, 1868.

The Regulation of Railways Act, 1889.

The above Acts, of course, as their name implies, refer to Railway Companies, and to certain Tramway Companies specially defined in the Acts.

The Stannaries Act, 1869,

The Stannaries Act, 1887,

which refer to mines worked under the jurisdiction of the Court of the Warden of the Stannaries.

Gas and Water Companies.

The Gas Works Clauses Act, 1847.

The Gas Works Clauses Act, 1871.

The Water Works Clauses Act, 1847.

The Metropolis Water Act, 1852.

The Metropolis Water Act, 1871.

Life Assurance, Building and other Societies.

The Life Assurance Companies Act, 1870.

The Building Societies Act, 1874.

The Building Societies Act, 1894.

The Friendly Societies Act, 1875.

The Friendly Societies Management Act, 1876.

The Industrial & Provident Societies Act, 1894.

The Trustee Savings Banks Act, 1863.

The Savings Banks Act, 1891.

The above refer exclusively to companies carrying on the business indicated in the titles of the Acts.

The Auditor should also be acquainted with :—

The Larceny Act, 1861, and

The Falsification of Accounts Act, 1875, which point out the penalties attached to the alteration, mutilating, or falsifying any books or papers, or circulating or publishing any written statement or account known to be false, although I hope that no one present to-night will ever be brought under these penalties.

Knowledge of Mercantile Law essential.

An Auditor is also, of course, supposed to know the general principles of mercantile law, as prescribed in the syllabus of the examination of the Institute.

Having made himself familiar with whichever of these documents applies to his audit, the Auditor must then commence the investigation of the accounts intrusted to him, and in the prosecution of his audit he should be exceedingly systematic in all his steps.

An Auditor has practically to guard himself against three classes of errors:—

Errors of omission.
Errors of commission.
Errors of principle.

Errors of omission.

To guard against errors of omission is really the most difficult part of an Auditor's work. When once an entry has been made in any of the books, it is to a certain extent a mechanical process to see that they are brought forward step by step until the revenue or profit and loss account and balance sheet is reached. But it is exceedingly difficult for an Auditor to ascertain if an entry that ought to have been made in the books has been kept out. Many persons used to contend that this is no part of an Auditor's duty, which is simply confined to ascertaining that the accounts as presented, either to the partners or shareholders of a company, as the case may be, agree with the books of account; but this was taking a very low view of the Auditor's duties, and which I am glad to say never met with favour from respectable practitioners. It is an Auditor's duty to see that the record of the transactions of the business whose accounts

Lecture IV.

are under his investigation show the actual result of the business, and should he have reason to suppose that these have not been properly recorded it is his duty to attempt, by any means in his power, to ascertain whether his surmises are or are not correct, and it is here where an Auditor has an opportuntity of showing his skill, and where experience is of the greatest assistance to him.

The Auditor of a company's accounts does not discharge his duty by merely examining the books of account without inquiry and without taking any trouble to see that the books themselves show the company's true position. He must take reasonable care to ascertain that they do so, otherwise his audit would be useless.

Errors of commission and Errors of principle.

Errors of commission are comparatively easy to detect, while errors of principle are, as a rule, ascertained, if they exist, after the balancing of the books. For example, when the books have been balanced and the statements drawn, it is then the duty of the Auditor to see that they are in accordance with the form prescribed either by law or by custom. In the case of a company the Auditor should ascertain that the authorised capital has not been exceeded, and that the company has not exercised its powers of borrowing beyond those authorised, as cases have occurred where a company has made an over-issue of debentures to the public, and an Auditor would be very rightly blamed if this were not properly reported by him to the shareholders. An Auditor should also ascertain that the funds of the company have not been invested in any securities forbidden by Act of Parliament or its own deed of settlement. In the case of a partnership, and specially where there is a sleeping partner, who looks to the Auditor to protect him, he should ascertain whether the drawings of the partners have exceeded the prescribed sums mentioned in the deed of partnership, whether their capital accounts are in accordance with the deed, and whether any special provisions referred to therein have been properly carried out. In the case of executors and trustees, the Auditor should ascertain whether the legacies have been properly paid, whether the annuitants receive their income, and that the investments are those authorised by the will, or, in the absence of special directions, whether the investments are such as are specially prescribed for trustees by Act of Parliament, and generally that the directions contained in the will of the testator have been carried out.

Auditor should be provided with list of Books.

It is advisable on commencing an audit to have a list of the books of account in use, and, if it be of the accounts of a business, the Auditor should make himself acquainted with its nature, and the system upon which it is conducted. Having done this, he then commences the details of the audit, and here I come to a subject which it is absolutely impossible for me to discuss at length, as although the books of every business are practically kept on the same system they all vary in detail.

The most complete form of audit is really that of a public company, and I will, therefore, confine my remarks as to details to the books of a company.

The same remarks are applicable with slight variation to those of a firm where the Auditor is instructed to make a thorough audit by his clients, but it will not be necessary to go into so much detail where instructions are given to only make a partial audit.

Many private firms, for example, are quite satisfied it the Auditor takes all their entries for granted, and merely require him to prepare therefrom a Profit and Loss Account and Balance Sheet. Frequently the books do not balance, and the Auditor is not even asked

Lecture IV.

to examine them for the purpose of discovering the error.

In the case, however, of a thorough audit, the books should balance exactly, and in order to do this it is frequently necessary for the Auditor to call over the postings from the Cash Book, Day Book, Invoice Book, and Journal to the Ledger for the purpose of discovering where the error lies.

Duty of Directors of a Company to prepare Accounts for Auditors.

In no case, however, is this necessary in the audit of a company's accounts, unless the Auditor is employed independently by the directors to prepare the accounts, as he may require that the books be correctly balanced before they are placed in his hands. The Articles of Association usually prescribe that the accounts to be presented to the shareholders shall be handed to the Auditor, and then he has simply to confirm or reject them within a given number of days. In practice this is seldom done. As a rule the accounts are discussed with the Auditor before being finally settled, and this is more convenient and more desirable in every way, as it might have a very disastrous effect upon the business of a company were the directors to present accounts to the shareholders which would be correct but for a trifling exception, with a comment by the Auditor that they are not perfectly correct.

As already stated it is not the practice for Auditors of a public company to call over the postings into the Ledgers, their correctness are usually taken for granted, but the Auditor must be entirely guided by his experience as to what he may take for granted, in fact anything he does assume to be correct is at his peril.

Vouching Payments.

It is sometimes a little difficult to know what are and what are not genuine vouchers, and sometimes it is impossible for a company to produce a document as a voucher, but the payment may be satisfactorily vouched by the Auditor in a different way. For example: if you know that the salary of a secretary is £300 a year, an Auditor does not require a separate receipt for £25 monthly in order to feel satisfied that the secretary has received his salary. If it is paid by cheque, the cheque can be produced, and if paid out of cash, there is sufficient proof in the absence of any document, even although the official may have left the service of the company before the Auditor commenced his duties.

A list of missing vouchers should be made and handed to the secretary or accountant of the company, with a request that they should be found, followed up by an intimation, if necessary, that the Auditor will not be able to give an unqualified certificate until they are either found or duplicates obtained.

It is no part of an Auditor's duty to reject a voucher on the ground that it does not bear either an impressed or an adhesive stamp, he is not an official appointed for such a purpose, and if he be satisfied that the payment has been properly made he should accept the voucher as evidence of payment.

Vouching Receipts.

To guard against omissions on the receipt side of the cash book is a matter of great difficulty. Fortunately, accounts are seldom presented to Auditors intentionally falsified in this respect, but should an Auditor have reason to believe that the receipts have not been fully accounted for he should try every means in his power to discover the extent of the fraud.

Example of fraud.

To give an instance of a fraud of this nature. I had to investigate the books of a firm for the purpose of ascertaining to what extent they had been robbed by their book-keeper.

This official commenced by taking a payment from one of the customers and not passing it to his credit in the cash book. This he afterwards did in several instances, consequently these customers appeared as debtors in the books for amounts they had already

Lecture IV.

paid. As time went on the danger of discovery became greater, and in order to protect himself he took the moneys of other customers and passed it to the credit of those customers from whom he had received money some months previously, leaving a fresh set of customers debtors. In the meantime he was gradually appropriating more moneys, and in order to record these transactions it was necessary for him to keep two sets of books.

When I first inspected the books I was much struck by the admirable manner in which they were kept; but the book-keeper absconded in a hurry, and left the duplicate set of books behind, which helped me in my investigation. Had this not been the case, there was absolutely no other means of finding out what moneys had been received without applying to every customer of the firm, and it is exceedingly possible the accounts would have been audited and passed without finding out a fraud of this description.

The first step to take to ascertain if any items of receipt are omitted is to inspect those subsidiary books which in the opinion of the Auditor will throw light on the subject of the cash takings. For example, the counterfoils of travellers' receipt books, porters' books, rough or counter receipt books, &c., should be examined and compared with the cash book, but a fraud of this nature is much more likely to occur in the books of an individual or small firm, where only one or two clerks are kept, than in the case of a large firm, or of a public company, where the clerks are, to a certain extent, a check upon each other.

Comparison of Cash Book with Bankers' Book.

Having practically audited the cash book, it should be reconciled with the bankers' pass book. It is not, of course, necessary to check one with the other in detail, as a rule; but, as I have said before, what may be unnecessary in nineteen cases may be necessary in the twentieth. It would be no answer for an Auditor to a body of shareholders to say he had not thought it necessary to check any item in particular, as it is for him to decide as to what may or may not be necessary. Lecture IV.

It is also, of course, entirely a matter of experience for an Auditor to decide as to what extent he should check the entries in various subsidiary books which are posted into the ledgers. As a rule, it is not usual to check the postings or to compare entries from the original invoices and other documents, but if the Auditor has the slightest doubt in his own mind that everything is not perfectly straightforward and correct, he should, at any rate, take some test cases, if he does not check the books through.

Having finished this portion of the audit, which is to a certain extent mechanical, he then deals with the results of the book-keeper's entries in the shape of the accounts to be presented to his clients.

The usual accounts presented to a company are a revenue or profit and loss account and balance sheet, or statement showing the financial position at the date on which the books were closed. Some companies issue a cash account, either in conjunction with the revenue account or without it. A cash account does not form any part of the book-keeping proper. It is merely an abstract of the cash book, and is, therefore, a statistical account, showing the total receipts on one side and the total expenditure on the other side. As it does not in any way refer to the periods during which the liabilities were incurred or the receipts earned, it is not in any way a guide as to the financial results of the period embraced by the accounts. It is quite possible a loss may have been incurred during the period, although the balance in hand at the end of the account is in excess of that shown at the commencement, for the reason that the receipts may include a much greater amount of Statements of Account.

Lecture IV. earnings of the previous period than was due at the close of the period, while the liabilities may be exactly the reverse, and be much heavier at the end of the period than they were at the commencement.

The certified accounts of a person in trade or of a firm, are usually a profit and loss account and balance sheet, and, perhaps, the capital accounts of the partners, while the accounts presented to executors and trustees, in the case of a first audit, would include a statement showing the financial position of the testator at the date of his death, the dealings with the estate by the executors from the date of the death of the testator to the end of the period under audit, and the financial position of the estate at the end of this period. In future audits the two latter statements only would be necessary, although, if there are several tenants for life, with securities specially hypothecated for the income of each, it is usual to present a statement showing the financial position of each of these trusts.

Audit of Revenue Account.

The principles for examination of the revenue or profit and loss account of a company, individual, or firm are practically the same, the object being simply to ascertain that the whole of the revenue taken credit for has been properly earned during the period, and, secondly, that the whole of the expenses connected with earning it have been properly charged on the other side, including the full amount for depreciation of perishable property.

The revenue account, to be perfectly clear, should be divided into three parts: the first one showing the gross profits earned; the second one showing the net profit, being the amount which, in the case of a company, would be available for dividend, subject, of course, to there being no deficiency in the previous revenue account, or, in the case of a firm, the balance available for distribution amongst the partners; while the third part should show how this net profit has been dealt with. Lecture IV.

It is seldom, as a rule, that an Auditor has to take any steps to find out that sufficient credit has been taken in the revenue account for earnings of the company, as a rule he has to guard against credit being taken for too much. For example, in the case of a trading company he should see that the entries last made in the books recorded only sales which had *bonâ fide* taken place within the period, and that they did not really occur in the first two or three days of the succeeding period.

Items of Expenditure.

It is, of course, impossible for me to discuss in detail all the various forms of expenditure, but an Auditor should, in every instance, take pains to ascertain that every charge belonging to the period under audit has been included in the revenue account, whether the same has been paid or not. The longer the audit takes place after the closing of the books the easier this becomes, as it can, of course, be ascertained by looking at the vouchers for the payments made after the close of the period, as to whether they should not be included in the indebtedness of the period under audit.

Where there is no profit, or the margin of profit shown by the accounts is only just sufficient to pay a small dividend, the Auditor has frequently great difficulty in inducing the officials of the company to include outstandings on various pretences. This he must be exceedingly firm about, but it is, of course, not only allowable but proper to listen to arguments of this nature, and, provided the Articles of Association or Act of Parliament sanction it, he may allow a portion of the expenditure to be treated as a credit in the balance sheet, and spread it over a number of years, charging only a proportion against the revenue account for the period. I may here mention that

Spreading Expenditure.

Lecture IV. — there is absolutely no authority for a company to spread the expenditure of any one year over succeeding years, unless expressly authorised by the Articles of Association. Where this clause has been omitted from the Articles, Auditors are frequently asked to treat these items as assets, on the ground that it is the custom of all companies to do so; but custom is not sufficient, and Auditors should point out to the directors the risk they run personally by declaring any dividend paid out of profits earned by treating accounts in this manner. As far as the law at present stands, they would be answerable to a liquidator for any dividend thus distributed, on the ground of its having been paid out of the capital of the company.

Stock-in-Trade.

In all trading companies, the stock-in-trade forms a very important feature in the revenue account and balance sheet. It is not, of course, part of the duty of an Auditor to take the stock—that is always done by one of the officials of the company; but it is certainly part of an Auditor's duty to inquire into the mode of taking stock, and ascertaining, by examination of the officials and otherwise, that it has been done in a proper manner. For his own protection he should require a certificate from a superior official of the company certifying to the value of the stock.

All stocks should be taken at cost price, never above it, and where the stock has been for some time on hand, and has suffered from deterioration, or the market has depreciated since it was bought, a proportion ought to be written off for depreciation in this respect. Depreciation also should be written off every description of perishable security held by the company or firm.

Depreciation.

Where property of this nature is of various descriptions, the question of depreciation of each class of property should be inquired into very carefully. For example, it would be considered by modern professional

Auditors exceedingly unscientific to write off a round sum as a percentage on leases, buildings, machinery, tools, and stock-in-trade. In the case of a lease, the sum must be arrived at by a proper table, and due regard must be had to the number of years it has to run. In the case of solid, substantial buildings, built on freehold land, a very small percentage would be sufficient. In the case of engines the percentage would be higher, but nothing like so great, again, as it would be on certain portions, such as "washers," or on workshop tools, &c.

Writing off.

For the purpose of ascertaining the proper amount to be written off in the case of factories, machinery, &c., I recommend to your notice two books which will be of interest to you, "The Depreciation of Factories," by Mr. Ewing Matheson, and "Factory Accounts," by Messrs. E. Garke and J. M. Fells.

Reserve.

It is a matter of no importance whether the amount decided upon be deducted from the property account, or whether it be added to or form the commencement of a "reserve," beyond the fact that there is a temptation to transfer from a "reserve" in order to pay a dividend, which does not occur when the depreciation has been actually written off the accounts before the balances are taken credit for in the balance sheet.

Difference between Reserve and Reserve Fund.

The term "reserve fund" is frequently misapplied and confused with "reserve." The latter is merely the surplus of the credit side of a balance sheet over its debtor or liability side, while the addition of the word "fund" clearly indicates either a special investment or at least a special hypothecation of some asset. A "sinking fund" is a sum invested outside a business, and allowed to accumulate at compound interest. The sum is, of course, charged against the revenue or profit and loss account, and a "sinking fund" account is opened in the ledger, to which the amount is credited. When the sum is invested a "sinking fund investment" account

Lecture IV. is debited and cash credited, and the "sinking fund" account is increased each year by the amount charged against revenue and the dividend or interest on the special sinking fund investments.

Interest. Where any sum has been borrowed by a company, the interest payable on the loan must, of course, be charged against the revenue account before the net profit is ascertained, as its payment is not dependent upon the profits.

A company or firm is, of course, at liberty to take credit for interest accrued up to the date of closing the books, although the sum may not be payable for some time; but, on the other hand, the expenditure must include accrued interest, including debenture and mortgage interest, on all loans.

Balance Sheet. The revenue account is usually prepared from the trial balance, which term you are, of course, acquainted with; and after all the items forming the revenue account have been eliminated, the remainder forms the statement usually called, for this reason, the balance sheet, or statement showing the financial position of the company or firm whose accounts are under audit. In auditing this account it should be the object of the Auditor to ascertain that the liabilities have not been understated, nor the assets over-estimated.

Nature of Balance Sheet misunderstood. The exact nature of a balance sheet has been very imperfectly understood by persons not conversant with accounts. Owing to the fact that the credit balances of the ledger transferred to the debit side of the balance sheet includes the liabilities, and the debit balances of the ledger transferred to the credit side of the balance sheet includes the balances of the accounts representing expenditure on property or assets, a custom arose of describing this account as a Statement of Liabilities and Assets. The mere fact that this account always balances exactly, shows that the popular name is incorrect. How can a surplus or reserve on one side be a liability or expenditure represented by nothing of value, or a loss on revenue be an asset? The plan now adopted by the leading Chartered Accountants is to leave out the words "Liabilities" and "Assets" at the top of balance sheets, and substitute the words "Dr." and "Cr.," and I strongly recommend you to follow this course, so as not to be a party to any deception towards those before whom may be laid a balance sheet either prepared or certified by you.

In the same manner as on the debtor side of the balance sheet of a company is put the capital of the shareholders, so is the capital of the partners in the case of a private firm; the business being, of course, indebted to them in their private capacities for the amount they have embarked in the enterprise.

Mortgaged Property.

When property has been mortgaged it should not, strictly speaking, appear in the balance sheet amongst the general assets. The proper way of stating it is for the sum borrowed to be placed amongst the liabilities with a statement that the lenders are fully secured by the particular property charged, the value of which should be stated, and the balance, being the amount which it is believed would be realised, only included in the assets. In practice this is very seldom done, and, where a company or firm is solvent, it is not of much consequence, but should a company not be solvent it is then of the highest importance that the form recommended by me should be strictly adhered to, as otherwise the accounts are exceedingly misleading. For example, assuming the capital of a company is £30,000, the liabilities £90,000, and the ordinary free assets £30,000, also that it possesses freehold property worth £90,000, mortgaged for £60,000, the balance sheet on being prepared with the mortgages amongst the ordinary liabilities, and the property as a free asset, would show a

Lecture IV.

deficiency of only £60,000. This would appear to an unsecured creditor as if, on winding up, he would receive sixteen shillings in the pound, whereas, if the account be properly prepared, it will be seen that there is really only a dividend of thirteen shillings and fourpence in the pound for the unsecured creditors. This will be seen more readily from the two following statements :—

Balance Sheets showing improper and proper way of stating Mortgaged Property.

STATEMENT No. I.

Capital	£30,000	Assets unencumbered	£30,000
General Liabilities	90,000	Freehold Property	90,000
Mortgages ...	60,000		
		Total Assets ...	120,000
		Balance Deficiency	60,000
	£180,000		£180,000

STATEMENT No. II.

Capital	£30,000	Assets unencumbered	£30,000
General Liabilities	90,000		
Mortgages £60,000		Surplus after paying off Mortgages, as per Contra	30,000
Freehold Property 90,000			
Surplus £30,000		Total Assets ...	60,000
		Balance Deficiency	60,000
	£120,000		£120,000

As I have already informed you when discussing the revenue account, it is necessary that the expenses should include the amounts due at the date of closing the books ; it follows necessarily, if this has been done correctly, that all the liabilities must be brought into the balance sheet, and I need not therefore discuss these items separately.

Balance Sheet should be clearly stated.

With reference to the balance sheet of a company the Auditor should impress upon the directors the necessity of making perfectly clear to the shareholders its financial position, and should not let there be any ambiguity as to that position. If the directors refuse to alter any statement of accounts proposed to be issued to shareholders, the Auditor has always the power of rectifying any omission or mis-statement by means of his certificate or report. For example, accounts are frequently presented to shareholders in which the last item on the credit side of the balance sheet is "Balance." This, of course, to any person understanding accounts, means the amount of the deficiency in consequence of the liabilities of the company being that much in excess of the assets, while an uninitiated shareholder, seeing this balance on the credit side, might think it meant a balance to the good. This the Auditor should decidedly object to, and require the Account to be more explicit.

Inspection of Securities.

Either on the conclusion of an audit, or previous to its completion, it is usual for the Auditor of a company or society, when the assets are represented by investments or property, to inspect the securities or title deeds of the same, to see that they are in the custody of the company, and have not been improperly made use of. For this purpose he should be supplied with a full list of the property, and appoint a time for the inspection. In the case of banks and financial companies, the securities held are sometimes exceedingly numerous, and it is quite impossible to check them in one day. In these cases the Auditor must take whatever steps he thinks desirable to ensure that some of the securities are not presented to him twice, and for this purpose, in some way or another, either by taking away with him the keys of the strong room or safe containing the securities, he must have the whole of them under his control, and they must remain

Lecture IV. so from the moment he commences the examination until he has concluded it.

If he has to check any securities of a company at their bankers, or at any place where they may be deposited out of the control of the company, he should by inquiry ascertain that they are not held by the persons in whose custody they are against any loan, and that they have no lien upon them.

Counting of Cash Balances.

Where large sums of money are in the hands of an official on the date of closing the books, it is usual for the Auditor to count them; but as this is sometimes resented by the official, the difficulty can be overcome by his paying the whole of it into the bank on the evening of the day on which the books are closed.

In examining the title deeds of property, unless the Auditor is acquainted with documents of this description, he should for his own protection receive a certificate from the solicitor to the company that they are in proper order, and not pledged to any mortgagee.

Auditor's Report.

Having completed the audit, it is usual for the Auditor to either confirm the accounts, or make a special report upon them. In many companies it is specially enacted in the Articles of Association that the Auditors shall make a report, in which case it is obligatory upon them to do so, although the ordinary certificate of the Auditor probably complies with the requirement.

Although all Articles of Association are still drawn stating that the accounts are to be presented to the Auditors, and returned by them within a specified time, either confirmed or reported upon, it is usual for the Auditors, if they object to the form of accounts, to make their suggestions to the directors, who generally acquiesce, for it is pretty certain that an unfavourable report in the accounts of a company might be exceedingly disastrous, and would certainly affect the value of the shares in the money market.

With the exception of railway companies, no form of certificate is prescribed.

Lecture IV.

Form of Auditor's Certificate.

I should, myself, very much like it to be settled by the Institute of Chartered Accountants what would constitute a thorough audit of every class of company, and for all Auditors' certificates to be in one or other of certain prescribed forms, but experience has shown how difficult, if not impossible, it would be to restrict Auditors in this respect, and at present the form of certificate is left to the Auditor. Supposing he is satisfied that the accounts are correct in every particular, I do not consider it of much consequence in what words his satisfaction is expressed. I, however, assert very firmly that an Auditor should never, either to please the officials of a company, or to further his own interests, attempt to protect them or him by an ambiguous certificate. Unless an Auditor indicates plainly in his certificate he is dissatisfied with the accounts, his clients have the right to expect things are correct in every particular. An Auditor's signature after the single word "audited" is the strongest he can give, and implies that without a single reservation the accounts are correct in every particular, and that the securities have been found in perfect order.

LECTURE V.

THE AUDIT OF THE ACCOUNTS OF BUILDING SOCIETIES.

Read before the Chartered Accountants' Students' Society of London, 2nd May, 1894.

Lecture V.

Responsibility of accepting invitation to Lecture.

To deliver an address on the Audit of the Accounts of Building Societies after the events of last year, which witnessed the collapse of so many of these societies, including the one whose later history has become notorious, is a task from which a lecturer might well shrink, knowing the criticisms to which he at the present time exposes himself.

Reasons for declining.

When, therefore, I received the invitation of your Society I naturally took some time to consider as to whether I should act on my first impulse and decline it, thus leaving the responsibility to someone else, or accept it with its consequent criticisms by those qualified to judge whether my views are or are not correct, as well as by those who, without any experience or even any common sense to guide them, take for granted that an Auditor is as much responsible for the mal-administration of the affairs of a society as are its directors. There are also many who, without going as far as this, consider that, while an Auditor may not be responsible for the acts of the directors, yet he is clearly to blame should he not at once detect any errors they may have committed, and give such information to the members as would enable them to rectify the results of such errors or effect such alteration in the management as would prevent a recurrence in future. **Lecture V.**

Reasons for accepting.

After duly weighing the arguments for and against accepting the invitation of your Society, I took the first course, as I felt that, if those who are considered experts on the subject of auditing are afraid to give their opinions to the public, there was not much hope of any practical legislation being effected when the powers and duties of Auditors, not only of building societies, but of public companies and societies of every description, are dealt with in Parliament, as must now shortly happen.

The evening of the annual meeting of the Institute of Chartered Accountants is therefore a fitting occasion for putting forward the views of professional Auditors as to their duties in relation to the audit of the accounts of building societies, but it must, of course, be understood that the remarks I am about to make are enunciated entirely on my own authority, and that neither the Institute nor any single individual member is pledged to their accuracy. My hearers will doubtless approve of the greater part of what I shall say, but many will probably only agree with me in part, in which case I hope that time will permit of our hearing their views when I have finished, as the great value of these meetings is the interchange of ideas on subjects interesting both to the members of the Institute who are already in practice as well as to the students, for whom these lectures are primarily intended.

Failure of the Liberator Building Society.

Since the failure of the Liberator Building Society many comments have appeared in the Press on the conduct of the directors and also of the Auditors, but as this is at present, and will be for some time, the subject of investigation by the Courts, it would not be proper—

Lecture V.

even were it pertinent to this address—to refer to them beyond calling attention to this fact, that whatever may be the ground of action against the directors—and one, at least, is accused of fraud of the most revolting and heartless description—no charge whatever has been made or even hinted at against the Auditors of participating in any way in the misapplication of the funds of the Institution; nor, even, has any improper motive been attributed to them. Their most bitter opponents only contend that they have failed either in taking a correct view of the duties of Auditors or in properly carrying out what they may have conceived was their duty.

Unfair comments on duties of Auditors.

Now, as to these duties there has been a great deal of hysterical writing, and, to judge from some of the criticisms, an Auditor for a fee of twenty or fifty guineas—and, sometimes, for even less—is expected to check in the minutest detail the transactions which it has required a staff maintained at a cost of several hundred or several thousand pounds to record. Other critics have, on the contrary, asserted that all an Auditor has to do is to satisfy himself that the accounts are in accordance with the books, and that, having done this, no further responsibility lies upon him.

Now, as is usual when parties go to extremes, the correct solution lies somewhere between the two views, and the duties of Auditors may be divided into two classes, those which an Auditor should perform in every case, and those which he should perform according to the special circumstances of each case which comes under his review. In the latter he is, of course, guided by his judgment, based on his education and experience.

Proper duties of Auditors.

As regards those duties which should be performed by an Auditor in every case, the audit of the accounts of a building society proceeds on the same lines as those which have been recognised by us for many years in the audits of every class of company or society. In the first place, the Auditor must be acquainted with the Act of Parliament under which the society is registered and the special rules which, under that Act of Parliament, form the constitution of the particular society. The Act under which Building Societies are nearly all now registered is the Building Societies Act, 1874, as amended by the Building Societies Act, 1894, and the special sections of the former Act which demand the attention of Auditors are the 15th—which regulates the borrowing powers of societies, and enacts that in a permanent society the total amount received on deposit or loan and not repaid by the society shall not at any time exceed two-thirds of the amount for the time being secured to the society by mortgages from its members; the 25th Section, which regulates the investment of the surplus funds; and the 40th Section, which requires the preparation of accounts and the auditing of the same. This last runs as follows;—

Lecture V.

Building Societies Act, 1874, Sec. 40.

40. "The secretary or other officer of every society under this Act, shall, once in every year at least, prepare an account of all the receipts and expenditure of the society since the preceding statement, and a general statement of its funds and effects, liabilities and assets, showing the amounts due to the holders of the various classes of shares respectively, to depositors and creditors for loans, and also the balance due or outstanding on their mortgage securities (not including prospective interest), and the amount invested in the funds or other securities; and every such account and statement shall be attested by the Auditors, to whom the mortgage deeds and other securities belonging to the society shall

Lecture V.

be produced, and such account and statement shall be countersigned by the secretary or other officer; and every member, depositor, and creditor for loans shall be entitled to receive from the society a copy of such account and statement, and a copy thereof shall be sent to the Registrar within fourteen days after the annual or other general meeting at which it is presented, and another copy thereof shall be suspended in a conspicuous place in every office of the society under this Act."

Building Societies Act, 1894.

The Building Societies Act, 1894, enacted that the Annual Account and Statement referred to in the section just given should be in the form prescribed from time to time by the Chief Registrar of Friendly Societies with the approval of a Secretary of State, and accordingly a form was issued on the 5th September, 1895, which is still in force. This form has received the severest condemnation from all qualified by experience to judge of such matters, and without doubt it will before long be altered for the better. The Act also made it compulsory on every Society to appoint as one of its Auditors a person who publicly carries on the business of an Accountant, but this is very little, if any, protection to members, as any unqualified person can by merely calling himself an Accountant make himself eligible for the appointment.

Chartered Accountants as Auditors.

Public opinion, however, is doing more than the Act of Parliament, and all building societies of importance are now selecting a Chartered Accountant as an Auditor, either alone or in conjunction with one or more member Auditors.

Building Societies were, some years ago, divided into two groups, called respectively "Terminating" and "Permanent." The former have practically ceased to exist, owing to the difficulty they naturally experienced in advancing their funds during the latter part of their existence, and I therefore to-night refer solely to the accounts of Permanent Building Societies.

Income of Societies.

The income of these societies is derived from subscriptions on shares, deposits, repayments of advances, amounts paid on redemption of mortgages, interest on investments, and miscellaneous small items, such as entrance fees, fines, sale of rules, &c.

The amounts paid up on the shares taken by members may be paid by weekly, monthly, quarterly, half-yearly or yearly subscriptions, monthly payments being the most usual. Shares thus treated are called "Subscription shares," while many societies in addition issue "Paid-up shares," on which the full amount is at once paid. The amount of these "Paid-up shares" is fixed by the rules, and they can usually be divided into parts for the convenience of those of limited means. The shares of building societies are on a totally different footing to those of companies, inasmuch as the former can be paid off by the societies to their members desirous of withdrawing, subject to the rules, while those of a company can only be disposed of by transfer to some other person.

Deposits.

Deposits are received from either members or non-members, and the rate of interest is fixed at the time of the advance. The amount of the deposits is limited, as already stated, to two-thirds of the amount lent on mortgage.

Repayments of Advances and other Receipts.

Repayments of advances are the instalments which are paid by the members in satisfaction of the amounts advanced to them, together with the interest, and are usually paid monthly in equal payments in accordance with the scale in force at the time of the advance. Amounts paid on redemption of mortgages, interest on investments, and miscellaneous receipts explain them-

Lecture V.

selves. When a society has had to take over a property upon which it has advanced through the default of the borrowing member, it will occasionally include among its receipts the amount realised on the sale of such property.

Expenditure.

The expenditure of building societies consists of advances on freehold and leasehold securities, the repayment of deposits and loans, the amounts withdrawn on investing shares, interest on deposits and loans, the expenses of management, and the interest paid to its members. The profits of a building society are derived from the interest on its advances, and on its investments, entrance fees, fines, &c., and when the directors have, at the conclusion of the financial year, prepared the statements of account which they propose to lay before the members, and which as already stated must be in the prescribed form, it is the duty of the Auditor or Auditors to check them.

Profits.

Duty of Directors, not of Auditors, to prepare Accounts.

Now, considering the audience I am addressing, many will think this remark of mine quite superfluous, but I have made it with intention, as from articles which have lately appeared in the public Press, and from answers which have lately been given by directors and others when under examination under the provisions of the Companies (Winding-up) Act, 1890, it would appear that there is a most erroneous impression existing, even in the minds of what I may term professional directors, that the Auditors of a company or a society are responsible for the preparation of the Balance Sheet, and that the approval of the Auditors relieves the directors of responsibility.

Although the law relating to accounts and their audit is of an exceedingly meagre description, in fact, so meagre and insufficient that those who have made it the business of their lives to attend to audits of companies and societies have not enough to guide them as to the full legal extent of their responsibilities and their powers, still the little there is tends conclusively to show that the preparation of the accounts of companies and societies is clearly the work of the directors and of the officials of the company or society, and that the Auditors have nothing whatever to do with such accounts until they have been formally passed by the board, and submitted to them for approval as agents on behalf of the shareholders or members.

Selection of professional Auditors by Shareholders.

The practice of having accounts audited by professional Auditors is one that has not been forced on the community by the Legislature, but has arisen through it having gradually dawned upon members that it was a foolish and mischievous practice to select as their Auditors those who did not even pretend to have any special qualification for the office beyond the fact that as members they were naturally interested with the other members in their joint adventure. Up to within the last quarter of a century the accounts of all companies, building societies, and similar institutions were audited solely by one or more of the members. Now, would it have been pretended for a single moment that these members were in any way responsible for the preparation of the accounts to which they affixed their signature as Auditors? Had directors in those days put forward the proposition that the approval of the Auditor relieved them of their responsibilities, I think everyone will at once admit the idea would have been scouted as absurd. In what way has this position been altered? I state most emphatically, in not one whit. The professional Auditor has gradually replaced the member Auditor, but there has been no alteration whatever, from a legal point of view, in his duties or in his responsibilities, beyond the natural consequence that more skill and experience is naturally expected from one who avowedly puts himself forward as an expert than

Lecture V.

from one who, however ready he may have been to accept such an appointment, seldom, if ever, claimed any special knowledge in accounts as the ground for his selection.

Auditors agents of the Shareholders, not of the Directors.

It is therefore clear that from my point of view the Auditor has in no case any kind of duty to perform as regards the directors, he is solely the agent of the members, for the purpose of ascertaining whether the statements submitted by the directors for their adoption at their annual meeting show a correct view of the transactions of the society during the period embraced by the accounts, and also a true and just statement of its assets and liabilities at the date up to which the accounts are prepared.

An Auditor will naturally, in his capacity as agent of the members, be prepared to discuss with the directors any question of policy or matter of principle as to the mode of submission of the accounts, but no matter to what extent this may be done, the accounts are those of the directors, and if they are wrong the directors must bear whatever blame may be attached to the issuing of incorrect statements, and they have no right whatever in mitigation to state that they relied upon the Auditors.

The incorrectness of the accounts placed before a meeting is, of course, a proper ground of complaint by members against their Auditor, should he have passed them, and an Auditor may, of course, be held liable for damages caused through either his neglect or incompetence.

Difference between duties of Accountants and Auditors.

These remarks, of course, do not apply to any Chartered Accountant who may be specially employed by the directors to prepare the accounts previous to their being submitted to the Auditors. In this case an undoubted responsibility rests upon the Chartered Accountant towards his clients, the directors, but to

Lecture V.

them solely, as the Chartered Accountant would naturally consider that, as regards the members, their interest would be guarded by their duly-appointed Auditor.

Directors' Auditor and Members' Auditor.

It must also be understood that in these remarks I am referring to Auditors who are acting on behalf of the members. In many building societies there are two classes of Auditors, viz., the directors' Auditor and the members' Auditor, and although I cannot point to any case, it would, in my opinion, be quite possible that a directors' Auditor may have no responsibility whatever to the members. In order, however, for this to be the case it must be quite clear on the face of the accounts that the directors' Auditor does not share the responsibility with the members' Auditor, and he may have special functions, such as the preparation of the statements on behalf of the directors, and ascertaining that they are correct; also a special examination into the value of the securities, for the purpose of preventing the directors from declaring a dividend in excess of what has really been earned, and thus protect the directors from being in any way held liable at any future time for improper payments of dividends.

I am, however, here merely stating a hypothetical case; I know of no instance where a directors' Auditor, so called, has sole responsibility towards the directors.

The usual practice in the audit of the accounts of building societies, where there is a directors' Auditor, is for the directors' Auditor to work in conjunction with the shareholders' Auditor, perform the duties in exactly the same way and share the same responsibility, in which case it is only the mode of election that makes the slightest difference between the members' and directors' Auditor.

List of Books.

Before commencing an audit for the first time, the Auditor should be provided with a complete list of the

Lecture V.

Books, both financial and statistical, in use in the office. He should also have a note-book, in which to record the details of the audit as performed by him, which will be a proof, if required at any future time, of the care and attention he may have devoted to his duties. This book should also contain queries raised by him, and the manner in which they have been answered by the officials.

Audit of the Income.

Now, the audit of the accounts of a building society differs in no way from that of any other audit, in that it is advisable to check the income from as many independent sources as possible, so as to be satisfied that all the amounts received have duly come into the books of account. The ascertainment of this fact is one of the greatest difficulties of an Auditor, and it is, of course, perfectly impossible for him in every case to find out should money be arrested before it comes into the society's office and embezzled by the official receiving the money. In the days of the amateur Auditor it was not looked upon as any part of an Auditor's duty to attempt a check of this nature, as he was supposed merely to deal with the cash admitted to have been received according to the books. So far as I am aware, this view of the duties of an Auditor is still correct, but I am pleased to say that Chartered Accountants long ago anticipated any legislation on this subject, and have considered it part of the duties of an Auditor to endeavour to ascertain that all moneys received have been accounted for, and not merely to concern himself with the expenditure of that which has been brought into the books.

At the same time, however, no responsibility could be attached to any Auditor were he, after taking ordinary precautions, to fail in detecting omissions through fraud. In many cases detection would be absolutely impossible, but in a building society, as well as in a bank, there is a very efficient check for ascertaining that the greater portion of the revenue has been brought to account, provided the persons most interested in the stability of the society, viz., the members, will, in their own interest, co-operate with their Auditor.

Examination of Members' Pass Books.

Previous to the commencement of the audit every member should be requested to send in his Pass Book to the office by a certain day for the inspection of the Auditors, and a notice to the same effect should be printed inside the cover of every Pass Book, so that, on the day appointed for the audit to commence, the officials of the society should have for the inspection of the Auditors a large proportion of the members' Pass Books. I hope that, in the next legislation in connection with building societies, it will be enacted that on a certain day, to be named, every member shall return his Pass Book to the office for examination by the Auditors, and that any member not doing so shall, in the event of any defalcations arising which could have been discovered had he complied with this rule, be not entitled to have any portion of his loss made good to him until those members who have complied with the request have been paid in full.

Pass Books should be marked by Auditors.

The balances of all Pass Books so returned to the office should be examined by the Auditors with the accounts of the members in the society's ledgers, and both should be marked by the Auditors, either by a stamp solely under the control of the Auditors, or by the initials of one of the Auditors. Were this practice universally adopted it would gradually become the custom for the members to look for the Auditor's check in their Pass Books at each balancing date, and they would naturally communicate directly with their representative in any case when, after forwarding the Pass Book to the office for the purpose of examination, they did not observe this mark on its return. Having

Lecture V. checked as many Pass Books as are available, the Auditor can then turn his attention to the books of account.

Subscription Cash Book. It is the custom of most societies to keep a "Subscription Cash Book," which contains the daily takings on account of members' shares, the entries in which book are copied daily, either in detail or in abstract form, into a General Cash Book. Whichever plan be adopted, the entries in this book should be checked by the Auditors into the General Cash Book. Most building societies also keep what is called a "Deposit Cash Book," into which is entered deposits as they are received over the counter. At the same time there is handed to the depositor a receipt for the amount of his deposit, which is taken out of a "Deposit Receipt Book," on the counterfoils of which are the usual particulars of their respective receipts. The entries on these counterfails should be checked by the Auditors into the receipt side of the Deposit Cash Book.

Deposit Cash Book.

The Deposit Cash Book also contains the payments made to depositors on account of withdrawals of deposits, and these entries should be checked either in detail or in total into the General Cash Book. As a rule, the Deposit Cash Book in a large building society is added up daily, and the daily totals are collected into the General Cash Book.

Checking additions. I may here state that in all cases where totals only of a subsidiary Cash Book are entered into another Cash Book, the checking of the additions of the items comprising the totals in the subsidiary books must first of all take place, otherwise the checking of the totals with the entries in the book into which they are made will be of no real value.

Vouching Income. This is a convenient place to refer to the vouching of the Cash Book, which, however, can be done at any time during the audit. As regards vouching the receipts, I have already referred to the great check there is upon the subscriptions of members by comparison of the balances shown in the members' Pass Books with the balances in the Ledgers, and the checking of the postings from the Cash Book into these Ledgers will, of course, be a very efficient check on the receipts of the society from this source.

In addition, however, the Auditor should check the counterfoils of the Receipt Books used by the society for acknowledgment of its other revenue, of which the principal one would be the receipts for deposits.

Vouching Expenditure.

As regards the vouching of the payment side of the Cash Book there should be produced to the Auditors proper receipts for all payments made to depositors on the withdrawal of portions of their deposits, and the original receipts cancelled should be produced when the whole of the deposit has been paid off. The amounts withdrawn on investing shares, the payments to tradesmen, the survey fees, commission, &c., should be vouched by the production of properly receipted accounts. This requires care, and, in addition to merely vouching the payments of the money, the Auditors should ascertain that they are entered in the Cash Book under their proper heading, and thus be ultimately posted to their proper accounts in the Ledgers.

Calling over the postings.

Having completed the checking of the subsidiary Cash Books into the General Cash Book, this latter book should then be checked into the Ledger—in other words the postings must be called over. Now, as to this, I have no doubt, from what I have read during the last few months, that the statement I am about to make will meet with opposition from many. In the case of a small building society there will be no difficulty in performing this part of the audit in the most complete way, but in the case of a very large building society, where the daily cash entries take up several pages, I say it is quite

Lecture V. impossible and unreasonable to expect that an Auditor should check all these postings ; but it is his duty, all the same, to satisfy himself that the postings are correct, and for this purpose he will ascertain what process has been gone through inside the office by those responsible for the preparation of the statement placed before the Auditor—in other words, what checking has already been done by members of the staff who are independent of the control of the cash.

Audit Committee.

Many building societies have what is called an audit committee of the board, whose duty it is to perform what may be called an inside audit, and if the Auditor, on inquiry, finds that an audit by a committee has been systematic, and that the members of this committee are entirely independent of the staff, more especially of the cashier, whose entries it would be their principal duty to check, he will feel justified in dispensing with a great deal of checking and leave himself more time for the larger questions of principle embraced in an audit. One of the differences between an experienced and an incompetent Auditor is the facility with which the former takes advantage of other people's checking, while the latter pursues a mechanical route, and is only able to deal with that which is immediately under his notice in the books which happen to lie open before him.

Having satisfied himself, either by means of calling over the entries himself or by his staff, or in some other way, that the postings into the various Ledgers are correct, the Auditor should then test the correctness of the additions in the Investing Ledgers, the Advance Ledgers, the Deposit Ledgers, and the General Ledgers.

Journal.

The Auditor can then turn his attention to the Journal, and the entries in this book should be gone carefully through by the Auditor himself, and not delegated to any of his staff, except one of great experience, as it

Lecture V.

is through this book that many transfers from one account to another are made, sometimes embracing large sums. As these would naturally appear in the Ledger Accounts with no explanation whatever, an Auditor can very easily pass an entry involving a question of principle which may have been dealt with in altogether a wrong way. The Journal should contain the entries charging borrowers with interest on their advances, entries transferring amounts from one Ledger Account to another, which, in the absence of explanation, should be inquired into by the Auditor, entries relating to losses on realisation of any property or asset, to the amount written off for bad debts, and innumerable other entries, including those in connection with the closing of the books.

Entries in Journal.

It is in the Journal containing these entries that the items most likely to require explanation will occur. The postings from the Journal should be checked into the General Ledger, and if, in consequence of its being known that the Auditors are in the habit of carefully scrutinizing the Journal, an attempt be made to conceal some transfer by not making the proper Journal entry, the Auditor will be able to discover this through the absence of the ticks in the Ledger Accounts containing them.

Varieties of checking tick

In the course of an audit it frequently happens that more than one tick has to be placed against the same items. It is, therefore, very desirable for different varieties of ticks to be used, each one denoting that a special part of the audit has been performed. For example, one class of tick should denote vouching; another, the calling over of postings; a third, that an addition has been checked; and a fourth, that a security has been examined. Ticks denoting the calling over of postings should be placed against the number of the pages and not against the amounts.

Lecture V.

Checking Ledger Balances.

Having completed the checking of the postings into the various Ledgers, there then remains the checking of the various Ledger balances into the Balance Sheet and the other statements prescribed by the Registrar and referred to by me later on. Nearly all building societies adopt a very commendable practice of keeping in a book called a Balance Book the full details of the balances of the various Ledger Accounts. In other words, this book contains in an extended form the Accounts and Balance Sheet referred to. This Balance Book should, of course, exactly balance, and until this is the case the Auditor should refuse to certify the accounts.

In the case of large trading companies it is frequently impossible to obtain a perfect balance, but this does not in any way apply to the books of building societies, and as an error in the balance may possibly be a balance of a number of errors of a very much larger amount, the Auditor must require the books to be worked to a perfect balance should the directors of the society wish him to give an unqualified certificate.

Minute Book.

The Minute Book of the society should also be inspected by the Auditor for the purpose of ascertaining what care has been bestowed by the directors before making advances on property, and he may also discover from the contents the opinion of the directors as to the values of certain properties representing the security for advances, also whether any properties have been taken over during the year through the default of borrowing members. The Auditor may also find a great deal of other information useful to him by the perusal of the Minutes.

Should, however, the directors refuse to allow the Auditor to make a general inspection of the Minute Book, there does not appear to be any authority to compel its production. The book containing the minutes of the directors is not a book of account, but should the

Auditor be of opinion any information in the Minute Book which would be of assistance to him in his duty is kept back from him by the directors, he could, of course, refer to this refusal in his certificate.

Lecture V.

The accounts usually presented to the members of building societies which require to be certified by the Auditors were formerly three in number, a Cash Account, Profit and Loss Account, and a statement of Liabilities and Assets. Many societies presented the Profit and Loss Account in two or more divisions, calling them different names, but practically, no matter how many different statements were submitted, they were all comprised under these three titles.

Forms of Statements.

The forms of Accounts prescribed by the Registrar of Friendly Societies, and issued on the 5th September, 1895, comprise also these three Accounts, and in addition certain Schedules, as follows:—

1. Receipts and Payments Account.
2. Revenue (including accretions to capital) and Expenditure Account.
3. Liabilities and Assets Account.
4. Schedules (three in number).

Receipts and Payments Account.

The Receipts and Payments Account is, as its name implies, a statement of the actual sums received and expended by the society, and is therefore an abstract of the Cash Book or Cash Books. It is an indication to the members of the amount of business done, as it shows the amount actually received on shares, the amount received on redemption of mortgages, in repayment of advances, the amount realised on sale of investments, and also the dividend actually received on investments, during the period; while on the other hand it shows the actual amount advanced on mortgaged securities, the amounts withdrawn on shares, deposits repaid, loans repaid, and expenses actually paid during the year; but beyond this it must not be taken as any guide to the

Lecture V. financial result of the transactions, and it must not be assumed that a society which has a small cash balance at the end of the year as compared with a large cash balance at the beginning of the year is in any worse condition, or *vice versâ* The statement which really shows the financial result of the business done during the period and the position of the society is the Revenue and Expenditure Account and the Statement of Liabilities and Assets.

Trial Balance.

Before these two accounts are checked, the Auditor should require to see what is technically known as the Trial Balance, and although he may be willing to commence his audit before this is actually taken out, yet he should not in any case sign the accounts until the Trial Balance has been agreed.

Before auditing the Revenue (including accretions to capital) and Expenditure Account, or Statement No. 2 of the Form prescribed by the Registrar, the following points should be borne in mind:—

Special Notes on Audit of Receipts and Payments Account.

The first column should show the Liabilities and Assets at the beginning of the year, and the last column the Liabilities and Assets at the end of the year. The total amount of each Liability and Asset respectively, under the several heads provided in the prescribed Form, only should be given in these columns; that is to say, the figures marked (*e*) (*f*) (*g*) (*h*) (*i*) (*k*) in the last column of the Revenue, &c., Account, and in the last column of each side of the Liabilities and Assets Account, should be the only figures in these columns.

The two intervening columns show how the last column is derived from the first: thus, in the first item in No. 2 Account—"Amount due to Shareholders"—the total amount due to Shareholders (including principal and interest) at the beginning of the year should be shown in the first column; Subscriptions of Shareholders, interest added, and any other details, constituting additions during the year, should be shown in the second column; Withdrawals of Shareholders, transfers from Share to Repayment Account, deductions for working expenses, interest paid, and any other details, constituting diminutions during the year, should be shown in the third column; and the total amount due to Shareholders at the end of the year in the fourth column. The last amount will be the difference between the second and third columns added to, or deducted from, as the case may be, the first column. Each of the items in the first column should be dealt with in a similar manner, and each should therefore balance, independently, across the Form.

Agreement of Balances.

The total balances at the beginning of the year (A.A.) should agree, and the total balances at the end of the year (D.D.) should also agree. It follows that the sum of B in the upper part, and C in the lower, will agree with the sum of C in the upper part and B in the lower. Should the balance in the previous year's Account have since been found to be incorrect, the corrected Balance should be shown in the first column of the Account, and an explanation of the discrepancy given on the Form itself.

Profit Balance

Should the society have at the beginning of the year a balance of unappropriated profit, and also at the end of the year a balance of unappropriated profit, either smaller or larger, the additions to profit and diminutions of profit should respectively be inserted in the second and third columns of the upper half of the return.

The Management Expenses charged in the third column of this Account should be the full amount incurred during the year, whether the transactions have been completed by the actual payment of cash or are outstanding at the end of the year.

Should the society have at the beginning of the year a balance of unappropriated profit, and at the end

Lecture V. of the year a balance of loss, the additions to profit and diminutions of profit should be inserted in the second and third columns respectively of the upper half of the return. The Undivided Profit Account will then be balanced, and the balance deficit carried down to column 2 of the lower half.

Deficiency Balances.

Should the society have at the beginning of the year a balance deficient, and also at the end of the year a balance deficient, larger or smaller, the additions to the deficiency should be inserted in column 2 of the lower half and the diminutions of the deficiency in column 3 of the lower half, and in this case no figures are required to be inserted opposite the item "Undivided Profit" in the upper half of the return.

Should the society have at the beginning of the year a balance deficient, and at the end of the year a balance of unappropriated profit, the additions to the deficiency and diminutions of deficiency should be inserted in the second and third columns respectively of the lower half of the return. The Balance Deficient Account will then be balanced, and the balance profit carried to column 2 of the upper half.

Cross Entries.

Cross entries to be transferred from one part of the Account to another should be avoided as much as possible. In general, items that appear in the Cash Account will only be required to be entered once in the Revenue, &c., Account. Items that are not cash but credits will in general be required to be balanced with a corresponding debit in another part of the Revenue, &c., Account.

The Cash paid in and out of the Bank should not be inserted in full in the second and third columns, but only the excess of the one over the other.

Interest on Advances.

Now, the principal item of revenue on the credit side of the Revenue and Expenditure Account is Interest on Advances, and the amount so taken to credit requires

Lecture V.

most careful scrutiny by the Auditor, as it is distinctly part of his duty to see that no item is included in respect of interest which has either not been received or, if earned but not received, is not covered by the security held by the society from the borrower.

The amount taken credit for in respect of interest can be investigated best by the Auditor when checking the balances from the Advance Ledger into the Balance Book, and I will therefore refer to it when dealing with the balances due on mortgage securities under the assets in the Liabilities and Assets Account.

Interest due from Borrowe in arrear.

It is clear, therefore, that it is part of the Auditor's duty to ascertain that nothing is taken credit for in respect of interest which is not likely to be received, and should the Auditor observe that interest is taken credit for and charged to a borrower who is not paying off the stipulated instalments, he must inquire very carefully into the transactions. Instances have been known where the interest due on the balances of borrowers who have not paid their instalments for years, and whose security is so doubtful that in some cases the building society has not even taken the properties into their own hands, or, where they have so taken it, yet are unable to realise it, has been calculated and charged to the borrower year after year and carried to the credit of the Revenue Account, and dividends have been paid to the members on the strength of this interest being ultimately realised. This is, of course, not only reprehensible on the part of the directors, but any Auditor passing accounts showing apparent profits of this nature must certainly be considered to have failed in his duty.

Interest on Investments.

As regards interest on investments, a building society is clearly entitled to take credit for interest accrued on its investments to the date of its making up its accounts, and as the investments of building societies are limited to those paying fixed rates of interest or

Lecture V. dividends, the calculations can be easily made, and must either be checked by the Auditor or he must be satisfied that this has been carefully done by having prepared for him a list showing how the interest is arrived at on each investment, and by his testing it as he may think proper.

Rent of Properties in hand.

Another item which should appear on the credit side of the Revenue and Expenditure Account is the rent received in respect of those properties which have been taken possession of by the society through default of the borrowers. Building societies did not as a rule disclose in their balance sheets the amount of the properties taken over, nor, in their Profit and Loss Accounts, the revenue received from them in a heading by itself, but the form prescribed by the Chief Registrar now requires this to be set out. There can be little doubt that it is in the interests of the public that the fullest information be given in the accounts of building societies, but at the same time it is a perfectly sound argument to state that, inasmuch as a disclosure of this nature to the members is a disclosure to the world, the calling special attention to the fact the society holds securities upon which there is likely to be a loss on realisation does to a certain extent discredit the good name of the society. Members, moreover, run this risk, that directors, knowing that publication would damage the society, may hesitate to take over the properties at all, and continue to leave the management thereof in the hands of persons in whom they may have lost entire confidence.

Reserve for Interest.

While it is quite proper to include in the Revenue and Expenditure Account income from properties in possession, the Auditor must be very careful that no interest on these advances and charged against the borrowers is credited to interest on advances, unless the whole of it is taken out on the other side of the Revenue and Expenditure Account as reserve, so as to cancel such interest credited. Should this not be done such a wholly unjustifiable practice must be resisted by the Auditor, and in the event of the directors not yielding on this point it is most clearly his duty to make the fact known to the members, and in such a way that it cannot possibly be misunderstood.

Miscellaneous Revenue.

Amongst the sundry revenue of a building society may be named the entrance fees, fines, payments for rules, &c., but as these in all cases will either have been paid before the close of the year or charged against the members' accounts, their checking presents features of no difficulty, and it does not come within the province of an Auditor to satisfy himself that every member has paid his entrance fee, or that fines have been levied whenever the society has become entitled to such fines, the remittance of such fines being entirely within the discretion of the directors as appertaining to their management.

Audit of Expenditure.

The audit of the expenditure side of the Revenue and Expenditure Account presents no great features of difficulty, the expenditure consisting principally of interest on deposits and loans, and the general expenses of management. The amount actually paid away in cash for these expenses will come through the Cash Book into the Ledger Accounts, but the Auditor has to satisfy himself that the interest accrued due to the date of closing the accounts both on deposits and on loans has been properly included and charged. He should also require to have produced to him a list of all outstanding accounts, and ascertain that all such are included in the expenditure side of the Revenue and Expenditure Account, and thus ultimately be found on the liability side of the Liabilities and Assets Account. In the event of there being properties in hand, the Auditor must also be satisfied that any expenses

Lecture V.

incurred in the maintenance of this property, including rents, rates, and taxes incident thereto, have been charged against this account and not added to the value of the property, which would have the effect of bringing in a fictitious asset into the Liabilities and Assets Account by improperly swelling the balances due from borrowers who are already unable to meet their obligations.

Liabilities and Assets Account.

I now come to the Liabilities and Assets Account, which is also a statement requiring the most particular attention of the Auditor. In the first place, he has to ascertain that the liabilities and assets are stated in accordance with the books of the society and with the form prescribed by the Chief Registrar; secondly, that the liabilities are all included; and, thirdly, that the assets are of the value attached to them, or, which comes to practically the same thing, that—if they are taken credit for in excess of their real value—there is a reserve on the other side for depreciation which, in the opinion of the Auditor, will be amply sufficient to meet any loss there may ultimately be on realisation.

Liabilities.

As regards the inclusion of all the liabilities in the Liabilities and Assets Account, this has to a certain extent been inquired into when auditing the Revenue and Expenditure Account, provided the Auditor has ascertained that the proper entries of outstandings have been made in the books and charged on the expenditure side of that account. It is, however, necessary to make a few special remarks in connection with their appearance in the Liabilities and Assets Account, and there are, of course, in addition, liabilities which have no connection with the Revenue and Expenditure Account.

Amounts due to Members and Depositors.

The principal amount on the liability side consists of the amounts standing to the credit of the holders of members' shares. This is, of course, ascertained from the balances of the Investment Ledgers. The next largest item will probably be the amount due to depositors, which is, of course, ascertained in taking out the balances from the Deposit Ledgers. In the case of a large building society these deposits are very numerous, and I do not consider that the Auditor can do more in the way of satisfying himself that the amounts due to depositors are brought into account than ascertaining that each entry on the counterfoil of the Deposit Receipt Book has been brought into the Cash Book and then posted into the Deposit Ledgers. Cases have been known of persons handing their money to be placed on deposit to an official of a society not properly authorised to receive it, and of such officer not accounting for it to the society. It is impossible for an Auditor to check misappropriations of this nature, and although in such cases it is quite possible that under certain circumstances it might be held that directors or trustees were responsible, I cannot conceive that such responsibility can be extended to an Auditor.

Limit to Deposits.

The Building Societies Act of 1874 enacts that deposits must not be received by any building society registered under that Act to an amount of more than two-thirds of the amounts secured by mortgages from its members, and it is part of the duty of the Auditor to ascertain that this provision has been duly complied with.

Loans.

Another item usually found on the liability side is "Loans." It is advisable that any amount borrowed from the society's bankers should be stated separately from the other loans, but should the directors decline to do this I am not prepared to say that the Auditor would be justified in making any comment thereon in his certificate. The interest accrued to the date of closing the books on deposits and loans should, of course, be included on the liability side of the Liabilities and

Lecture V.

Assets Account, and the Auditor must endeavour to satisfy himself that this has been properly calculated and that none has been omitted.

Miscellaneous Liabilities.

Any amounts due to tradesmen, also directors' fees, and sundry small items of this sort, should be included on the liability side, and any reserve which it may have been advisable to create, either for loss likely to arise on the realisation of any of the assets, or a general reserve, which would be available, say, for the equalisation of dividends, will appear on this side of the statement. There are two classes of reserve: one where the amount of the reserve included amongst the liabilities is specially invested in realisable securities, and the other where it is merely a reserve represented by the surplus of assets over liabilities.

Difference between Reserve and Reserve Fund.

In the former case it is usually styled a "Reserve Fund," and, in fact, this is its proper designation; in the latter case the word "Fund" should never be added to the word "Reserve." Although this is very frequently done, it is, in my opinion, wholly unjustifiable. A "Reserve" is not necessarily a "Reserve Fund," and where the words "Reserve Fund" are used there should be an amount on the assets side of the Liabilities and Assets Account of an exactly equivalent amount, showing the special investments representing this fund.

Undivided Profit.

The last item on the liability side of the Liabilities and Assets Account consists of the balance of the assets over the liabilities, and practically represents the amount of undivided profit—including, perhaps, the non-distributed profit of previous years as well as that of the period under audit. The form prescribed by the Chief Registrar describes the balance as "Undivided Profit," and requires the amount to be shown distinctly in two divisions, namely, the Reserve Funds and the undivided profit. This balance of undivided profit is not to include prospective interest. All premiums, bonuses, or commission deducted from, or paid as a consideration for, advances are of the nature of prospective interest, and should not be taken account of as assets, neither should the purchase of appropriations, being merely the redemption of a liability incurred by the society.

Lecture V.

Assets.

The principal asset of a building society is the amount due to the society in respect of the mortgages which are held by the society as a security for these advances. This asset represents the balance remaining unpaid of the advances on mortgage, including the premiums payable to date, in respect of which the repayments are, or should be, regularly made. The Auditor must satisfy himself that the balance due or outstanding on these mortgage securities does not include prospective interest. If it be the custom of the society to make any advances to non-members, it is certainly advisable that these amounts should be separately stated, and the Building Societies Act, 1894, requires that these advances should be divided into separate divisions according to the amounts. For example, mortgages where the debt does not exceed £500 have to be separately stated, and those between that amount and £1,000, those between £1,000 and £3,000, those between £3,000 and £5,000, and those above the latter amount, have also to be separately stated, and the Auditor has the right to require this classification to be made on the face of the account.

Balances due on Mortgages.

Mortgages in possession or in arrear.

The number of mortgages in each of these divisions referred to has also to be stated on the face of the Account, and in addition the mortgages (if any) on property of which the society has been upwards of twelve months in possession, the particulars of which have to be given in the second part of the Schedule, as referred to hereafter, and also on mortgages where the repayments are upwards of twelve months in arrear,

Lecture V.

and the property has not been upwards of twelve months in possession of the society, as shown by Part 3 of the same Schedule.

Responsibilities of Auditor as regards Mortgages.

In respect to the asset of "Balance due or outstanding on Mortgage Securities," the Auditor has several important duties. Although I can quote no legal authority for my statement, it may, I think, be taken that the Auditor cannot be held responsible for any error he may make in connection with these duties if he exercises all reasonable and proper precaution in looking after the interests of the members. For example, it may be stated that it is the duty of the Auditor to ascertain that properties, the deeds of which are deposited by the borrowers, are of sufficient value to cover the advances, should it be necessary to realise any of them through default in repayment, but this cannot be held to mean that the Auditor is to make for himself a valuation of each of these properties. It is, of course, undoubtedly the duty of the directors, when each proposal to borrow has been entertained, to have placed before them full and satisfactory evidence that not only is the market value of the property at that time equal to the proposed advance, but that there is sufficient margin to make the society perfectly safe should a large depreciation take place, from any cause whatever.

Limitation of his duty.

The duty of the Auditor is, in my opinion, confined to his satisfying himself to the best of his ability that the directors are in the habit of exercising care before they advance the moneys of the society, that is to say, he should inquire into the practice of the office, and if it appear to him from the Minute Book, or from inquiry of the secretary or manager, that it is the invariable rule of the directors either to employ a proper valuer to inspect all properties submitted as security, or to ascertain for themselves, by means of a committee of their own number, that there is not only security, but a fair margin for a depreciation in value, in my opinion the Auditor has fully performed his duty. Lecture V

Insurance of Property.

Again, the Auditor should satisfy himself that it is the practice of the directors to ascertain that all houses or other buildings forming part of the security are properly insured; this he can only do as a matter of general principle, it is certainly outside his province to inquire as to whether this necessary precaution has been exercised in the case of every security. As already indicated, it is not part of his duty to interfere in any way with the management of the society; this is entrusted solely to the directors by the members, who have the opportunity at each annual general meeting of displacing certain members of the Board should they be dissatisfied; while, on the other hand, they can, by reinstating the directors who retire by rotation, evince their confidence in those who have the administration of their affairs.

Reserve.

In dealing, therefore, generally with the asset of the advances due on mortgages, the Auditor must satisfy himself as far as he can that the whole amount is likely to be received, or, if not, that a sufficient reserve has been created to allow for any probable loss. The best test is to ascertain whether the instalments are paid at their due dates; or if they are in arrear, or in those cases where the Auditor observes irregularities in paying the instalments, he should inquire into the position of the borrowers, and as to the steps the society are taking to recover the arrears. Having done this, he should then satisfy himself that the reserve is sufficient, and if not should recommend that a larger amount be reserved, and in the event of it not being agreed to he must call attention to the fact in his certificate.

Freehold and Leasehold Investments.

The next item in the Liabilities and Assets Account requiring notice is "Freehold and Leasehold Investments." When such is there the Auditor should

Lecture V.

satisfy himself as far as he can that the freeholds are of the value at which they stand in the books, and in the case of the leasehold investments that a proper amount has been written off for depreciation. Should this not have been done, this is also a matter for the Auditor to refer to in his certificate.

Consols and other Investments.

The amount taken credit for Investments represented by Consols, Stocks, &c., also requires the careful attention of the Auditor. For this purpose a list should be prepared showing the names of the different investments, the price at which they stand in the books, and the market price as ascertained from the Stock Exchange authorised list on the day on which the books are closed. Should the investments have depreciated, a reserve should be created to allow for such depreciation, as it is clearly wrong for the directors to distribute a dividend relying on the value of investments when the market price is lower than that taken credit for. On the other hand, it is not desirable to take credit for any appreciation in the market value of the securities, but to leave them at cost price, and only take credit for the profit on an investment when it is sold. By the Building Societies Act, 1874, a society may, so far as its rules permit, invest any portion of its funds not immediately required for its purposes upon real or leasehold securities, or in the public funds, or in or upon any Parliamentary stock or securities, or in or upon any stock or securities payment of the interest on which is guaranteed by authority of Parliament, and by the Act of 1894 the powers of investment have been extended so as to include power to invest in or upon any security in which trustees are for the time being authorised by law to invest.

Cash at Bankers.

The cash at the bankers, and in hand, should also be verified; in the case of the cash at bankers, the balance shown in the Pass Book would probably not be the same as that shown in the Cash Book, owing to the fact that all the cheques drawn by the society on the last day, or within the last few days before the closing of the books, may not have been presented for payment; while, on the other hand, the society would probably not have received credit from the bank for cheques paid in on the last few days. A Reconciliation Statement should be prepared agreeing the two balances, but it is not now considered sufficient for a professional Auditor to be satisfied with the production of the Pass Book. It is now the practice for the Auditor to attend at the bank, and to be there shown the Ledger Account of the society in the books of the bank, or to obtain from the bank a letter addressed to the Auditor, certifying as to the balance shown in their books. The cash in hand should be counted by the Auditor, and for this purpose he should attend at the hour at which the society closes its books, or just before that time the whole of the cashier's balance should be paid into the bankers.

Cash in hand

Miscellaneous Assets.

The other assets demanding attention are the lease of the offices in which the business may be carried on, furniture, &c. No comment by me is needed on these items, beyond stating that a proper depreciation should be charged against the Revenue and Expenditure Account at the end of each financial period, leaving the balance representing these assets at the value which may fairly be taken credit for, looking upon the society as a going concern.

Deficiency.

Should the society not have been successful, and there be a deficiency from the commencement of the society's existence to the date of closing the books, the balance representing this deficiency will, of course, be on the asset side of the Liabilities and Assets Account, in accordance with the present absurd and misleading practice of requiring the statement of assets and liabilities of a company or society to show the same

Lecture V.

total on each side. As this is, however, the universal practice, the Auditor has no power to alter it, but experience shows that amongst those not accustomed to balance sheets it is not by any means clear to members of a society whether the balance shown on the balance sheet is a deficiency or a surplus, unless accompanied by explanatory words.

Schedules.

The Building Societies Act, 1894, requires that, in addition to the sub-division of the ordinary mortgages from members on the face of the Liabilities and Assets Account, a schedule shall be appended to the Accounts issued to members, divided into three parts, as follows :—

(1.) Mortgages, where the repayments are not upwards of twelve months in arrear, and the property has not been upwards of twelve months in possession of the society, and where the debt at the date of the accounts exceeds £5,000.

(2.) Particulars to be set forth in the case of property of which the society has been upwards of twelve months in possession.

(3.) Particulars to be set forth in the case of a mortgage where the repayments are upwards of twelve months in arrear, and the property has not been upwards of twelve months in possession of the society.

Statistical not Financial Statements.

These schedules must, like the accounts, be prepared for the Auditor by the officials of the society, and submitted to them with the accounts. They can, of course, being mere statistical statements, and not part of the book-keeping system, be merely checked by the Auditor to the best of his ability, but he should certainly compare each schedule with the corresponding one of the preceding year, and ascertain why any mortgages have been removed from the latter. If the society has

Lecture V.

not any mortgages exceeding £5,000, nor any mortgages in arrear, nor any property in possession as required to be given in the schedule, the word "*Nil*" should be inserted in each part.

Inspection of the Securities

Having completed the audit of the accounts proposed to be submitted to the members, there remains one of the most important of the Auditor's duties, viz., the inspection of the documents representing the securities.

These documents consist principally, if not entirely, of the deeds of mortgage held by the society as a security for their loans, which, in the case of large building societies, number many thousands. It is a statutory duty imposed upon the Auditors of every building society by the Building Societies Act, 1894, to certify that they have inspected the mortgage deeds and also state the number of deeds produced and inspected by them.

Absurd views as to extent o Auditor's duties.

The duties of an Auditor with relation to the inspection of securities is, at the present moment, a subject of controversy. Many persons go so far as to say that, not only has the Auditor to inspect the deeds, but to satisfy himself in each case that the loan is fully covered by the security. I have no hesitation in stating that it is perfectly impossible for an Auditor to do this, for however desirable it may be for the members of a society to know that this has been done, the carrying it into practice would involve an enormous expense. At the present moment I think it is universally acknowledged that the most efficient Auditor a building society can have is a Chartered Accountant, but to carry out the views of some of those who have lately criticised their duties in connection with building societies, the Chartered Accountant must be either at liberty to employ a solicitor and a valuer, or else he must possess himself the qualifications and experiences of three professions.

Lecture V.

In the first place the mortgage deeds when produced to him would have to be examined one by one to ascertain that the title is good, and that the property when first of all lent upon was of the value of the advance, and that at the date of the Auditor's examination it had not depreciated in value, or at any rate not below the value which, after giving credit for the instalments already paid, left the society still secured. Conceive what this would mean not only where the securities are many thousands in number, but where there are only two or three hundred. It requires very little reflection to see that the time this operation would take, even supposing the Auditor were competent to do it by himself, precludes its possibility, and were he to call in the two experts, the solicitor and the surveyor, already referred to, the members would, undoubtedly, refuse to pay the fees, and consider the remedy worse than the disease.

His proper duties.

The duty of the Auditor in this respect is, in my opinion, confined to his satisfying himself, firstly, that proper care has been exercised by the directors and officials in ascertaining that the securities were full securities when the advances were made; secondly, that the securities are still in possession of the society; and, thirdly, that they have not unduly depreciated, or if they have that a proper reserve has been made.

The following method of examination of securities covers, in my opinion, the Auditor's duty to the fullest extent.

Register of Advances to be produced.

As regards the mortgage deeds held by the society to cover advances, a register containing the particulars of each advance should be placed before the Auditor. Each advance should have a number, and a corresponding number should be placed on the conveyance to the society. A schedule of all the title deeds should be set out, also the amount of the advance, the period for

Lecture V.

which it is made, followed by several columns, the first one giving the heading for the year in which the advance is made. In the column opposite each advance the Auditor should place his initials, and the same process would be repeated in following years.

Deed Boxes should be opened in presence of Auditor.

The boxes containing the deeds should be opened in the presence of the Auditor, not more than one box being opened at the same time. As a rule these boxes are kept in the strong rooms of the society's bankers, and can only be opened by at least two different keys, held by two of the trustees. Occasionally a third key of a different lock is held by the secretary. Each box as opened should be emptied, and the deeds as checked should be replaced in the box. The boxes should then be re-locked in the presence of the Auditor, and the keys handed back to the trustees or their representatives. Each security should bear a distinct number, which should correspond with the register of deeds, and the number of this register should be placed in the Balance Book against the name of each debtor. As the deeds should only be able to be taken out in the presence of the trustees or their representatives, the Auditor can, in the case of those deeds which have previously been submitted to him, satisfy himself that they are the same which were shown to him on a former occasion by means of his own private mark placed against the numbers of the deeds. As regards the deeds held for advances made since the date up to which the previous accounts were audited, and the date of closing of the books, that is to say, made during the period embraced by the audit, they should be carefully examined by the Auditor, and the actual conveyances executed by the borrower to the society should be opened. From each of these the Auditor will obtain the amount of the advance and observe the due execution by the borrower. The conveyance should be

Deeds for new Advances.

Lecture V.

numbered, and against the number the Auditor should put his private mark or stamp, and the deed should then be placed in a parcel with the other title deeds of the property and deposited in the box. It is certainly not within the province of the Auditor to attempt to investigate, even if he be sufficient lawyer to do so, the title deeds themselves.

A still better plan is for the Auditor to affix his private seal outside a package containing all the deeds of each security. The production of the packages with the seals unbroken would be an absolute proof of their not having been tampered with. In those cases where the deeds had been required for reference or for some other purpose they would be carefully re-examined by the Auditor, made into a parcel, and re-sealed by him.

Deeds in hands of Solicitor.

It usually happens that some deeds are missing, the reason being that they are in the hands of the solicitor for some purpose. A note should be taken of these, and before the Auditor ultimately signs the accounts he should require their production. Occasionally a further advance is made by a society upon the same title deeds; this is either secured by a separate document, or by an endorsement on the original conveyance to the society; but in either case the actual conveyance or endorsement, with the execution by the borrower, should be produced to the Auditor.

Deeds representing Investments.

The title deeds representing the freehold and leasehold investments of the society should be inspected by the Auditor in the same manner; that is to say, either his private mark againtst the conveyances he has previously seen should be shown to him, or, in the case of a fresh purchase, the actual conveyance to the trustees of the society should be inspected. Should any of these investments consist of house property, the Auditor should satisfy himself that they are insured for

Lecture V.

the full amount, and should have produced to him the last receipt for the premium paid to the fire insurance company.

Verification of Consols and other Investments.

The documents representing the other investments of the society, such as Consols, stocks, or other securities authorised by Section 25 of the Building Societies Act, 1874, or by Section 17 of the Building Societies Act, 1894, should be inspected. In the case of Consols, a form for the express purpose can be obtained from the Bank of England, on which the society should fill up the names of the persons in whom the Consols are invested, also the nominal amount of Consols held, with the request that a certificate as to its correctness may be issued by the Bank to the Auditor. In the case of stock registered in the books of the Bank of England a similar form can be obtained, and in the case of stock registered in the books of other bankers a letter should be addressed to the bankers requesting them to give the same information direct to the Auditor.

Before leaving the bank the Auditor should ascertain, by application to the officials, that the securities in their possession are held merely for safe custody, and that they hold no charge or lien upon them, unless such is disclosed by the accounts, when the Auditor must ascertain that the charge or lien is not in excess of the amount stated.

Auditor's Certificate.

After the inspection of the securities has been completed, there then remains to be settled the certificate of the Auditor. By Section 2, Sub-section 2, of the Act of 1894, every Auditor in attesting the annual Account or Statement shall either certify that it is correct, duly vouched, and in accordance with law, or specially report to the society in what respect he finds it incorrect, unvouched, or not in accordance with law, and he has also to certify that he has, at that audit, actually inspected the mortgage deeds and other

Lecture V.

securities belonging to the society, and to state the number of properties with respect to which deeds have been produced to and actually inspected by him.

Form prescribed by Chief Registrar.

There is affixed to the form prescribed by the Chief Registrar a form of Auditor's certificate, to which no objection can be raised, but there is no reason why the Auditor should adopt this form.

If the accounts are, in his opinion, correct in every detail, the certificate can be contained in very few words; but, should the Auditor not be satisfied with them, two courses are open to him. He may allow the directors to alter their statements of account to suit his views, or he may, in his certificate, call the attention of the members to those items in the accounts which, in his opinion, are inaccurate or not clearly understood.

The former is the course usually adopted by Chartered Accountants, as if the Auditor's recommendations are agreed to by the Board the credit of the society is not injured, as it would be were the accounts to be published with a qualified certificate thereon. It is an unselfish course to adopt, as the members have no means of knowing how much they have benefited by their Auditor's experience and, perhaps, by his firmness, and few outside our profession know how much anxiety and trouble we often go through before unqualified certificates are given by us, and what a very different appearance the original statements submitted by the directors bear to the ones ultimately placed before the members.

With the issue of his certificate the Auditor's work is complete. It is desirable he attend the annual meeting, when the accounts he has audited are submitted, and when his functions cease, to commence, however, again, should he be re-elected to the office for the ensuing year.

This annual re-election of Auditors is one of the

Lecture V.

great blots on the present system of company and building society administration, but I do not consider it comes within the province of my address this evening to comment on past or future legislation.

Crisis through which Auditors are passing.

You will, however, I feel sure, allow me, in conclusion, to say a few words on the crisis through which Auditors are, undoubtedly, at present passing. Although it is over thirty years since the Limited Liability Act, under which nearly all companies now in existence are registered, came into force, no statute has been added defining the duties of Auditors. At the present moment a company may be registered whose directors can not only present accounts without having them audited, but they need never even present accounts at all. In the absence of legislation, Auditors have had to work in the dark, and it is not surprising there should be a great divergence of views as to their duties.

Weakness of the Legislature.

When the present or any future Government choose to take the matter in hand, they will find in the members of the Institute of Chartered Accountants a body, not only capable, but willing to carry out whatever duties it may be decided appertain to Auditors. Give us also the power and authority, and we will wield it. When once, however, an audit has been entrusted to one of our body on behalf of the members of a company or society, let us hold it until deposed by those members. Do not allow a board of directors, whom an Auditor has displeased through doing his duty, to replace him by one of their nominees on the suggestion of one of their own friends in the body of a meeting, as is done at present, the existing practice of Auditors having to be re-elected annually rendering this easy.

The Charter of the Institute should be upheld.

Let the Charter granted to us by the Privy Council in 1880 after long deliberation be upheld. It may be true, in fact I admit it is true, that some incapable Auditors are numbered in our ranks. This is because it

Lecture V.

was felt to be unfair to exclude anyone who at the date of the Charter was in practice; but they are going one by one, and every year makes us as a body more efficient, the Charter requiring that those who aspire to enter the Institute shall have a long special training.

Those who have been articled to our members since the date of the Charter come from the same class as do those who are now at Woolwich, Sandhurst, and the Inns of Court. They have been educated at the same class of schools, and, in addition, they have had a special education in the duties of Auditors.

Absurdity of the term Public Accountant.

They have, therefore, in my opinion, a right to rely upon the upholding of our Royal Charter, but the Building Societies Act, 1894, which has undoubtedly done much for members of building societies, contained the weak enactment that one at least of the Auditors must be a person who publicly carries on the business of an Accountant. What is the use of such a clause? For years persons without the slightest qualification or training have been publicly carrying on the business of an accountant. Anyone can call himself a public accountant, and it makes no difference in his favour if he be a member of a society. Fifty societies could be registered to-morrow under the Limited Liability Acts, which would probably have little difficulty in inducing the Board of Trade to allow them to drop the word "limited," and thus enable them to pretend they were specially incorporated.

The society in England and Wales whose members possess the qualifications of Auditors is the society in whose head-quarters I am now addressing you. Let legislation tell us a little more clearly what our duties are, make us independent, and we will carry them out—I say more, it is we alone who can carry them out.

LECTURE VI.

THE INVESTIGATION OF THE ACCOUNTS OF COMMERCIAL UNDERTAKINGS PREVIOUS TO THEIR CONVERSION INTO PUBLIC COMPANIES.

Read before the Chartered Accountants' Students' Society of Edinburgh, 19th February; the Glasgow Institute of Accountants' Debating Society, 20th February, and the Chartered Accountants' Students' Society of London, 26th February, 1890.

Lecture VI.

Introductory Remarks.

As I am the first English Chartered Accountant who has been invited by your Society to deliver an address in Scotland, it will not be out of place for me to commence by saying how much I appreciate the honour you have done me, and to express the hope that it is only the commencement of friendly relations between the members of the profession in both countries, and that the day is not far distant when we shall all be members of one body, the Associations of Chartered Accountants now existing in London, Edinburgh, Glasgow, and Aberdeen being branches of one society, in place of their being separate institutions at at present.

English Chartered Accountants.

Although professional Accountants have been recognised in England for over half a century, still it

Lecture VI.

was not until 1870 that the first society formed for the advancement of their interests, known as the Institute of Accountants, was founded, and this was followed in 1872 by the Society of Accountants in England and several provincial societies. It was not, however, until 1880 that the Privy Council granted a Charter to the senior institute, which resulted in the amalgamation of all the English Societies, previous to which date the practising professional Accountants in England and Wales could not really consider themselves as being members of a recognised profession.

Scotch Chartered Accountants.

In Scotland, however, the profession is of considerably older standing, the first Charter having been granted to the Society of Accountants in Edinburgh in 1854, the Institute of Accountants and Actuaries in Glasgow in 1855, and the Society of Accountants of Aberdeen in 1867, and in consequence the Scotch Chartered Accountants have obtained a certain class of professional work, notably that of acting as Judicial Factors, Curators *bonis* to lunatics and minors, Factors *loco tutoris*, Factors *loco absentis*, also as agents for large landed proprietors, which, up to the present time, has not yet been acquired by the English Chartered Accountants, English landlords still retaining the far more costly method of having local agents, maintaining separate establishments in each district in which their estates are situated.

Students' Societies.

As the Charters were granted as much in the interest of the public as of the members of the profession, they naturally provided for the proper education of those to be admitted to membership, the proof of such education being tested by examinations. It was only natural, therefore, that the Charters should be followed by the institution of Students' Societies, and it must be pleasing to all members of the profession, who take a real interest in its welfare, to watch the growth of these Societies, and to do everything in their power to assist those who are likely to be their successors.

Lectures to Students.

With this object, many members of the profession have given lectures on various subjects to the Students' Societies. The Chartered Accountants' Students' Society of London have hitherto confined their lectures to professional subjects, having regard to the Intermediate and Final examinations of the Institute. I am glad, however, to observe that, in addition to obtaining lectures from members of the profession, the Chartered Accountants' Students' Societies of Scotland have been fortunate in securing addresses from others eminent in their respective subjects, such as barristers-at-law, solicitors, actuaries, and University professors. The instruction derived from these lectures cannot fail to be of the greatest usefulness to the Students in their future career, having regard to the variety in the businesses carried on by the undertakings whose accounts they will probably have to investigate in later life.

Investigation for Company purposes.

The investigation of the accounts of commercial undertakings, previous to their being incorporated as Public Companies under the Companies Act of 1862, and subsequent Acts, is to a certain extent a new branch of our professional work.

It is true that almost from the passing of this Act advantage was taken by some of the old-established and well-known private partnerships to register themselves under its provisions, yet it is only within the last three or four years that company promoters have turned their attention to this particular line of business.

This is, perhaps, owing to the remarkable success attendant upon the conversion of some of the best-known brewery partnerships into public companies, the investing and speculating public having so eagerly competed for the possession of their capital, but more to the formation of those companies which, although professedly

Lecture VI. incorporated for the purpose of investing in the debentures of existing companies, yet soon found it more profitable to assist in the formation of companies, and have become practically "Promoting Companies," although they prefer to style themselves Debenture and Assets Companies.

Private Syndicates.

Private syndicates having this object in view have been in existence for many years, but the first company which originated this class of business on a larger scale, in conjunction with influential names, was registered in 1883, more for the purpose of purchasing assets of insolvent estates, with a view to their gradual realisation at a profit.

This was subsequently followed, in 1885, by an offshoot of the company, with practically the same board, which at once commenced business by inviting subscriptions for debentures of new undertakings, and it has subsequently been followed by many others in the last two years, who openly announce that they are incorporated for assisting in the formation of public companies.

System adopted by Promoters.

Previous to the existence of these companies, the ordinary promoter had a limited *clientèle*. Several of the large financial and commercial houses who were in the habit of placing loans for Foreign Governments, and bonds for foreign railway companies, occasionally made a departure and offered the capital of commercial undertakings, but as a rule they regarded with suspicion the agents who brought them schemes for proposed companies. The usual plan, therefore, was for the promoter to attempt to launch his company by means of advertisements in the newspapers and the circulation of a large number of prospectuses through the post to supposed investors and speculators. If he had the means he did this at his own expense and risk, if not, he would form a small syndicate, sometimes inducing the printer of the prospectuses and the advertising agents to enter into the speculation, by receiving little or nothing if the company were not successfully floated, and a heavy reward, which had to be borne by the company, in the event of its being successfully launched.

Secret Contracts.

This method of company promotion necessitating many secret arrangements, which ultimately caused so much scandal, led to the passing of the 38th Section of the Companies Act of 1867, which required the dates and the names of the parties to contracts of every description to be disclosed in the prospectus of the company. As a result of this section many promoters, advertising agents, and others who had entered into these speculative arrangements found themselves in the Bankruptcy Court.

Since the formation of the financial companies just referred to, a new field has been opened for the promoter, and it cannot be denied that the companies which have been brought out under their auspices within the last few years have been of a very far superior class to those which were launched in the last speculative mania, which existed about eight or ten years ago, and this is principally owing to the number of sound commercial undertakings which have taken advantage of the proposals made by company promoters to convert their businesses into public companies.

Conversion o private concerns into Companies.

There are many advantages gained by the conversion of firms and individuals owning large trading concerns into companies, the principal one being that the liability of those interested in the business becomes limited instead of unlimited, as is the case of members of firms.

It is specially important in the case of those who may have inherited a partnership in an undertaking, but who take no part in the management of the business, also for those who wish to retire from business,

Lecture VI.

leaving the management of its affairs to others, but who still wish to retain their capital in the concern, either for the profits or for the sake of assisting those to whom they leave the goodwill and the management of affairs.

Frequently, also, a partner may not only wish to retire from the business but to withdraw his capital also, in which case, if the existing partners are not able to provide the amount, it would be necessary to find a new partner or partners, and this might, perhaps, be impossible, or for many reasons very undesirable. In all such cases the conversion of a sound trading concern into a company is perfectly legitimate.

Advantages to be gained.

The interest also of a large holder of shares can be disposed of in parcels, and divided at the will of the holder, which can rarely be done in the case of a partner having a large capital at his credit in the books of a firm, there being, as a rule, no limit to the number of the holders of shares in a company. The members of a firm have, as a rule, the right to object to the introduction of another partner, although, perhaps, such introduction may not affect in any way the profits they receive from the business; such right of objection does not exist in the case of a company unless specially authorised by the Articles of Association. The shares also of a company can be mortgaged, whilst it is, as a rule, impossible for a partner in a firm to procure an advance on his interest.

Retirement of Partners.

In the case of a partner retiring, or on the sale of a business to other persons, it is almost impossible to obtain the value of the "goodwill," more especially if the members of the old firm decline to allow their names to be used by the purchasers. In the case of a company taking over an established business, it is usual for the vendors to receive a far larger amount for the goodwill than could be obtained from private purchasers. As much as ten years' purchase is sometimes given by a company, whereas it is very seldom that under ordinary conditions a sum equivalent to more than two or three years' purchase can be obtained from partners or private purchasers.

Death of Partners.

On the death of the sole proprietor of a large business, it is exceedingly difficult for his executors and trustees to dispose of his interest; and if, under the terms of the will, they choose to carry on the business, they of course run the risk of being involved in personal liability. This is of course obviated if the business be turned into a company, and fully paid-up shares or debentures be accepted by the executors and trustees for their interest.

Certificate of Profits by Chartered Accountant.

Before an established business is thus converted, it is now the recognised practice for the books to be submitted to a Chartered Accountant, for the purpose of his giving a certificate as to the result of the transactions in the past.

New enterprises are launched on the names and position of the directors who appear on the prospectus, in conjunction with the certificates of engineers, or of other experts, as to the probability of their success, also on the strength of a statement put forward by the directors in the prospectus as to the estimated profits likely to be derived from an investment in the shares; but within the last few years the investing and speculating public have learnt, some through bitter experience, that estimates cannot be relied on, and that, when possible, it is desirable to obtain some definite statement of the transactions of the past, on which estimates for the future can be reasonably based. They have, therefore, come to regard it as a matter of course that the accounts of an established business shall be investigated by a Chartered Accountant, and to find a certificate in the prospectus embodying the result of his investigations. This is, practically, so firmly established that it would be almost useless for a first-class board of directors to attempt to obtain capital, even for a well-known business, in the absence of a Chartered Accountant's certificate.

On receiving instructions to investigate the accounts of a commercial undertaking for the purpose of giving a certificate, which will enable it to be converted into a Public Company, there are several points to be considered by the Chartered Accountant before he commences his actual investigation.

In the first place, he should clearly understand on whose behalf he is acting, what kind of certificate is required of him, and what use is going to be made of his certificate when granted.

Should the investigation have to be made on behalf of the partners of a firm, who intend simply to register their firm as a company, without offering any of the shares or debentures to the public, then the responsibility of the Chartered Accountant is practically limited to the actual professional work of making the investigation correctly, and he can practically limit the nature of the investigation in accordance with the instructions of his clients.

His responsibility would also be equally limited were he instructed by the partners of two or more firms, who intend to form a company, to take over their respective businesses and carry them on under a board of directors and shareholders formed exclusively of the partners, and who did not intend to issue any shares or debentures to other parties. Should it not be, however, the intention of the firm or firms to take the whole of the shares and debentures, but to offer part of the share capital, or none of the share capital but debentures, to the public, the responsibility of the Chartered Accountant is practically as great as it would be were a public issue made of the shares.

As a rule, a Chartered Accountant's certificate is principally required when the capital is offered to the public by means of an advertised prospectus, in which case it is essential he should know, not only who are his actual clients, but also all who are associated with the promoter, as it is scarcely going too far to say that there are many promoters with whom he should at once refuse to have any connection, and it would be wise to decline the investigation altogether. The Chartered Accountant may be absolutely certain from the past careers of these men that, however apparently respectable the business may be, the accounts of which it is suggested he should investigate, some subterfuge will be made use of, in endeavouring to obtain the capital, with which a Chartered Accountant who values his reputation should not run the risk of being associated.

It may be argued that this would press unduly harshly on a respectable firm who were desirous of converting their business into a company, but it would really have the contrary effect, as, when they ascertained the reason of the Chartered Accountant's refusal, they would seek a more respectable channel for the purpose of introducing the shares of their company to the public.

Assuming, however, that the preliminary inquiries are satisfactory, the Chartered Accountant should then ascertain how many years' accounts it is proposed should be examined, and he should be supplied with copies of Profit and Loss Accounts and Balance Sheets for the period. If these accounts have been audited he should ask to be supplied with the reports and other documents, if any, which accompanied the Statements of Accounts when sent in by the Auditors.

Should statements not have been periodically prepared, a much greater responsibility is thrown upon the Chartered Accountant, as it will then be necessary

Lecture VI.

for him to prepare the Profit and Loss Accounts and Balance Sheets himself, a much more responsible and lengthy task than to audit the accounts prepared by another Chartered Accountant and presented to him merely for his authentication.

Prospectus of proposed Company.

The Chartered Accountant should apply for the prospectus of the proposed company, which, when obtained, should be carefully perused by him, and if he sees anything objectionable therein, not only referring to his own special department, but in any other particular, he should at once point this out, and, if necessary, inform the promoters he cannot allow the prospectus to be issued, with his name attached, without modification.

Should the promoter not fall in with his views, the Chartered Accountant should withdraw before commencing the investigation, as it would be manifestly unfair to the partners of the business proposed to be converted into a company were he to commence the investigation, and to raise objections afterwards to clauses in the prospectus which were submitted to him previous to his clients incurring any expense.

As regards the number of years over which the investigation extends, it is not for the Chartered Accountant to prescribe the period.

Accounts should be brought to as late a date as possible.

It, however, clearly comes within his province to require that the Statements of Accounts referred to in the prospectus shall be brought down to the latest possible date, and he would clearly be a party to a deception, if not to an actual fraud, were he to issue an unqualified certificate of the profit of past years, up to any period, if the transactions of the subsequent period had resulted in a falling-off.

The Chartered Accountant would, however, be perfectly justified in limiting his investigation and issuing his certificate for a very short period immediately antecedent to the date on which the company is to take over the business, even, say, for one year, had the business of the previous year resulted in a far lower profit; but if during the investigation he discovered that some special reasons had caused the trading of the period under investigation to result in an exceptional profit which would probably not occur again, then it would be clearly his duty to require a longer period to be investigated and reported on by him, and he should explain that unless this were done he would have to qualify his certificate in such a way as perhaps to render it practically useless.

It is also clearly the duty of the Chartered Accountant, before putting his client to the expense of investigation, to ascertain that it is possible for him to give a certificate, as again it would not be fair to commence the investigation and then have to report that it could not be completed owing to the absence of certain information, without which his experience shows him would render it impossible for him to arrive at a definite statement of profits. For example, supposing a trading concern had been in existence for fifty years and a large amount of capital was employed in stock, and no stocktaking had ever been made during this period, it might be absolutely impossible to prepare a Profit and Loss Account for the last five or ten years. The most a Chartered Accountant could do under these circumstances would be to give a certificate of the amount of the sales for a given period and then leave it to the directors to settle, either on their own responsibility or with the assistance of special trade experts, what would be the probable profit on the turnover, and it would be the duty of the Chartered Accountant to inform his clients that in the absence of stocktaking it would be impossible for him to prepare a Profit and Loss Account, and then to leave them to decide as to the steps they will take.

Lecture VI.

Method of conducting Investigation.

As regards the method of conducting the investigation into the accounts of a business which it is proposed to convert into a company, and to offer the shares or debentures to the public, the Chartered Accountant must, of course, be entirely unfettered by any instructions as to what is and is not absolutely necessary to inquire into. His responsibility is to the unknown persons, who at a later date may, on the strength of his certificate, be induced to apply for shares and debentures; consequently there are no persons who can give instructions to whom he owes any allegiance, and should any attempt be made to influence him during his investigation he should at once resent it, and make his clients clearly understand that until his examination is completed, and he is prepared to issue his certificate, he only wishes to hold intercourse with those who have charge of the books which he is investigating.

Full extent of Investigation.

It does not, of course, come within the province of my address to discuss fully the details connected with investigations of this class. You have your own instructors in book-keeping, auditing, and general investigations, and considering the vast range of the businesses undertaken by the trading institutions which have already been, and those which are likely to be, converted into public companies, it would be practically impossible to discuss details in an address of this sort.

It must depend entirely upon the experience of the Chartered Accountant, having regard also to the special class of business whose transactions are recorded in the books he is investigating, as to how deep his inquiries are to extend, and this will greatly depend, of course, upon the manner in which the books are kept.

Advisability of taking Notes.

There are, however, a few special items which it is well to call attention to. Before I refer to these, however, I will state the desirability of preserving most carefully any notes that may be taken during the progress of an investigation. Any queries raised, although perhaps asked and the answers thereto given verbally, should be recorded, and where necessary reference should be made to the entries in the books provoking the inquiry.

These notes should of course be eventually endorsed and put away with the papers, as the Chartered Accountant should be prepared, even years afterwards, to answer any questions that may be put to him as to how he obtained certain results.

We all know from experience that a company may be launched successfully, have a prosperous career for many years, yet eventually go into liquidation, and questions might be raised in the course of the liquidation impossible to answer without a great deal of trouble in the absence of these notes taken at the time of the investigation, although the books of account might be available.

List of Books in use.

Should the Chartered Accountant have to obtain information necessary for his investigation, not included in the books, it is desirable he should put his request in a letter, and require the answer to be given him in the same manner. He should also, previous to the commencement of the investigation, be furnished with a complete list of the books of the business, both financial and statistical.

He should also keep notes of all books and papers examined by him, so that when he has completed his investigation and delivered his report he will have with his papers a complete record of the investigation, and will be able, if necessary, years afterwards, to give a clear explanation of the manner in which he has arrived at his results.

Original

Original documents should be consulted by the

Lecture VI.

Documents should be called for.

Chartered Accountant as far as possible. The larger the business, the less likelihood there will be of intentional fraud, as those who might not scruple to mislead, were the entries in books entirely under their own control, naturally shrink from placing themselves in the power of their staff, which would necessarily be the case were they to give instructions for entries of an improper nature.

The Chartered Accountant must, however, in his investigation, be always on his guard, as it is difficult to suggest a position of greater professional responsibility than the one he accepts in the circumstance under consideration.

I am not, of course, implying he should enter upon his duties with a feeling of distrust of the documents placed before him, or of those with whom he is brought into contact. On the contrary, I attach the greatest importance to his at once securing the good offices of the staff, by approaching them in a genial spirit. By this means he is far more likely to discover if anything be amiss than he will be should he treat those upon whom he may have to rely for information in a brusque manner, as, instead of trying to assist him, they will possibly throw difficulties in his way.

Stock-in-trade.

In the case of a trading company, care must be taken to ascertain that the stock at the commencement and at the end of the period under investigation has been properly taken and valued, and, moreover, that it has been taken and valued at both periods on precisely the same basis.

It does not, of course, come within the province of the Chartered Accountant to take stock, either by measurement or by weight. At the commencement of the period it would probably have been taken by the *employés* of the firm, but it is desirable that the stock at the end of the period, which would probably be the date on which the company is to take over the business, should be taken by independent experts. Although it would probably be valued for the purpose of arriving at the price to be paid by the company, the stock, for the purposes of the accounts, must, as already stated, be taken on the same basis and valued in the same manner as at the commencement of the period. Lecture VI.

Certificate of Stock-in-trade.

If the value placed upon the stock is the cost, the Chartered Accountant should require a certificate, either from an independent person or from an official of the firm on whom he feels he can place reliance, as to the quantity of each class of the goods in stock, and he should then, if possible, test the cost price, both at the commencement and the end of the period, by comparing the items in the inventory with the original invoices. If the stock has been valued at cost price, subject to an allowance for depreciation, he should ascertain that the same percentage upon the various classes of stock has been allowed at the commencement and end of the period.

A correct valuation of the stock is, of course, of the greatest importance in the investigation of the accounts of a trading concern, as when it is heavy it is obvious that a very little manipulation as to values could increase the apparent profits to an enormous extent.

Relation of Gross Profit to Sales.

The percentage the gross profit bears to the sales should be ascertained, and should be compared by the Chartered Accountant with that made by similar trading concerns, and the result would probably be of great assistance to him in ascertaining that the stock has been properly valued.

He should also ascertain that the stock at the end of the period is marketable. The stocks of many trading concerns are subject to freaks of fashion, and what may be of value one month may be rendered almost unsaleable the next month in consequence of

Lecture VI. the introduction of something new which supersedes it in public demand. Any loss which has arisen in this manner must be charged against the Profit and Loss Account, regardless of remonstrances. Credit may, of course, be given for any amount of a similar character clearly proved to have been wrongly included among the assets at the commencement of the period, but I use the word clearly advisedly, as after an interval it would, in the majority of cases, be impossible to ascertain the nature of the stock for such a purpose.

Sales. The amount taken to credit for sales in the Revenue Account must be scrutinised, first of all, for the purpose of ascertaining that a full allowance for trade discounts has been deducted, and, secondly, for the purpose of ascertaining that the sales are *bonâ fide*.

Discounts. The prices invoiced to customers are frequently subject to two discounts, one in consideration of immediate payment, the other the discount allowed to the trade off the prices quoted in trade circulars or price lists. These trade discounts vary from a small rate to as much as 40 or 50 per cent., and it is obvious that when the trade discount is large the sales of a large business may be most unwarrantably swelled, in a Profit and Loss Account, if an allowance be not made for this discount, while, apparently, there may be nothing incorrect in the statements submitted.

The sales may be improperly increased if a firm, with the intention of deceit, press their travellers to obtain from their customers large orders for goods which they would not, in the ordinary course, receive until the period after which the books have been closed.

Goods on sale or return. The Chartered Accountant must also ascertain that the sales, especially those made in the last few months, are *bonâ fide* sales, that is to say, that the goods have not been sent out subject to an understanding with the customers that under certain circumstances they may be returned. The value of goods sent out "on sale or return" should not be included, therefore, amongst the sales, but only the value of that proportion which had been actually disposed of, the balance in the hands of the customers held on behalf of the firm would, of course, be included in the stock.

Consignments.

Consignments abroad must also be separately stated, and only the value of the goods actually disposed of taken credit for, and the Chartered Accountant should require to see acknowledgments in writing in every case, both from the holders of goods on sale or return and from the consignees, of the value of the goods they have disposed of and the value of those on hand.

It must also be remembered that, as a rule, goods of this description are invoiced at the selling price, and care must be taken, therefore, that the cost or valuation price is ascertained before the amount is added to the stock.

Sales by instalments.

Occasionally goods are sold, the delivery of which is to be made by instalments. The Chartered Accountant must ascertain that no amount is taken credit for in respect of the goods which will have to be delivered after the date on which the books are closed, unless he makes reference to this in his report.

Care must be taken that the Profit and Loss Account does not take credit for any item of income which may possibly not eventually be received without a proper reserve has been made and charged in the accounts. In the case of a bank or financial firm, a very large income could be shown on paper, were interest charged at a high rate on a number of bad and doubtful debts. This may sound too improbable to be likely to happen, but it has occurred in several well-

Lecture VI. known instances in the case of companies where dividends have been distributed on the strength of the supposed revenue, as shown in the published accounts.

Expenditure. The expenditure side of the Profit and Loss Account must, of course, be carefully scrutinised by the Chartered Accountant, and he must ascertain that each item includes all the outstandings at the end of the period in respect of that item.

Commission on Sales. Where the revenue of a business has been derived through the means of travellers or agents, who are paid by commission, care must be taken that the whole of the commission due in respect of the amounts not collected, but yet taken credit for in the Revenue Account, has been properly charged.

Omission of Liabilities. It is sometimes exceedingly difficult to ascertain that all the liabilities have been charged against the Profit and Loss Account, and it is quite possible, in anticipation of a business being converted into a Company on the strength of a Profit and Loss Account, for liabilities to be concealed altogether by the partners, and not brought into the books at all. It is, of course, impossible to lay down any rules to prevent omissions of the kind being overlooked, and the discovery of a fraud of this nature will depend almost entirely on the skill and experience of the Chartered Accountant.

If he has the slightest suspicions, he must be guided by circumstances as to the best means of verifying or dissipating them, and although liabilities may be omitted from the books of account, still there may be other documents in the office which may put him on the right track. Letter books, for example, are, of course, available for his inspection, and he would also be able, without exciting any suspicion, to ascertain from the firms in the habit of supplying the business whether all their invoices have been entered in the books.

Moral and legal responsibilities of Chartered Accountants.

It may possibly be argued that the responsibility of a Chartered Accountant is simply confined to ascertaining that the statements are in accordance with the books of account, and that he cannot be blamed should omissions have been made therefrom. With regard to the legal responsibility this is probably true, but I am sure that no one in this room would agree that legal responsibility is all we have to consider. I am proud to say I could mention many instances where my professional brethren in London have thrown away valuable business sooner than have their names connected with doubtful enterprises or persons, and I am sure that were I as well acquainted with the Scotch Chartered Accountants I should find they have an equal regard to their moral obligations.

Unlikelihood of Revenue being omitted.

The Chartered Accountant may practically take it for granted that a Profit and Loss Account placed before him for examination is not likely to have any omissions from the Revenue. In respect, therefore, to the credit side of this account he need not take the same pains as an auditor to guard against omissions. His duty is practically confined to ascertaining that too much has not been taken credit for, and that what is taken credit for appertains only to the period under investigation.

Absence of Profit and Loss Account.

Should the books of a business not have been kept on a proper system of double entry, and a Profit and Loss Account has to be compiled, which is not the result of book-keeping, it is possible that a statement of receipts and expenditure, or an abstract of the cash account, may be placed before the Chartered Accountant. This, of course, must not be accepted by him and certified as a Revenue Account, for a Receipts and Expenditure Account, being merely an abstract of the cash received and paid during the time, does not include either the amounts due to creditors or the

Lecture VI. amounts due by debtors at the commencement and end of the period. It would, therefore, be the duty of the Chartered Accountant to only make use of this statement for the purpose of assisting him in the preparation of a proper Profit and Loss Account, and it would be necessary for him to ascertain the amounts due by debtors, the amounts due to creditors, and the value of the stock at the commencement and end of the period.

If he cannot do this from the material supplied, he must be careful to show in his report that the Income and Expenditure Account, although it may extend over many years, is not a satisfactory document, as the average annual profit deducted from this account cannot be accepted as being as reliable as a Profit and Loss Account.

Leasehold Property.

The Chartered Accountant must also ascertain that when leasehold property forms part of the assets of a business that a sufficient proportion has been charged against the Profit and Loss Account in respect of each lease for the period under investigation.

Should the Chartered Accountant be investigating the accounts of a mine to be taken over by a company, he should ascertain that the royalties in respect of the minerals raised have been charged, also, of course, dead rent; the latter, being a fixed annual payment, is easily determined, but in order to ascertain the royalties it would be necessary to check the quantities of ore or mineral raised, on which the royalty is based, so as to be sure that all is brought into account.

Depreciation

The amount to be charged against the Profit and Loss Account for the period under investigation in respect of what is known amongst Chartered Accountants as "Depreciation" requires careful attention. When a firm, whose business it is proposed shall be converted into a company, has a considerable portion of its capital invested in leasehold property, patents, plant and machinery, or any class of wasting security, the greatest care must be exercised by the Chartered Accountant, and it may be necessary for him to require those instructing him to call in the assistance of other experts. **Lecture VI.**

In considering questions, however, of this nature, the result to be arrived at is the same, namely, that the period embraced in the accounts under investigation shall be charged with the exact proportion applicable to the period, so that the balance left, which would be included among the other items on the credit side of the Balance Sheet, really represents the value of the property in question at the date on which that statement is made out.

Leases and Patents.

In the case of a lease or a patent, the amount to be ascertained is easily arrived at, the price paid for each being in both cases for a fixed term of years.

The Chartered Accountant must not entertain any objection to this method of dealing with this class of security on the ground that the lease or the patent may be renewed, unless there is produced to him actual proof that the firm are legally entitled to the renewal, and that it does not depend on any person's favour or caprice, or the result of an application to the Court, which may be opposed.

Buildings, Plant and Machinery.

The amount to be written off buildings, plant, and machinery is often a most difficult question, and, in the case of a business where a large amount of the capital is thus employed, the total value of the plant and machinery should be divided into sections classified according to their lasting capabilities, each section bearing a different rate for depreciation. For example, an asset represented by buildings on freehold land would be subject to a very trifling deduction, and possibly none at all, if the cost of maintaining the

Lecture VI.

buildings in a high state of efficiency were charged against the Profit and Loss Account.

Heavy machinery also would be subject to a comparatively small rate of depreciation, but then regard must be had to the fact as to whether the machinery is not only in first-class condition, but also whether or no it has been superseded by machinery of an improved nature.

Boilers, Workmen's Tools, &c.

Other machinery, and articles used in conjunction with machinery, such as boilers, will be subject to a much higher rate of depreciation, and driving bands to a still higher rate, while tools for workmen might have to be charged entirely against the revenue of the year, or the expenditure on them be at most spread over two or three years.

In dealing, however, with accounts containing particulars of property of this nature, it is very desirable that a civil or mechanical engineer, or some other expert familiar with the special class of machinery used in the business, be called in to assist the Chartered Accountant.

Interest on Loans, &c.

Where interest is payable by a firm in respect of any outstanding loans or on ordinary trading accounts care must be taken that the accrued interest to the date of the closing of the books is brought into account.

Bad Debts.

The amount to be charged against the Profit and Loss Account in respect of the loss likely to arise on the realisation of outstanding debts is also of great importance, and for the purpose of arriving at a proper conclusion as to how to deal with these a schedule containing the dates of the contraction of the various debts included amongst the assets of the company should be prepared.

This schedule must be considered item by item, and the total amount of all debts admitted to be bad, and a percentage in respect of the doubtful debts, must be charged against the Profit and Loss Account, provided they have been incurred during the period under investigation.

Extraordinary Expenditure.

Occasionally the Chartered Accountant will find that in accounts placed before him for investigation certain expenses have been eliminated on the ground that they were very exceptionable and not likely to occur again. These should be very carefully gone into by the Chartered Accountant, and should he be of the same opinion and allow them to be left out of the Revenue Account he must specially call attention to this omission in his certificate, and under no circumstances whatever must any item of expenditure be eliminated without special attention being called thereto.

Interest paid to Partners.

Certain items may, however, properly be omitted from the expenditure side of the Profit and Loss Account, provided the Chartered Accountant calls attention thereto in his certificate. "Interest paid to partners on account of their capital" may properly be left out in this way, for, as the object of the Profit and Loss Account is to show what profit will probably be available for shareholders in the event of the concern being turned into a company, it is evident that interest on the capital employed would, in the case of a company, be only payable out of the profits by way of dividend. I am, of course, supposing that the capital of the intended company is equal to or superior to that of the capital of the partners.

Should the capital of the partners have been insufficient to carry on the business of the company without the assistance of loans, the interest payable on these loans might also be properly omitted, if the capital of the proposed company is sufficient to conduct the business without recourse being had to loans.

Interest on Loans, &c.

Interest paid by the firm, either for temporary loans

Lecture VI.

or for discounting bills, may also be omitted in the charges against revenue if the proposed capital of the company will be sufficient to carry on the business without these temporary loans and discounts; but in all of the above cases, as already stated, the certificate issued by the Chartered Accountant must state specifically every item of expenditure thus omitted, that is to say, that the profit certified is clearly understood to be exclusive of such charges.

Balance Sheet not usually investigated.

In the majority of investigations of this nature, the balance sheet or statement showing the financial position of the concern at the date up to which the books are investigated is not as a rule referred to in the Chartered Accountant's report, or in fact scrutinised by him very closely. So long as the books are worked to a perfect balance, so that the Chartered Accountant may feel satisfied that the Profit and Loss Account is correct, that is all, as a rule, he cares about, for the reason that the assets are not generally taken over at the value they stand in the books, but are specially valued by experts, for the purpose of demonstrating to the intending shareholders that the price they are to pay is represented by the full commercial value, while the liabilities are also agreed at a fixed amount, and scheduled to the agreements which have to be eventually adopted by the company.

In certain cases, however, the assets and liabilities are taken over by the new company at the respective values placed upon them in the accounts, subject to certain allowances which are settled by the Chartered Accountant.

It is, therefore, desirable, in order to make my address complete, to refer to certain points which would come under the notice of the Chartered Accountant, although, as previously stated, I wish to trouble you with as little detail as possible.

Amounts due to Creditors.

As regards the amount due to creditors, the Chartered Accountant must be careful to ascertain that all those on open account have been included, for, as regards the amount due to creditors on bills of exchange, these must certainly have been properly recorded, unless they have been intentionally omitted.

For the purpose of ascertaining if any creditors on open account have been omitted, it is desirable to scrutinise the invoices in respect of the payments made and shown in the Cash Book, subsequent to the date on which the books were closed, and ascertain that the value of all the goods in respect of which payments have been made, but delivered previous to the date on which the books were closed, are included amongst the liabilities.

Bills Discounted.

Should any of the bills receivable of the firm have been discounted, the Chartered Accountant should go carefully through the list of these bills and endeavour to ascertain by means of inquiry whether the bills are likely to be met at maturity, and whether any loss is likely to be sustained by the new company.

Assets.

The assets must, of course, be carefully scrutinised, and if they are to be taken over by the new company in accordance with the Chartered Accountant's certificate, he must be careful to ascertain as near as he can their proper value at the date at which it is proposed they shall be transferred to the company.

Investments.

In the case of investments, either in Government securities or stocks and shares of joint stock companies, the Chartered Accountant would, of course, consult the official stock and share list, made up to the evening of the day on which they are to be transferred. In the case of those investments which are not quoted, he should either obtain the assistance of a stockbroker or else arrive at his valuation by scrutinising the last published accounts of the companies.

Debtors.

The amounts due from debtors can only be properly

Lecture VI.

arrived at by scrutinising the particulars of each debtor's account, special reference being had to the nature of the account, regularity of the payments, and the age of the balance. The Chartered Accountant must, of course, see that a proper allowance is made for loss likely to arise on realisation.

Amounts due from Branches, &c.

The amounts due from branches, agents, or travellers should be acknowledged in writing by the parties stated to be so indebted; but, in addition, the Chartered Accountant must satisfy himself that the parties are able to pay the amount admitted to be due by them.

Undesirability of Chartered Accountant being responsible for Valuations.

It is most undesirable that assets, such as freehold and leasehold property, buildings, plant, machinery, &c., should be taken over by the company on a Chartered Accountant's certificate. It is impossible for him to arrive at their value in any other way than by taking into consideration the price originally given, subject to a percentage for depreciation, and although it may be perfectly satisfactory to the partners of a firm, or even to the shareholders of a company, to be provided with a balance sheet so prepared, yet it is not suitable that a company should take over the assets ascertained in this manner, and valuers should be called in to value as between the vendors and the proposed company. The Chartered Accountant should not, of course, attempt to fix any values except those arrived at in the manner above indicated.

When it is left to the Chartered Accountant to settle the statement of assets and liabilities, he must be careful to exclude from the assets any nominal or fictitious assets not represented by value; for example, if the goodwill of the business is represented on the credit side of the balance sheet at any value, this must certainly be eliminated. The proper method of dealing with goodwill is for the average profits to be ascertained, and for the number of years' purchase thereof to be agreed between the vendors of the business and the proposed directors.

Estimates.

Occasionally a company is formed to purchase a small business, and the prospectus put forward states that it is expected that, with the addition of capital, a much larger business will be done. The Chartered Accountant must be exceedingly careful that improper use is not made of his certificate, of high profits made by the small business, to influence capital, as it by no means follows that, because a small business is a profitable one, the connections of the firm are good enough to employ a large capital to the same advantage.

In the same manner, where a business has been newly started and it is proposed to transfer it to a company, the Chartered Accountant should not allow too much stress to be put in the prospectus with reference to his certificate of the profits, as frequently a new business may have a special point of novelty to influence a large sale, which, when the novelty is worn off, may at once decline. In fact, new businesses are altogether unsuitable for conversion into companies, as no proper average can be ascertained until the business has been at least a few years in existence, and the Chartered Accountant should, if asked to give a certificate of the profits of a business which has only been in existence for a short time, put a special clause in his certificate protecting both himself and the public.

Unsuitability of new Businesses for conversion.

Foreign Commercial Undertakings.

In addition to a large number of businesses in the United Kingdom that have been within the last few years converted into public companies, a large number of commercial undertakings, both in America and on the Continent of Europe, have been transferred to companies, and many millions of English capital have been within the last two or three years invested in this class of security.

Lecture VI.

Investigations conducted Abroad.

Investigations of undertakings abroad demand more than the average precaution, and should the Chartered Accountant not make the investigation himself, but entrust it to a partner, a member of his staff, or another Chartered Accountant, he must be exceedingly careful in the choice of his representative. The question is not merely a matter of investigating the books of account but in out-of-the-way districts in America, and also on the Continent, it requires, in addition to professional skill, both physical and mental strength, which is not necessary in our own country.

When the investigation is abroad and in a language not understood by the Chartered Accountant, he must be exceedingly careful in the choice of his interpreter, and before deciding upon one must, after the names are suggested to him, ascertain that he has no connection whatever with, or is on any terms of intimacy with, the person whose books have to be investigated.

Supervision over Account Books Abroad.

Fortunately, a system of supervision by the Government over books of account exists in most of the countries in the Continent of Europe which is not known in England, and it may surprise many to hear that the standard of book-keeping amongst commercial people is far higher on the Continent of Europe than in the United Kingdom.

It is impossible to discuss in any detail the precautions which ought to be taken by the Chartered Accountant in the examination of books of account abroad, and in arriving at a proper conclusion as to whether the profits for the period under examination are of the proper average, and not for some reason or other unduly high. To ascertain this it is absolutely necessary, unless he be acquainted with the language of the country, that he should have with him a member of his staff, or someone else in whom he has confidence, who could make inquiries for him in the neighbourhood, apart from the mere investigation of the accounts.

Amalgamation of Firms in a Company.

Companies are now frequently formed to take over the business of two or three firms carrying on the same class of transactions, in which case it is usual for the same Chartered Accountant to investigate the accounts of all the firms. It is necessary that before setting forth the results of his investigation he should see that the accounts are placed upon a similar basis, for example, that the stocks of all are valued by the same person and in the same manner, or if they are taken at cost price, subject to a percentage for depreciation, that the percentage is in all cases exactly the same.

Report of Chartered Accountant.

On completing his investigation, the Chartered Accountant has, of course, to issue a report or certificate, and this naturally requires careful consideration. Provided the period under investigation is of sufficient duration to form a proper estimate upon, the most satisfactory certificate for a Chartered Accountant himself to issue is one merely to the fact that he has examined the books of the firm or firms proposed to be incorporated into a company for the period, and certifies to the annual average net profits. This certificate, however, must distinctly, in my opinion, be accompanied by a qualified statement, should the business show a decline during the latter part of the period over that of the earlier part. For example, supposing the net profits of a business had increased £5,000 annually for the period under investigation, say, five years, beginning at £20,000, and increasing to £40,000, it would be quite proper for the Chartered Accountant to give a simple certificate of average without any other details. Supposing, however, the business had made £40,000 the first year, and decreased £5,000 per annum, so that in the last year the profits were £20,000, the average would be the same, but in my opinion the Chartered

Certificate of average Profits.

Lecture VI. Accountant would have no right to give a simple certificate. He should require the profits for each year to be set out in detail, so that intending investors may see that, although the average may be good, the business is a declining one.

Certificate of Chartered Accountant should be confined to facts.

The Chartered Accountant should, in his report or certificate, strictly confine himself to statements of fact, and never allow himself to be persuaded to include estimates for the future, no matter how satisfied he may be that the business is progressive. The most satisfactory certificate, from a professional point of view, is a simple statement of the net profits for the period under investigation. There can be no objection to amplify this certificate by the statement of the percentage this net profit bears to the capital of the partners, or even to the registered capital of the company.

Should the Chartered Accountant be asked to give a certificate of the percentage the net profit bears to a partial issue of the capital, he must only acquiesce after he is satisfied the partial issue is sufficient to discharge all the payments the company will have to make after the allotment of shares, and leave sufficient working capital to carry on the business on at least as extensive a scale as in the days of the firm, otherwise his certificate might be most misleading.

Under no circumstances whatever should a Chartered Accountant give a certificate as to the possible dividend a company might earn were the business to increase either in a ratio corresponding with an increase of capital, or to attain to a certain volume. A statement of this nature might be justifiable for the Board of Directors, but never for the Chartered Accountant, who should, as I have already stated, strictly confine himself to a certificate of fact.

Promoters.

The position the Chartered Accountant occupies, with regard to the promoter of a company formed to take over a business, the accounts of which the Chartered Accountant has investigated, will not, I think, be out of place in this address.

Lecture VI.

Occasionally the promoters are the persons owning the business themselves, in which case they of course pay all the expenses incidental to the formation of the company, but if this be not the case the promoter is either one of the financial companies already referred to, or a professional promoter, when a profit has, of course, to be made by him to recompense him for his trouble and perhaps risk in launching the Company.

For the owners of the business to be the promoters themselves, is, of course, the most satisfactory for all parties concerned, especially for the future shareholders, and provided the Chartered Accountant has in the course of his investigation found everything to be perfectly satisfactory, and that profits have been earned in a *bonâ fide* manner to justify the amount of capital proposed to be invited from the public, there can be no possible objection to his assisting the vendors in finding directors and other officials, and there can be, to my mind, also no objection to his receiving a suitable fee for his assistance, in addition to his fee for making the investigation.

Assistance by Chartered Accountants in formation of Companies.

It is now frequently the practice for persons owning businesses to approach Chartered Accountants in the first instance to ask if they can assist them in converting their business into a company, and if this position be accepted by the Chartered Accountant it is then his duty to give his clients the full benefit of his experience; there can, therefore, be no objection to his giving them also the benefit of his commercial and financial connection in placing the shares and debentures of the company.

In the case, however, of a professional promoter being employed, the relationship between him and the

Lecture VI. Chartered Accountant has to be more carefully considered. Frequently the promoter has the selection of the Chartered Accountant for the investigation, very often this is left to the proposed board of directors, and frequently the Chartered Accountant selected is the one who has for years audited the accounts of the business proposed to be taken over.

I do not myself see any objection to the Chartered Accountant assisting the promoter in the same manner as I have already stated he may assist the members of a firm when they are the promoters, subject to the same conditions; but he must be perfectly open in all he does, and not receive anything in the shape of fees not known to the vendors and the directors.

Should not give Certificate if financially interested in promotion.

When a Chartered Accountant takes upon himself to introduce a business to a promoter, and expects a commission for the introduction, then I am clearly of opinion that under no circumstances should he make the investigation or give a certificate upon which the public would be invited to subscribe for shares. There may be really no wrong in his doing so; but however conscientiously he may act he is liable at any future time to have reasons imputed to him, and it is, therefore, desirable another Chartered Accountant should be entrusted with the investigation.

There can be no possible objection, however, to his being the Auditor of the company, and his name being placed upon the prospectus as Auditor, and with a view to securing this there can be no objection to his being allowed to name another Chartered Accountant to perform the investigation, with the stipulation that he shall retire after giving his certificate, and not allow himself to be nominated for the auditorship.

Chartered Accountant should approve Prospectus.

It is not any part of the Chartered Accountant's duties to inquire into the arrangements made between the vendors and the promoter. Having completed his investigation and issued his certificate, his work is completed, with the exception of his approving the prospectus proposed to be issued, and ascertaining that the clause referring to his certificate is in accordance with facts. Should any objection be raised to his approving the prospectus, the Chartered Accountant should point out to the promoter and the proposed directors the risk they run of his being compelled in his own interests to give public notice, either through the newspapers or in any other way he may be advised, of his name having been made use of in an improper manner.

Lecture VI.

Responsibility for name appearing on Prospectus.

A Chartered Accountant does not, in my opinion, by allowing his name to appear upon the prospectus of a new company as Auditor, in conjunction with the names of the directors, bankers, solicitors, and other officials, render himself liable, either legally or morally, for the statements in the body of the prospectus, even although they refer to the transactions of a business taken over by the company, should his name not appear in the body of the prospectus as having given a certificate. He would, of course, be liable were he aware of any statement being incorrect.

It will be evident from the preceding remarks that the responsibility of Chartered Accountants in connection with these investigations is of a serious nature, but I venture to express the opinion that time will show that the certificates which have been given by members of the profession, both in Scotland and England, during the last few years, and published in the prospectuses of companies, have been granted conscientiously after careful investigation and deliberation, and that the confidence which has been reposed in them by investors has not been misplaced.

LECTURE VII.

THE OFFICIAL DUTIES OF CHARTERED ACCOUNTANTS.

Read before the Manchester Chartered Accountants' Students' Society, 4th May, 1891.

Lecture VII.

Private Duties.

The duties of a Chartered Accountant may be divided into three classes, viz., Private, Public, and Official.

By private duties I mean such as are due by a Chartered Accountant to his client when he is instructed to perform an audit or an investigation on behalf of a private association, a firm, or on behalf of individuals, either in their business or private capacity. His duty is then strictly confined to carrying out the instructions of his clients to the best of his professional skill and ability; when he has performed these his responsibilities are at an end.

Public Duties.

The public duties of a Chartered Accountant have reference to those cases where he acts on behalf of persons who give him general but not definite instructions, and who leave him to carry them out according to his own ideas, in the full belief that he will do his duty in the interest of all concerned, and hold him responsible for so acting. These duties are such as are undertaken by accepting the appointment of Auditor of a public company, of voluntary Liquidator of a company, of

Auditor of the accounts of a deceased person's estate on behalf of those interested, either in the division of the estate or in the income derived from investment of the same, and of an Arbitrator, while the official duties are those appertaining to offices or appointments held under the Courts of Justice, whether of the Chancery Division or the Queen's Bench Division of the High Court of Justice, or under the County Courts, and under the Board of Trade. It is with the last class of duties that my lecture is concerned.

Official Duties

The appointments under the Chancery Division of the High Court of Justice are those of Receiver, Receiver and Manager, Provisional Liquidator, Voluntary Liquidator under supervision of the Court, and Liquidator; the appointment under the control of the Queen's Bench Division of the High Court of Justice is that of Trustee in Bankruptcy. Under the Board of Trade a Chartered Accountant may receive the special appointment as a skilled Accountant to assist a debtor against whom a Receiving Order under the Bankruptcy Act of 1883 has been made, in the preparation of his statement of affairs, and also to assist the directors or other officials of a company, after an order for winding it up has been made by the Court, in the preparation of a statement of affairs. He may also be appointed the Special Manager of the business of a debtor from the date of the Receiving Order until the appointment of, or rather certification of, a Trustee, or the approval of a scheme, and also the Special Manager of a company after a Winding-up Order has been made by the Court.

Appointments under Court.

Under Board of Trade.

The duty of a Receiver is usually to protect property, pending an action which is to decide as to which of the parties are to take possession of the property at the termination of the action. The Receiver should, as a rule, be a person not interested in the action, and for that reason it is becoming usual for

Receiver in Chancery.

Lecture VII. solicitors to nominate a Chartered Accountant, instead of, as formerly, one of the parties interested, although this is sometimes done in a friendly suit, or where the person proposed is of such standing and responsibility that there can be no risk in conferring the appointment upon him.

The duties vary considerably according to the class of property to be protected. Where it consists of estates, leasehold or household property, the duty of a Receiver is to collect and receive the rents. In other cases he may have to collect dividends, book debts, and income of every description.

Appointment of Receiver.

The appointment rests in the discretion of the Court, and there appears to be no definite rule as to when a Receiver will or will not be appointed. The Court decides after hearing the special grounds for the appointment in each case where a Receiver is asked for.

Receivers have been appointed in the following cases:—

(1) In the case of Infants, where a proper case has been made out that it is necessary to protect the estate.
(2) Executors and Trustees.
(3) Pending litigation as to Probate.
(4) In actions between Mortgagor and Mortgagee.
(5) In cases between Debtor and Creditor.
(6) In cases of Public Companies.
(7) In cases between Vendor and Purchaser.
(8) In cases between Covenantor and Covenantee.
(9) Between Tenant for Life and Remainderman.
(10) In Partnership cases.

There are also several other cases, such as in matters of Lunacy, and in the case of Tenants in Common, &c., which are not likely to be entrusted to

Chartered Accountants; their appointment is, in fact, in England and Wales almost solely confined to Receiverships in the case of Public Companies or in Partnership disputes or dissolutions.

Lecture VII.

It is not necessary here to go into the cases in which the Court will and will not appoint a Receiver beyond giving the above instances, as with that the solicitors are more immediately concerned, our practice being confined to duties after it has been decided a Receiver shall be asked for, and our consent has been given to act if appointed.

Consent to act

On agreeing to accept the appointment of Receiver, a consent has to be signed, which is of course drawn up by the solicitors, and an affidavit of fitness has to be produced to the Court, together with the consent. This is, as a rule, drawn up by the solicitors, but as they occasionally in cases of great urgency ask us to send one on I here give the usual form. The deponent must be a solicitor:—

Affidavit of fitness.

"IN THE HIGH COURT OF JUSTICE.

"CHANCERY DIVISION.

"MR. JUSTICE ———

"IN THE MATTER of the Companies Acts, 1862 to 1890, and in the Matter of the——— Co., Ltd.

"I,
of
in the solicitor,
make oath and say as follows:—

"I know, and am well acquainted with
of Chartered Accountant,
the person proposed to act as Receiver in this matter, and have been acquainted with him for years and upwards.

"The said is a Fellow (or Associate) of the Institute of Chartered Accountants in

Lecture VII.

England and Wales, and has been in practice as a Chartered Accountant since the year .

"The said is a person of thorough business habits and capabilities, and of the highest integrity, and in my opinion he is a fit and proper person to be appointed Receiver of the above-mentioned company."

Practice in Chambers.

The application for a Receiver is made to a Judge in Court, but the appointment is usually left to one of the Masters attached to the Judge in Chambers. As a rule the Master appoints the nominee of the petitioner, whose solicitor draws up the Order, the affidavit of fitness, and the consent to act. The solicitor also produces an affidavit showing the assets which will be under the control of the Receiver, which will be a guide to the Master in his settling the amount ot security the Receiver will have to give. When the amount has been fixed the Receiver should at once obtain from the Guarantee Society who usually acts as his surety in these matters what is called a "Cover Note," which is practically an undertaking on behalf ot the Society that they will be responsible for the Receiver until the formal bond has been executed.

Receiver's Security.

When a Receiver has been appointed in Court by a Judge, the Petitioner usually undertakes to be responsible for the Receiver's acts until the security has been completed, and the duties commence immediately. In ordinary cases these do not commence until the Order has been signed. The Receiver should, however, be careful to ascertain the moment his responsibilities commence, otherwise he may find himself held liable for not taking immediate steps to guard the assets.

Preliminary Duties.

The first duty is to draw up a complete list of the property vested in the Receiver, and take possession, cash, cheques, and easily convertible property being of course first secured. When responsible persons are already looking after other property, it is usual for the Receiver to allow them to continue as his agents after first giving them notice of his appointment, but he must be guided entirely by the different surroundings in each Receivership, as he is the only person responsible to the Court, and is liable for the acts of any of his agents. A notice should be at once sent out to all persons indebted to the estate demanding payment at the due date, and giving notice not to pay to any other person save the Receiver or his properly accredited agent.

Limitation of Duties.

Unless the Order appointing the Receiver confer special powers upon him, he must be careful to obtain the leave of the Court before attempting to exceed his authority, which is merely to collect and get in the assets. For example, in the case of a Receiver appointed on behalf of the debenture-holders of a company, he can apply to shareholders whose calls are in arrear to pay the amounts due to him, but he must not attempt to enforce the payment of these calls by an action at law without taking out a summons for leave to proceed against the parties.

Receiver's Accounts.

The accounts of a Receiver have to be kept in a prescribed form, the receipt side showing the number of item, the date when cash received, the names of persons from whom received, on what account received, and the amount; while the payment side must show the number of item, the date when cash paid, the names of persons to whom paid or allowed, and the amount paid or allowed. But other books have, of course, to be kept, for the Receiver's own convenience and use, according to the nature of the estate administered by him. He must be careful to obtain a voucher for every payment made by him, and most Chartered Accountants now adopt the plan of having voucher guards with an endorsement printed to contain single vouchers, and

Lecture VII. numbered to correspond with the payment in the Receiver's official cash account. The receipt side of the cash account has also to be vouched, and the Receiver should therefore take care to obtain evidence that he has brought into account all the revenue, or, when he has been unable to collect it, to be able to show that he has done his best to do so.

Passing Accounts in Chambers.

The order appointing the Receiver prescribes the date of the year up to which the accounts have to be prepared, and directs that within a certain date afterwards they have to be filed in the chambers of the Judge. The draft account is handed by the Receiver to the solicitor having the conduct of the proceedings, who makes two copies, one for filing, and prepares the affidavit for the Receiver to make, verifying the account. The account and vouchers are left in chambers, and an appointment is made for their examination, which is attended by the solicitor, and, if necessary, by the Receiver or someone in his office acquainted with the details. In the meantime the costs of the solicitor are taxed, and the amount inserted in the account, as is also the remuneration of the Receiver, which is usually a percentage on the receipts, or, in a very heavy matter, an annual fee is agreed upon. For many years the practice in chambers was to allow a Receiver a commission of 5 per cent. on the amounts collected by him, but there is now no scale of remuneration recognised, each case being decided on its merits. When the account has been finally passed, the Receiver pays the balance in his hands either into Court or disposes of it in the manner prescribed by the order appointing him or by some subsequent order. The accounts are carried into chambers and passed in the same way each year while the Receivership lasts, and the final accounts also, previous to the Receiver being discharged. Should any of the capital of the estate be distributed during the Receiver-

Remuneration of Receiver.

ship, or if for any other reason the Receiver find the security he has given is in excess of the property he is responsible for, he can take out a summons for his security to be reduced. An affidavit in support has of course to be filed, and if the Master be satisfied he can reduce the amount he will obtain the Judge's sanction.

Investment of Funds.

As a rule a Receiver distributes the revenue half-yearly or annually, but when the estate is the subject of a suit it may remain in his hands for years. He has then to invest it in accordance with the terms of the order appointing him, and he must, of course, be careful only to select such investments as are named in the order. He must also be careful to observe the terms of any notices which may be served upon him during his continuance in office as to the retention and distribution of the fund, and not to pay anything away until the notice has been withdrawn, or he has obtained an order of the Court.

Discharge of Receiver.

When the parties to the suit have obtained a final decision of the Court, or have agreed their differences, application is made to the Court to discharge the Receiver, who thereupon prepares his final account, has it taken into chambers in the same way as has been done yearly during his appointment, has his final remuneration settled, pays over the balance, and obtains his release.

Receiver and Manager.

The Office of Receiver and Manager is not one frequently conferred by the Court, for the reason that in making the appointment the Court practically takes the management of the concern into its own hands, whereas, in the case of a Receiver only being appointed, the management remains undisturbed, and the Court assumes no responsibility.

In order to procure the appointment of a Receiver and Manager, the parties desiring it must present very

Lecture VII. strong affidavits to the Court, so as to prove to its satisfaction that it is highly essential in the interest of the parties concerned that the existing management should be displaced, and that an independent and responsible person should assume it.

It is evident, therefore, that such an appointment will not be made where it is intended the proposed official shall carry on the business for an indefinite period, and, therefore, the Court will only make the appointment with the view of a winding-up and a sale of the undertaking, the proceeds of which are to be held until it has been decided to whom they are to be paid.

Appointed on behalf of Debenture Holders.

An appointment can be made (with the consent of the company) though debentures are not due, and no interest is in arrear, where the debenture-holders of a company have a floating security, and execution has been levied upon goods of the company comprised in the security, and other actions against the company are pending.

The Court has also, on the application of the only debenture-holder of a company, appointed by consent the managing director as Receiver, and also Manager, of its business pending realisation, with a view to its being sold as a going concern, upon terms as to wages and current expenses, accounts, and immediate realisation.

Duties as Manager.

The appointment of a Manager implies that he has power to deal with the property over which he has been appointed, and to appropriate the proceeds in a proper manner. In his capacity as an officer of the Court he must, upon any question arising as to the character or details of the management, apply to the Court for directions. His sole responsibility is to the Court, and no orders of any of the parties interested can interfere with this responsibility.

Should the property to be managed be abroad, the Receiver and Manager can usually obtain authority to appoint as his agent someone resident in the country where the property is situated. In this case he must be very careful in his selection of the agent, as, of course, he will be responsible for his agent's acts, and also for his receipts and disbursements. Whatever may be the nature of the business to be managed, the Receiver and Manager must issue most stringent instructions to the members of his own staff who may attend to the matter, and also to those already connected with the business whom he may elect to continue in his service. A Chartered Accountant, as a rule, places one of his managing clerks at the head of the staff to represent him during his absence, and requires all orders for goods purchased to be signed by him, and all proposed sales, contracts, &c., to be submitted to him, leaving any matter of special importance to be submitted through this managing clerk to the Receiver and Manager himself. A Statement of Affairs should be at once prepared, showing the position of the business at the time of the appointment, and an inventory be taken of all the plant, machinery, stock, &c. A break should, of course, be made in the books of account, or a fresh set of books be opened.

Necessity for great precaution.

Statement of Affairs.

In none of his official appointments has more care to be taken by the Chartered Accountant than in acting as Receiver and Manager. He frequently comes upon the scene where internal dissension exists between the persons who previously had charge of the business, and he, therefore, feels that he cannot place reliance on what is told him ; it is consequently necessary for him to show very great firmness.

Personal Liability of Receiver.

The appointment is, as a rule, only necessary when a concern is hard pressed for means, and the Receiver and Manager must be careful only to incur liabilities in respect of absolute necessities, and then only when he is satisfied he is fully secured, as he is *primâ facie*

Lecture VII.

personally liable for goods ordered in the course of such business, and the fact of his signing after the name of the concern his own name, with "Receiver and Manager" attached thereto, to written orders for goods is not sufficient to rebut this presumption.

Making Advances.

Frequently money has to be advanced, and for this purpose the Receiver and Manager should apply to the Court for leave to borrow any money required. For this purpose it is advisable he should obtain the consent of persons holding any charges, so as to be fully secured before them.

He must also be careful to employ an independent solicitor, on whom he can rely, and he should have periodical statements prepared by his own staff for his guidance.

Accounts.

The Receiver and Manager's accounts have to be carried in half-yearly in the form prescribed by the Court, and in the same manner as those of an ordinary Receiver, and his final accounts are also carried in, passed, and his discharge granted in a similar way.

Voluntary Liquidator.

The appointment of Liquidator in a voluntary winding-up is conferred by the shareholders of a company by resolutions passed at an extraordinary general meeting, and the duties are either to wind up the company and distribute the assets, or at once to sell the assets to a new company formed for the express purpose of purchasing them from him. In the latter case, the appointment of Liquidator is a purely formal one, while in the former he has to conduct the company through its various stages of liquidation.

Method of appointment by Special Resolution.

A Liquidator of a company incorporated under the Act of 1862 can be appointed either by a special resolution or an extraordinary resolution. In the former case a notice has to be sent out to all the shareholders calling an extraordinary meeting in strict conformity with the Articles of Association of the company, or, if there be no Articles, in accordance with Table "A," and the shareholders pass a resolution to wind up and appoint a Liquidator, by a majority of not less than three-fourths of the members who are entitled to be present in person or by proxy and to vote. The notice must contain the intention to propose the resolutions, and these resolutions must be confirmed by a majority of such members entitled to vote who may be present and vote in person or by proxy at a second meeting, and there must be an interval of fourteen clear days between these two meetings or the resolution is not a valid one.

By Extraordinary Resolution.

When a Liquidator is appointed by an extraordinary resolution his appointment can be carried at one meeting, but in this case the notice of the meeting must contain the resolutions proposed to be passed, and one resolution must be to the effect that "it has been proved to the satisfaction of the company that it cannot, by reason of its liabilities, continue its business, and that it is advisable to wind up the company." Another resolution must be to the effect that, if the preceding resolution be passed, then a Liquidator will be appointed, and the Liquidator proposed is sometimes named in the notice. The remuneration of the Liquidator can also be settled at that time, or it can be left to a subsequent meeting, or to a committee of shareholders appointed for that purpose.

Voluntary Liquidation under Supervision.

After the Liquidator has been appointed, any creditor or contributory can present a petition in the Chancery Division for the voluntary liquidation to be continued, subject to the supervision of the Court, which gives creditors, contributories, and the Liquidator power to apply to the Court during the course of the winding-up.

Commencement of Winding-up.

The liquidation of a company is deemed to commence at the time of the passing of the resolution,

Lecture VII. or, in the case of a confirmatory resolution being required, from the passing of the confirmatory resolution.

The effect of such resolution is that the company ceases to carry on its business, except, and so far as may be required, for the beneficial winding-up. All transfers of shares, except those made with the sanction of the Liquidator, are void, and any alterations in the status of the company taking place after the commencement to wind up are also void, but the company continues under its Liquidator in its corporate state. Immediately on his appointment the Liquidator should take possession of all the property of the company, including its books of account, and unless the business be of such magnitude that it is necessary to continue the winding-up for a time in the offices of the company, he should at once remove everything to his own offices, and make arrangements for disposing of the offices of the company, and discharging the clerks.

Taking possession.

It is advisable, in the case of a winding-up requiring some technical knowledge, for the Liquidator to select one of the officials of the company whose opinion is most to be trusted, and who has the best knowledge of the business, and add him to his own staff for the purpose of the winding-up. On removing the business of winding-up to his office, a notice of change of the registered address should be at once filed with the Registrar of Joint Stock Companies, and the Liquidator should insert a notice of the resolutions passed for winding the company up, and of his appointment, in the *London Gazette*, or, in the case of Scotch or Irish Companies, in the *Edinburgh* or *Dublin Gazette* respectively.

List of Contributories.

A Liquidator in a voluntary winding-up has as full powers as are given to a Liquidator under a compulsory winding-up, and, therefore, in that capacity his first duty is to settle a list of contributories of the company. This list is prepared from the Register of Members, and is divided into two parts, the first part containing the names of those who are contributories in their own right, and the second part the names of those contributories who are representatives of, or liable for, the debts for others, and the following is the form usually adopted :—

Serial No. in List.	Name.	Address.	Description.	In what Character included.	Number of Shares (or extent of Interest).	Date when included in the List.

Having prepared a list of contributories, the Liquidator should send a notice to each of them informing them that they had been placed on the list, and that unless they appear at his offices on a certain day, named by him in the notice, they will be finally settled on the list.

Settling the List.

On the day appointed the Liquidator receives all the contributories who choose to put in an appearance, and he hears any objections they may have to their being settled on the list.

He should take careful notes of the objections, and come to a decision. He should afterwards give formal notice to the contributories whose names are settled on the list.

Should any contributory who attends before the Liquidator be dissatisfied with his decision, he has a right to appeal to the Court.

After the list of contributories has been settled, the Liquidator should, of course, require the payment of any calls in arrear, so as to put the contributories all on the same footing, and if necessary make a call on those shareholders who have not paid up in full. In making a call the Liquidator may take into

Lecture VII. consideration the probability that some of the contributories may fail, wholly or partly, to pay their calls.

Powers of Liquidator without sanction of Court.

A Liquidator in a voluntary winding-up can, without the sanction of the Court, exercise the following powers :—

(*a*) Bring and defend actions.

(*b*) Carry on the business of the company, so far as may be necessary for the beneficial winding-up of the same.

(*c*) Sell the property of the company.

(*d*) Execute in the name of the company all deeds, receipts, and other documents, and for that purpose to use the company's seal.

(*e*) Prove and take dividends in the matter of a bankruptcy or sequestration of a contributory.

(*f*) Draw, accept, and endorse any bill of exchange or promissory note in the name and on behalf of the company; also to raise upon the security of the assets of the company any requisite sum or sums of money.

(*g*) Take out in his official name letters of administration to any deceased contributory, and do in his official name any other act necessary for obtaining payment of sums due from a contributory or his estate, and which cannot be conveniently done in the name of the company.

(*h*) Do and execute all such other acts and things as may be necessary for winding up the affairs of the company and distributing the assets.

Extraordinary Powers.

The following extraordinary powers are conferred on a Liquidator :—

(*a*) To apply to the Court to determine any

question arising in the matter of the winding-up, or to exercise, as respects the enforcing of calls, or in respect of any other matter, all or any of the powers which the Court might exercise in a compulsory winding-up.

(*b*) To summon general meetings, for the purpose of obtaining the sanction of the company by special or extraordinary resolution, or for any other purposes.

(*c*) With the sanction of an extraordinary resolution, pay any classes of creditors in full, or make such compromise or other arrangement as the Liquidator may deem expedient with creditors or persons having any claims against the company.

(*d*) With the like sanction, compromise calls, debts, and questions affecting the assets ot the company.

Notices to Creditors.

The Liquidator should advertise for claims to be sent to him within a certain date. It is usual to allow about a month or six weeks for this purpose, and as soon as the day has passed, and it is pretty certain there will be sufficient to pay a dividend to the creditors, the Liquidator should examine these claims and give notice of admission to creditors whose claims are admitted, or formal notice of rejection to creditors whose claims he thinks should not rank against the company.

Reserves before declaration of Dividends.

Before declaring any dividend the Liquidator must be careful to reserve a sufficient amount to cover the costs of his solicitor, his own remuneration, and the preferential claims, such as amounts due to mortgagees or debenture holders, interest, also salaries, rates and taxes, &c. He must also allow for the costs of any pending litigation, but, as a rule, it is not advisable

Lecture VII. for a Liquidator to pay any of the creditors until all litigation has ceased, and the solicitors' costs ascertained and agreed.

It is not usual for solicitors' costs to be taxed in a voluntary liquidation, but should a Liquidator consider them too high, and cannot induce the solicitors to agree to a deduction, he can require them to tax their bill.

Preferential Payments.

The assets must be distributed *pari passu*, subject to the following payments, which have to be made in full, except when there is a deficiency, when they rank *pari passu* as between themselves:—

Rates.

(*a*) All parochial or other local rates due from the company at the date of the commencement of the winding-up, and having become due and payable within twelve months next before that time, and all assessed taxes, land tax, property or income tax, assessed on the company up to the 5th April next before the commencement of the winding-up, and not exceeding in the whole one year's assessment.

Salaries and Wages.

(*b*) All wages and salary of any clerk or servant in respect of services rendered to the company during four months before the commencement of the winding-up, not exceeding £50.

(*c*) All wages of any labourer or workman not exceeding £25, whether payable for time or piecework, in respect of services rendered to the company during two months before the commencement of the winding-up.

(*d*) Where any labourer in husbandry has contracted for payment of a portion of his wages in a lump sum at the end of the year of hiring, he has priority for the whole or part of such sum as the Court may decide to be due under the contract, proportionate to the time of service up to the commencement of the winding-up.

Before making any return to the shareholders, they must all be put upon an equal footing; for example, supposing some have paid calls in advance, it is possible some of these calls may have to be returned to the shareholders, in other cases calls in arrear may have to be enforced.

Annual Meeting of Members.

Should the liquidation continue for more than a year the Liquidator has to summon a general meeting, at the end of the first year and of each succeeding year from the commencement of the winding-up, or as soon thereafter as may be convenient, and lay before the meeting an account showing his acts and dealings, and the manner in which the winding-up has been conducted during the preceding year. The Liquidator has to file at Somerset House the list of members as it exists on the fourteenth day after the meeting within twenty-one days after the meeting.

Final Meeting.

When the affairs of the company are fully wound up the Liquidator has to make up an account showing the manner in which the winding-up has been conducted and the property of the company disposed of, then summon a general meeting, for the purpose of having the account laid before the members, and giving them explanation on any item in the account they may require. This meeting is summoned by notice inserted in the *London Gazette* one month previous to the meeting.

Dissolution of Company.

After the meeting a return on the prescribed form has to be sent to the Registrar of Joint Stock Companies, and at the expiration of three months from the registration of this return the company is deemed to be dissolved.

Lecture VII.

Liquidator under Companies (Winding-up) Act, 1890.

The Companies (Winding-up) Act, 1890, effected a great revolution in the winding-up of companies compulsorily by the Court. Previous to the 1st January, 1891, after a winding-up order was made by a Judge the appointment of Official Liquidator was made in his chambers, the nominee of the petitioner being usually appointed. The new Act, however, assimilated the practice which has existed in bankruptcy since 1883, an official called the Official Receiver in Companies' Liquidation becoming at once Provisional Liquidator, and he takes possession of the property in the same manner as an Official Receiver in Bankruptcy does of a debtor's estate. The new Act also prescribed that the directors or some official of the company shall prepare a statement of affairs showing the financial position of the company at the date of the winding-up order, and this statement is issued to the creditors and contributories by the Official Receiver, together with his report on same.

Meetings of Creditors and Contributories

The Official Receiver issues the report and accounts, together with forms of proofs and proxies, to the creditors and contributories of the company, together with a notice convening the meeting. There are two meetings held on the same day, both presided over by the Official Receiver, the meeting of creditors being held first, and any creditor, whether he has proved his debt or not, is entitled to be present at the meeting, but only creditors who have proved their debt and have lodged their proofs with the Official Receiver before the time named in the notice convening the meeting are allowed to vote, with the exception of those to whom the creditors give a special proxy or a general proxy to vote on their behalf.

Procedure thereat.

At this meeting the Official Receiver takes the chair and reads out a list of creditors from the proofs, asking those creditors, or creditors represented, if present, to answer to their names, while his assistant records the names present and the amount of the debt each creditor proves for.

The directors and chief officials are required to be present at this meeting. Their names are read out by the Official Receiver, so that they may answer if present. In important matters the Official Receiver, directly after his appointment as Provisional Liquidator, summons a meeting of directors and a few of the principal creditors for the purpose of deciding if the business shall be carried on by him, or whether it is in the interest of the company not to do so. He acts accordingly, and if he has carried on the business, reads out a statement showing the result of the trading to the meeting of creditors.

Selection of Liquidator by Creditors.

He then makes any observations to the creditors he thinks proper relating to the promotion of the company, if it be a new one, and perhaps expresses his opinion as to the conduct of the promoters and officials, and gives generally the history of the company. He also replies to any questions that may be put to him by the creditors, and intimates that it is now their business either to pass a resolution instructing him to apply to the Court to appoint a Liquidator, or to leave the liquidation in his hands.

It is then open for any creditor present to move a formal resolution authorising the Official Receiver to apply to the Court for the appointment of a Liquidator, and, following the old practice in Chancery, the Official Receiver asks the petitioning creditor if he wishes to nominate any person.

Selection by Contributories.

Later on in the day a meeting of contributories or shareholders is held, at which the contributories who sign their names, stating the number of shares they hold, are entitled to be present and vote. The Official Receiver presides, and informs the meeting of the

Lecture VII. result of the creditors' meeting, when it is open to them to pursue exactly the same course in the appointment of Liquidator, or pass a resolution requesting the Official Receiver to apply for the appointment of some other person as Liquidator, or to leave the liquidation in his hands. Should the meeting of contributories pass a different resolution to the one passed at the meeting of creditors, the matter is then brought before the Judge of the Chancery Division to whom winding-up business is assigned, who takes into consideration as to whether there is a probability of the creditors being paid in full or not. If it does not appear pretty certain that the creditors will be paid in full, he usually appoints as Liquidator the creditors' nominee; but, if he is satisfied the creditors will be paid in full in any event, he usually appoints the nominee of the contributories.

Security of Liquidator.

When the Liquidator has been accepted by the Board of Trade, he receives an intimation of the fact and the amount of the security he is required to give; he has then to notify his appointment to the Registrar of Joint Stock Companies, and takes over the winding-up from the Official Receiver. He is, of course, entitled to all the books and papers of the company in the possession of the Official Receiver, and he also receives the proofs of debt which may have been handed to the Official Receiver by the creditors. The proving of debts by creditors was only introduced by the Act of 1890, and the proofs are somewhat in the same form as those used under the Bankruptcy Act of 1883. The Official Receiver makes a list of these proofs, and takes a receipt from the Liquidator on handing them over.

Proofs of Debt.

For the purpose of the duties relating to the proofs the Liquidator may administer oaths and take affidavits.

It is the duty of the Liquidator, on the first day of every month, to file with the proceedings a certified list of all proofs received by him during the month, and it is also his duty, within three days after receiving notice from a creditor of his intention to appeal against a decision rejecting his proof, to file the proof, with a memorandum of its disallowance.

According to the Act, a proof must be either admitted or rejected within twenty-eight days after its receipt by the Liquidator, but the Court has power to extend the time.

Duties of Liquidator with sanction of Court or Committee.

A Liquidator may, with the sanction either of the Court or of the committee of inspection, carry on the business of a company, or bring or defend any legal proceeding in the name and on behalf of the company, or make compromises or other arrangements with creditors, contributories, and other persons, and may without such sanction execute such other things as may be necessary for winding-up the affairs of the company and distributing its assets. He may with the same sanction employ a solicitor or other agent to take any proceedings or do any business which he is unable to take or do himself.

Without sanction.

The Liquidator may, without the sanction of the Court or committee of inspection, exercise all the powers I have previously enumerated as those of a voluntary Liquidator, except those of bringing and defending actions and carrying on the business of the company, but the exercise of these powers is subject to the control of the Court, and any creditor or contributory may apply to the Court with respect to any exercise or proposed exercise by the Liquidator of any of these powers.

Companies' Liquidation Account.

Previous to the Companies (Winding-up) Act, 1890, Official Liquidators opened an account at the Bank of England in the name of the company, cheques upon which were drawn by themselves and the Chief Clerk of the Judge to whose chambers the winding-up was attached,

Lecture VII. but now an account, called the "Companies' Liquidation Account," is kept by the Board of Trade at the Bank of England, and Liquidators have now to pay direct into this account all moneys received by them, and are furnished by the Board of Trade with certificates of its receipt. If, however, the Liquidator is carrying on the business of the company, the Board of Trade will, on the application of the committee of inspection, authorise the Liquidator to keep a separate banking account.

List of Contributories.

A Liquidator prepares a list of contributories and appoints a day for settling the list in the same manner as I have already mentioned is done by a voluntary Liquidator, but in notifying to any person that he has been settled on the list the Liquidator has to state that any application for the removal of a name on the list, or for a variation of the list, must be made to the Court by summons within twenty-one days from the date of the service on the contributory.

Calls.

Should a Liquidator think it necessary to make a call on the contributories, he must, where there is no committee of inspection, obtain the leave of the Court, but where there is a committee he must summon a meeting by sending to each member a notice, in sufficient time to reach him not less than seven days before the day of meeting, containing a statement of the proposed amount of the call and the purpose for which it is intended. Notice of the intended call and the intended meeting of the committee of inspection must be advertised once, at least, in a London newspaper, and, when the winding-up is not in the High Court, in a local newspaper. Contributories may attend this meeting and make statements, or they may address a letter to either the Liquidator or the committee. These personal statements and letters have to be considered before the call is sanctioned. The sanction of the committee must be given by resolution passed by a majority of the members present, and a copy of the resolution or of the order of the Court (where there is no committee) must be forthwith served upon each of the contributories included in the call, together with a notice from the Liquidator, specifying the amount due from the contributory.

Meetings for Conference.

Should a Liquidator wish to confer with the creditors or contributories, he may call meetings for the purpose of ascertaining their wishes in any matter. The notices must be sent out not less than seven days before the day of meeting. A copy of any resolution passed at these meetings has to be sent by the Liquidator to the Registrar of the Judge or the Registrar of the County Court. Forms of general and special proxies must be sent with each notice, and proxies to be valid must be lodged with the Liquidator not later than four o'clock in the afternoon of the day before the meeting.

Liquidator's Cash Book.

Another novelty introduced by the Act of 1890 is the audit of the Liquidator's Cash Book by the committee of inspection, which is to be done not less than once in every three months. At the expiration of six months from the date of the winding-up order, and at the expiration of every succeeding six months until his release, the Liquidator has to send to the Board of Trade a copy of his Cash Book in duplicate, together with the vouchers and copies of the certificate of audit by the committee of inspection. With the first accounts he must also forward a summary of the company's statement of affairs in the prescribed form, showing thereon in red ink the amount realised, and explaining the cause of the non-realisation of such assets as may be unrealised. These accounts must be verified by affidavit. With the accounts must be sent a summary, which, when approved by the Board of Trade, has to be printed, and a copy sent addressed to every creditor and contributory, and stamped for transmission to the Board of Trade for issue by the Board.

Lecture VII.

Record Book. The Liquidator has to continue the Record Book commenced by the Official Receiver, and record therein all minutes, proceedings, and resolutions passed at meetings of creditors and contributories or of the committee of inspection, and the Record Book has to be submitted to the committee every three months, with the Cash Book already referred to.

Remuneration of Liquidator. The remuneration of a Liquidator is, unless the Court otherwise order, fixed by the committee, and is in the nature of a percentage, partly on the amount realised, after deducting the sums (if any) paid to secured creditors out of the proceeds of their securities, and partly on the amount distributed in dividends. Where there is no committee, the Liquidator's remuneration is settled by the Registrar, and may be the same as that of the Official Receiver acting as Liquidator.

Preferential payments. After payment of the fees and actual expenses incurred in realising or getting in the assets, the assets are liable to payments in the following order of priority :—

(1) The taxed costs of the petition, including the taxed costs of any person appearing on the petition whose costs are allowed by the Court.

(2) The remuneration of the Special Manager (if any).

(3) The costs and expenses of any person who makes, or concurs in making, the company's statement of affairs.

(4) The taxed costs of any shorthand writer appointed to take an examination; provided that, where the shorthand writer is appointed at the instance of the Official Receiver, the cost of the shorthand notes shall be deemed to be an expense incurred by the Official Receiver in getting in and realising the assets of the company.

Lecture VII.

(5) The Liquidator's necessary disbursements, other than actual expenses of realisation heretofore provided for.

(6) The costs of any person properly employed by the Liquidator with the sanction of the committee of inspection.

(7) The remuneration of the Liquidator.

(8) The actual out-of-pocket expenses necessarily incurred by the committee of inspection, subject to the approval of the Board of Trade.

When the Liquidator has completed the winding-up, he should give notice of his intention to apply to the Board of Trade for his release to all the creditors who have proved, and to all the contributories, sending with the notice a summary of his receipts and payments.

Trustee in Bankruptcy.

A Trustee in Bankruptcy is usually appointed at the first meeting of creditors of a bankrupt, at which the Official Receiver or his representative presides. He is usually nominated by a creditor, and, if more than one Trustee be proposed, it is generally left to the vote of the meeting, but the meeting may decide to leave the appointment to the committee of inspection.

Until the appointment of a Trustee the estate is vested in the Official Receiver, who has the administration of the estate until a Trustee has been appointed by the creditors and duly certified by the Board of Trade, when the estate passes from the Official Receiver to the Trustee.

Security of Trustee.

After the Official Receiver has reported to the Inspector-General in Bankruptcy, a communication is sent to the Trustee of his appointment, and informing him the amount of security the Board of Trade require him to give.

This security is now almost universally given by one of the many Guarantee Societies, and the Trustee,

Lecture VII. on receiving this intimation from the Board of Trade, at once makes the necessary arrangements with his Guarantee Society, who give a cover note pending the preparation of the policy, which cover note the Board of Trade accept as sufficient security, and at once place the certificate of the Trustee's appointment on the file of the Court, giving the Trustee notice thereof.

Objections by Board of Trade to appointment. The Board of Trade may, however, object to the appointment upon any of the following grounds :—

(*a*) That it has not been made in good faith by a majority in value of the creditors voting.

(*b*) That the person appointed is not fit to act as Trustee.

(*c*) That his connection with, or relation to, the bankrupt, or his estate, or any particular creditor, makes it difficult for him to act with impartiality in the interests of the creditors generally.

(*d*) That he has not complied with the requirements of the Bankruptcy Act, 1883, Section 162, or of any order of the Board of Trade made thereunder.

(*e*) That in any other proceeding he has been removed under Section 86 (2) of the Act from the office of Trustee.

(*f*) That he has failed or neglected, without good cause shown by him, to render his accounts for audit for two months after the time when they should have been so rendered.

Taking over Estate from Board of Trade. The first duty of a Trustee is to apply to the Board of Trade for the Estate Cash Book, Record Book, proofs of debt, and any other papers that may be in the possession of the Official Receiver which should pass to the Trustee. There is usually a little delay in this, as the Official Receiver has to make up the Estate Cash Book, and before he hands it over to the Trustee he

Lecture VII.

requires him to pay any balance there may be due to the Board of Trade.

On being put into possession of the estate, the Trustee must then make himself fully acquainted with the position, and for that purpose he should at once obtain an office copy of the statement of affairs, which is supplied from the Court. He should then make an appointment at his office for the bankrupt or bankrupts to attend on him, when he should go through this statement and take full notes of the bankrupt's replies.

Disclaimer of Leases, &c.

Under the Bankruptcy Act of 1883 there was a very serious obligation of having to disclaim leases and other onerous covenants within three months after a Trustee's appointment, but Section 13 of the Act of 1890 has substituted a period of twelve months for such a purpose, which is more reasonable than the provisions of the former Act.

Ordinary powers of Trustee.

The following powers are conferred on a Trustee without his requiring the permission of the committee of inspection :—

(*a*) Sell all or any part of the property of the bankrupt (including the goodwill of the business, if any, and the book debts due or growing due to the bankrupt) by public auction or private contract, with power to transfer the whole thereof to any person or company, or to sell the same in parcels.

(*b*) Give receipts for any money received by him, which receipts shall effectually discharge the person paying the money from all responsibility in respect of the application thereof.

(*c*) Prove, rank, claim, and draw a dividend in respect of any debt due to the bankrupt.

(*d*) Exercise any powers of attorney, deeds, and other instruments for the purpose of

Lecture VII.

carrying into effect the provisions of the Act.

(*e*) Deal with any property to which the bankrupt is beneficially entitled as tenant in tail in the same manner as the bankrupt might have dealt with it.

Powers to be exercised with consent of Committee.

With the permission of the committee of inspection the Trustee may—

(*a*) Carry on the business of the bankrupt so far as may be necessary for the beneficial winding-up of the same.

(*b*) Bring, institute, or defend any action or other legal proceeding relating to the property of the bankrupt.

(*c*) Employ a solicitor or other agent to take any proceedings or do any business which may be sanctioned by the committee of inspection.

(*d*) Accept as the consideration for the sale of any property of the bankrupt a sum of money payable at a future time, subject to such stipulations as to security and otherwise as the committee think fit.

(*e*) Mortgage or pledge any part of the property of the bankrupt for the purpose of raising money for the payment of his debts.

(*f*) Refer any dispute to arbitration, compromise all debts, claims, and liabilities, whether present or future, certain or contingent, liquidated or unliquidated, subsisting or supposed to subsist between the bankrupt and any person who may have incurred any liability to the bankrupt, or the receipt of such sums, and generally on such terms as may be agreed on.

(*g*) Make such compromise or other arrangement

as may be thought expedient with creditors in respect of any debts provable under the bankruptcy.

(*h*) Make such compromise or other arrangement as may be thought expedient with respect to any claim arising out of, or incidental to, the property of the bankrupt, made or capable of being made on the Trustee by any person, or by the Trustee on any person.

(*i*) Divide in its existing form amongst the creditors, according to its estimated value, any property which from its peculiar nature, or other special circumstances, cannot be readily or advantageously sold.

Advertisement of appointment.

The Trustee should at once insert an advertisement of his appointment in a local paper, and forward a fee of five shillings to the Board of Trade for them to advertise his appointment in the *London Gazette*.

With regard to the manner in which the winding-up of a bankrupt's estate is carried on, it varies, of course, in different offices, but the following plan is suggested: A register of creditors should be kept in alphabetical order, the names, addresses, and occupations of the creditors appearing in the statement of affairs being first inserted, and there should be columns for the amount which appears in the statement, the amount of the claim as notified to the Trustee, and the amount as per proof of debt, with particulars of the bills of exchange and any other securities mentioned in the statement of affairs or in the proof of debt.

Proofs of Debt.

The proofs should be gone through and checked with this register of creditors, and any names omitted from the statement of affairs should of course be added to the register of creditors. This register would also

Lecture VII. act as a creditors' address book, and notices of alteration of address should be recorded here.

Strictly in accordance with the Act all proofs should be gone through by the Trustee, and either admitted or notice of rejection given within twenty-eight days, but in practice this is not strictly adhered to, as it is frequently impossible to come to a decision within the specified period.

An estimate has to be made by the Trustee of the value of any debt proved which by reason of its being subject to any contingency, or for any other reason, does not bear a certain value, but any person aggrieved by the Trustee's estimate has an appeal to the Court.

Bankruptcy Estates Account.

The Trustee is required to pay all money received by him into the Bank of England to the credit of the "Bankruptcy Estates Account," kept there by the Board of Trade, and the necessary power to accompany each payment can be obtained from the office of the Inspector-General in Bankruptcy. The Trustee is also required to pay to the same account—

(*a*) Dividends under his control which have remained unclaimed for more than six months.

(*b*) Unclaimed or undistributed moneys arising from the property of the debtor under his control after a final dividend.

Local Bank.

The committee of inspection may authorise the Trustee to keep an account with a local bank for the, purpose of carrying on the debtor's business, or obtaining advances, or because of the probable amount of the cash balance, or if they satisfy the Board of Trade it is for the advantage of the creditors.

Committee of Inspection.

For the purposes of assisting the Trustee in the administration of the Bankrupt's property the creditors qualified to vote may at their first or subsequent meeting appoint from among themselves, or the holders of general proxies or general powers of attorney, a committee of inspection, which must consist of not more than five nor less than three, and the committee should meet as they from time to time appoint; strictly speaking, and in the absence of any official appointment, they should meet at least once a month, but in small bankruptcies, and in large ones after the first pressure of business has passed, the Trustee only summons a meeting of the committee when matters of importance have to be discussed. The Trustee should keep a minute book of the meetings of the committee of inspection, in which all formal business should be properly recorded, and he should obtain the signature of the chairman at the following meeting to these minutes.

Trustee's Record Book.

The important matters referred to in these minutes, together with all other acts done by the Trustee, have to be recorded in a book, supplied by the Board of Trade at the date of the appointment of the Trustee, called the Trustee's Record Book, which book is to be sent to the Board of Trade, together with the Trustee's quarterly statement, for their inspection.

A member of the committee may resign his office by giving notice in writing to the Trustee, whose duty is then to summon a meeting of the creditors for the purpose of filling the vacancy.

Audit of Trustee's Accounts.

The Record Book and Cash Book kept by the Trustee, together with the vouchers, have to be submitted to the committee of inspection not less than once in every three months. The Cash Book is to be audited by the committee and duly certified.

The Trustee, at the expiration of six months from the date of the Receiving Order, and at the expiration of every six months until his release, has to send to the Inspector-General in Bankruptcy, Board of Trade, a duplicate copy of the Cash Book, together with the

Lecture VII. vouchers and copies of certificates of audit by the committee. With his first accounts he has to send in addition a summary of the debtor's statement of affairs, showing in red ink the amounts realised, and explaining the cause of the non-realisation of the remaining assets. Where a Trustee has neither received nor paid any sum of money since the last audit, he must forward to the Board of Trade an affidavit of no receipts or payments.

General Meetings of Creditors.

Should any important matter occur which the Trustee is unwilling to take the sole responsibility of, he should summon a general meeting of creditors and take their directions. When he does so he must send to the Official Receiver a copy of the notice convening the meeting. At any of these meetings the creditors may be represented either by a general or a special proxy, which is to be lodged with the Trustee not later than four o'clock on the day before the meeting, and this proxy is to be filed with the proceedings.

Public Examination of Debtor.

The Trustee is entitled to take part in the public examination of the debtor, and, should he have been unable to obtain from the debtor any information he may require, he should take the opportunity, when the debtor is on oath in open Court, to examine him. Should he consider it necessary to be represented by counsel, he should apply for leave to employ one.

Employment of Solicitor.

A Trustee must be careful not to employ a solicitor without first obtaining in writing the consent of the committee of inspection, or in those cases where there is not a committee of inspection and the Official Receiver acts as a committee, he should obtain his consent on the proper form, otherwise he may be disallowed the costs. A Trustee must also not pay any costs before they have been taxed and the allocatur obtained.

Property of Bankrupt not divisible.

The following property is not divisible by a Trustee amongst creditors :—

Lecture VII.

(1) Tools, wearing apparel, bedding of the bankrupt, his wife, or children, to a total value of £20.

(2) Property held on trust for others by the bankrupt, and which is earmarked.

(3) The right of next presentation to a benefice.

(4) Personal earnings not in the nature of an income.

(5) Such property, being in the nature of an income, as the Court may allow the bankrupt to retain, notwithstanding an order attaching the bulk of it.

(6) Property which goes to the holder of a negotiable instrument within the rule *ex parte Waring*.

Declaration of Dividends.

A dividend should be declared by the Trustee, and distributed within four months after the conclusion of the first meeting of creditors, unless he satisfies the committee of inspection there is a sufficient reason for postponing its declaration to a later date. The Trustee must, of course, be careful to reserve what will be necessary to cover the costs of administration, including his solicitor's costs and his own remuneration, and he must also pay those debts which have priority, such as parochial or other local rates, assessed taxes, land tax, property or income tax, wages and salaries of clerks or servants, as defined in the Preferential Payments in Bankruptcy Act, 1888.

Order of distribution of realised Assets.

The assets, after payment of the actual expenses of realisation, must be applied in the following order:—

(1) The actual expenses incurred by the Official Receiver in protecting the property, and any expenses incurred by him, or by his authority, in carrying on the business of the debtor.

(2) The fees, percentages, and charges payable

Lecture VII.

under Table B. of the scale of fees, and any other fees and expenses incurred or authorised by the Official Receiver.

(3) The fee upon the copy of the Cash Book when forwarded for audit.

(4) The petitioning creditor's deposit.

(5) The deposit lodged on application for interim receiver.

(6) The special manager's remuneration.

(7) Petitioner's taxed costs.

(8) The remuneration and charges, if any, of the person appointed to assist the debtor in the preparation of his statement of affairs.

(9) Any allowance made to the debtor by the Official Receiver.

(10) Shorthand writer's taxed charges not already allowed under (2).

(11) The Trustee's necessary disbursements other than actual expenses of realisation heretofore provided for.

(12) The costs of any person properly employed by the Trustee with the sanction of the committee of inspection.

(13) Any allowance made to the debtor by the Trustee with the sanction of the committee of inspection.

(14) The remuneration of the Trustee.

(15) The actual out-of-pocket expenses necessarily incurred by the committee of inspection, subject to the approval of the Board of Trade.

Notices to be Gazetted.

Before declaring a dividend, the notice of his intention must be gazetted by the Trustee, and notice has to be sent to each creditor mentioned in the Bankrupt's statement of affairs who has not proved his debt. After the declaration, notice has to be sent to every creditor who has proved, showing the amount of the dividend, when and how it is payable, and a statement as to the particulars of the estate.

When the Trustee has realised the whole of the estate he prepares his final accounts, including among his expenses the cost of printing them and of sending out the requisite notices, &c., has them audited, and sends a copy to the creditors, informing them of his intention to apply to the Board of Trade for his release. He sends a copy of the notice, with evidence of having sent a copy to each creditor, to the Board of Trade, together with a copy of the accounts and an application for his release. If no cause is shown why this should not be granted, the Trustee receives a certificate of his release from the Board of Trade.

Assisting Debtor in preparation of Statement of Affairs.

When a Receiving Order has been made against a debtor, he has to make out and submit to the Official Receiver a statement of his affairs within three days after he has filed his own petition, and within seven days after a Receiving Order has been made on the petition of a creditor. As, however, it is only in very small cases indeed that the statement of affairs can be prepared in so short a time, the Official Receiver will, on application made to him giving sufficient grounds, extend the period, and in heavy matters he will grant an extension from time to time, as Official Receivers naturally attach the greatest importance to the statement of affairs being as correct as possible.

Forms to be used.

The form in which this statement is to appear is described in the Bankruptcy Rules, and blank forms for filling in by the Debtor are supplied to him by the Official Receiver. In all cases where a Debtor can prove, to the satisfaction of the Official Receiver, that he is not able to prepare his own statement, the Official Receiver will authorise him to employ a Chartered Accountant to assist him in the preparation of this

Lecture VII. statement, and the fee of this Chartered Accountant is allowed to come out of the assets as a prior charge.

Origin of Professional Accountants.

It will not be out of place here to state that it was the preparation of these statements of affairs, under the Bankrupt Law Consolidation Act of 1849, that brought professional Accountants into prominent notice before the commercial world, and some of the most eminent members of our profession built up their reputation solely in connection with the statements they prepared under this Act.

In those days the passing of the bankrupt's examination was contingent upon a favourable report being made by the Official Assignee as to the accuracy of the final accounts; and, as a bankrupt was liable to be opposed by any individual creditor on the grounds that the accounts were incorrect or insufficient, and the fact was established, the bankrupt was not allowed by the Court to pass his examination.

The Bankruptcy Act of 1883 is, to a certain extent, a return to the practice prevailing under the Act of 1849, and it is the practice of the Official Receiver, when appearing before the Court, at the time of the application for the bankrupt to pass his public examination, to report to the Registrar as to the manner in which the debtor has prepared his statement.

Employment by Debtor of Professional Accountant.

For the purpose of obtaining the assistance of a Chartered Accountant, the debtor must sign a formal application in writing to the Official Receiver that he is unable to prepare a statement without professional assistance, and he usually names the Chartered Accountant he wishes to assist him. This is then signed by the Official Receiver, and the remuneration is either fixed at the time, or, in the case of a heavy matter, his remuneration is left to be settled hereafter by the Official Receiver, and, as the fee is fixed according to the time occupied by the Chartered Accountant and his clerks, it is, of course, desirable that a full account of the time occupied and the nature of the work performed be recorded.

Must be for expert, not ordinary work.

The professional assistance rendered must be the assistance of experts, and not of mere bookkeepers, and should the books of accounts be in arrear, involving ordinary writing-up and posting, this work must be performed by ordinary clerks at ordinary clerks' salaries, and must not be done by the Chartered Accountant and his clerks except with special leave from the Official Receiver, otherwise the time devoted for mere clerical work may be struck out when the charges are submitted.

As the forms are supplied by the Board of Trade it is not necessary for me to discuss the form in which the accounts are to be submitted, and they will not present any difficulty whatever to a skilled Accountant.

The statement, however, accounting for the deficiency, which is scanned most closely by the Official Receiver before issuing his report, requires occasionally skill and experience in its preparation, as frequently the necessary information will not be found in the books of accounts at all, and it requires a cross-examination of the debtor to elicit the true facts.

Statement of Affairs of Company after Winding-up Order.

A novelty was introduced into the Companies Act of 1890 laying an obligation upon the persons who at the time of the winding-up order were the directors and secretary, or other chief officials of the company, to submit a statement of affairs in the same manner as bankrupts have long been compelled to do.

The forms on which this statement has to be prepared are given in the particulars appended to the Act, and include a deficiency account.

The statement is to be submitted within fourteen days from the date of the order, or within such extended

Lecture VII. time as the Official Receiver or the Court may for special reasons appoint. It must be made out in duplicate, one copy having to be verified by affidavit and placed on the file of proceedings; and the director or official who is made responsible for the preparation of this statement, not feeling himself competent to prepare it, can apply to the Official Receiver for his sanction to obtain professional assistance, but he must at the same time submit a statement of estimated costs and expenses which it is intended to incur.

The fee of a Chartered Accountant or any other person employed to assist in the preparation of this statement of affairs is allowed and paid by the Official Receiver out of the assets of the company, but these costs and expenses are not allowed if they have not been previously sanctioned by the Official Receiver.

Prepared in two forms.

The statement is prepared in two forms—(1) as regards creditors, (2) as regards contributories—for the purpose of showing both classes interested in the winding-up of the company what dividend or return, if any, they are likely to receive.

In the same manner as in bankruptcy the forms are supplied, and, as no special difficulty will be found by a Chartered Accountant in complying with the requirements of the Act, it is unnecessary to discuss the numerous schedules referred to therein.

Special Manager of a Bankrupt's Estate.

The Official Receiver of a debtor's estate may, on the application of any creditor, and if satisfied that the nature of the debtor's estate or business, or the interest of the creditors generally, require it to be carried on by an independent person, appoint a Special Manager to act until a Trustee is appointed, and with such powers, including any of the powers of a Receiver, as may be entrusted to him by the Official Receiver.

It is almost an universal practice for a Chartered Accountant to be appointed to this office. The Official

Receiver has an absolute discretion as to whether or not he will make the appointment, and no appeal lies from his decision to the Court.

On giving the usual security, and receiving his appointment, the Special Manager must remember that the estate is not vested in him but in the Official Receiver, but he has, of course, full authority to sell any of the stock-in-trade in the ordinary course of business, but before parting with any other asset he must obtain leave from the Official Receiver.

He should also at once ascertain whether the expenses incidental to carrying on the business can be diminished in any way, as he is not likely to carry on the same amount of business as was done by the debtor previous to the Receiving Order.

Appointment a personal one.

The appointment of Special Manager is practically a personal one, and he is supposed to employ the managers and clerks that were in the occupation of the debtor, and only employ his own staff for the purpose of keeping the accounts required by the Board of Trade, and for attending to his correspondence as Special Manager.

Should payments have to be made out by the Special Manager before he realises any of the estate, he should obtain an advance from the Official Receiver, or, if the latter has no funds in hand, the Special Manager applies to the Official Receiver for leave to borrow, and gives a first charge on the estate for such loan or any advances made by himself.

Special Manager's Cash Account.

The Official Receiver supplies the forms of cash account to be kept by the Special Manager. The cash account has to be prepared to the end of each week, and forwarded forthwith to the Official Receiver, together with a cheque for the total amount received, without any deduction whatever, and the Special Manager receives back from the Official Receiver a

Lecture VII. cheque for his disbursements. For his own protection, as also for the protection of the Official Receiver, the Special Manager should frequently confer with the Official Receiver, as they practically work together, and, to a certain extent, share joint responsibilities.

Special Manager of a Company.

The Official Receiver, in his capacity as Liquidator or Provisional Liquidator, may, if satisfied that the nature of the estate or business of the company, or the interests of the creditors or contributories generally, require the appointment of a Special Manager, apply to the Court to appoint a Special Manager of the estate or business of the company.

Affidavit in support of application for appointment.

The application to the Official Receiver for him to apply to the Court must be supported by affidavit showing—

The nature of the business of the company;

The estimated value of, and short particulars of, the assets of the company, stating what part of such assets is unencumbered;

The estimated amount of the unsecured debts;

The grounds upon which the appointment is considered necessary;

The benefits proposed to be derived from such appointment;

The name, address, and fitness of the proposed Special Manager;

The powers with which he asks to be entrusted;

The proposed remuneration;

The consents of a substantial number and value of the unsecured creditors to the appointment being asked for will also be required. Such consents must be in writing, and show the names and addresses of the creditors and the amount and consideration of their debts.

Remarks on Official Duties

I have, of course, been only able, in the limited time necessarily placed at my disposal for an address of this sort, to touch in a very brief and perfunctory way on the official duties of Chartered Accountants; but I think I have said enough to have impressed upon you the very responsible nature of these duties, and the consequent importance to you, while you are preparing for your future career, to make yourself acquainted with them, at the same time studying most carefully the Acts of Parliament under which the appointments referred to in my address are conferred upon Chartered Accountants, the rules attached to such Acts, and the various text books which have been published on the subject, some of which are recommended by the Council of the Institute of Chartered Accountants in the syllabus published from time to time for the guidance of articled clerks.

Necessarily brief.

Those members of the profession itself who have honoured me with their attendance to-night will doubtless have observed the great difference the Acts of Parliament passed within the last ten years have made in our profession.

The Bankruptcy Act of 1883 can, I think, only be described as a direct attack upon the profession. The Companies (Winding-up) Act of 1890 was looked upon by many of us as a further blow, but I think this Act was not so much an attack upon us as an attempt to support and strengthen the Board of Trade Department, which had not produced the financial result anticipated for it by the framer of the Act of 1883.

No necessity for creating Official Receiver's Department.

The working of this Act has also shown that there was practically no necessity for the creation of an Administrative Department of the Board of Trade. The creation of the Inspector-General's Department by itself would not only have been welcomed by the majority of practising professional Accountants, but, by giving the Government the use of all the balances standing at the credit of estates, have proved remunerative to the Government.

Lecture VII.

The Bankruptcy Act of 1869 gave full powers to the creditors in the administration of a bankrupt's affairs, and this, with the assistance of the Inspector-General's Department of the Board of Trade, would to my mind have made the old Act of 1869 about as perfect a Bankruptcy Act as could be devised. In the same way there was no necessity whatever for the creation of the Administrative Department of the Board of Trade under the Companies (Winding-up) Act of 1890. All the abuses of a liquidation could have been got rid of by a short Act putting the audit of Liquidators' Accounts under the Inspector-General in Bankruptcy.

However, the Acts are passed, and there can be no doubt that the profession have suffered in one way while they have gained in another; for, although there has been a great loss of professional work, especially in bankruptcy, there can be no doubt that which has been transacted since the passing of the Act of 1883, and that in connection with the liquidation of companies, has been and will be of a more satisfactory character, and the public now distinctly view with favour liquidation of the estates of companies and debtors being entrusted to Chartered Accountants.

Responsibilities of Chartered Accountants.

One reason for this is that both the Acts I have just referred to require us to know our duties, and do not allow us to consult solicitors without special leave, thus throwing very heavy responsibilities upon us. The Acts also require accounts to be kept and submitted periodically for audit in such a manner that it would be almost impossible for anybody outside our profession to undertake such duties. In fact, these two Acts have brought our profession very much nearer in practice to that of the Scottish Chartered Accountants, and this, I need scarcely say, is a step in the right direction. The more responsibilities that are thrown upon any profession, the more dignified does that profession become; and whatever loss there may have been of official appointments since the Bankruptcy Act, 1883, and the Companies (Winding-up) Act, 1890, that which remains is of a higher class, and what we have lost will be more than made up by the gain in the most important part of our practice, namely, that of auditing, as the practice now of employing Chartered Accountants as Auditors by public bodies, firms, and individuals is rapidly on the increase. The duty of an Auditor, however, does not come within the scope of the official duties covered by my address this evening.

In addition to the official duties I have referred to, there are many more which could, with great advantage to the public, and, consequently, with advantage to the profession, be conferred on Chartered Accountants.

Public Trustees.

For many years the desirability of appointing a Public Trustee was brought forward and discussed in Parliament, the present practice of appointing as Trustees under wills relatives who may have no capacity or desire for the duty, and who only accept the post by reason of their feeling it their positive duty to do so, being found to be very unsatisfactory. In the case of small estates, where the income of the corpus goes entirely to the wife and children of the testator, it is only natural a near relative should undertake the distribution of the income, and look after the investments free of charge, but, in large estates, the practice of a member of the family, who may, perhaps, have no pecuniary interest whatever in the estate, having to perform the duties without any remuneration, is most unfair.

Chartered Accountants as Trustees under Wills.

Several companies have been formed within the last few years which undertake to act as Trustees under wills, but they have not been in existence a sufficient time to form any opinion as to whether the public are likely to avail themselves of their proposals, but I am strongly of opinion that were it to be known that

Lecture VII. Chartered Accountants as a body were open to act as Executors and Trustees under wills at a fair remuneration for the time and trouble taken, and were prepared to give proper security for the strict performance of their duties, that the profession would gradually acquire these appointments. A Chartered Accountant who understands his work is essentially a business-like and practical man, and more capable than any other professional or commercial man to undertake the duties. There is no need of a Government official, and it is difficult to see where this rage for creating new Government departments is to cease. At one time there is a cry for the Government to take over the railways, another the waterworks. We shall probably hear of someone introducing a Bill into Parliament for the Government to take over all the joint stock and private banks, and making all the officials Civil Service clerks. However, it does not come within my province this evening to prophesy but to deal with facts.

Judicial Trustees.

The Judicial Trustees Act, 1896, gives power to the Court, on application by a person creating, or intending to create, a trust, or by or on behalf of a trustee or beneficiary, to appoint a Judicial Trustee of such trust.

There can be little doubt that Chartered Accountants will be the most suitable persons for selection for the appointments of Judicial Trustees, and the public will probably appreciate the advantages of making use of this Act by appointing Chartered Accountants, who are subject to control, in place of inexperienced relatives.

Concluding Remarks.

I much regret that I have been compelled to deal with the duties of official appointments of Chartered Accountants in one address, as, of necessity, I have only been enabled to discuss them in a very elementary manner, and only give a general outline of the duties. You will, however, have gathered from what I have said that many of them not only require practical acquaintance with commercial matters of every description, but a somewhat large acquaintance with the law under which the appointments are held. Certainly, as regards the law, as I have already stated we are expected to have a far greater knowledge than had the Accountants who helped to found the Institute of Chartered Accountants and their predecessors.

I do not mean to say that we have to perform any duties whatever that ought to be performed by solicitors, but the two principal Acts of Parliament referred to in my address have distinctly prohibited us from consulting solicitors in the manner that we used previous to these Acts coming into force.

We must not complain, however, of the additional study and responsibility thus thrown upon us, as the competition in all professions becomes keener and keener, and if those who are now students find they have more to learn before they are admitted members of the profession, and are required to gain further experience after they are admitted members before they can practise, they must console themselves with the reflection that if they had chosen any other profession they would have had to apply themselves with equal diligence to mastering its duties and responsibilities.

LECTURE VIII.

THE LAW OF PARTNERSHIP.

Read before the Northern Institute of Chartered Accountants, 15th March, and the Leeds and District Chartered Accountants' Students' Association, 16th March, 1893.

Lecture VIII.

Chartered Accountants and their Legal Education.

It is only natural that as a profession increases in importance and recognition that heavier responsibilities are attached to it, rendering necessary a higher education on the part of those who aspire to join it. A quarter of a century ago a knowledge of book-keeping and the method of the analysis of accounts was all that was expected of professional accountants, but the class of work undertaken by them gradually widened, and it became necessary that, in addition to being experts in accounts, they should be familiar with the principles and practice of certain branches of law. When the Institute of Chartered Accountants established its intermediate and final examinations for pupils serving under articles to its members, a knowledge of commercial law was considered an important part of its curriculum, and the law of partnership, on which I have to address you to-night, is a branch of this legal portion of your examinations.

Roman Law of Partnership.

Partnership has been recognised from the earliest times, but the law at present in force in England differs very considerably from the Roman law, upon which so much of our English law is based. The Roman law of partnership dealt only with the claims of partners as between themselves, every transaction by a partner being considered as his private business, so far as regarded the persons he entered into business transactions with, and third parties had no direct remedy except against the individual partner with whom they contracted, he merely having his rights against his co-partners.

Definition of Partnership.

Inasmuch as there are many varieties of partnership, no one, so far as I am aware, has been able to define the term so as to include all these. But for the purposes of this address it can be considered as the relation which subsists as the result of a contract, usually a duly executed deed of partnership, but not necessarily so, between persons who have agreed to share the profits of some business, or profession, or speculation.

Constitution of a Partnership.

In order to constitute a partnership between two or more persons, there must be an agreement between them, but not necessarily in writing, and in either case special arrangements can be made as to the nature of the partnership. For example, one partner, although sharing profits and losses, may have no right to interfere with the management of the business, or he may have no right to dissolve as an ordinary partner has, or he may not be entitled to share in the goodwill of the business on a dissolution.

In the event of there being no deed of partnership, or any agreement in writing, the question as to whether a partnership exists, or any dispute between the partners, must be ascertained from their words and conduct, and, even where a written contract has been entered into, it may be modified by a verbal agreement between all the partners.

Unless an intention to the contrary can be shown, persons engaged in any business or adventure, and sharing the profits derived therefrom, are partners as

Lecture VIII. regards that business or adventure. In fact, as regards the question as to whether persons are really partners or not, it is really answered by deciding their intention on the consideration of the agreement into which they have entered.

Joint Capital not necessary.

It is not essential to the existence of a partnership that there shall be any joint capital or stock. When two persons horsed a coach and divided the profits between them, each finding his own horses, the other having no property in them, they were held to be partners. An agreement to share gross returns does not constitute a partnership. Where two persons joined in the purchase of wheat with the intention of paying for it and dividing it equally, it was held that they were not partners.

Again, where the lessee and the manager of a theatre shared the gross receipts equally, the manager paying the expenses out of his share, it was held there was not a partnership.

Agreement to become Partners.

A partnership also is not created between persons who are only contemplating a future partnership, or who have only entered into an agreement that they will at some future time become partners, until the arrival of the time agreed upon between them. When one person contemplates joining another who is already in business, and agrees that the business shall be carried on upon certain terms not themselves creating a partnership, stipulating for an option to become a partner either at a specified time or at any time he may choose, a partnership is not created until the person having the option has exercised it.

Persons who agree to become partners may be partners, although they contemplate signing a formal partnership deed and never sign it; but, if they are not to be partners until they sign the formal deed, and they do not so act as to waive the performance of such condition, they will not be partners until it has been performed. **Lecture VIII.**

The case of *Cox* v. *Hickman*. Until 1860 it was held that all persons who shared the profits of a business incurred the liabilities of partners, although a partnership between them might never have been contemplated, but in that year the case of *Cox* v. *Hickman* was taken to the House of Lords, who decided that those who share the profits of a business do not incur the liabilities of partners unless the business is carried on by themselves personally, or by others as their real or ostensible agents.

Bovill's Act. In 1865, an Act of Parliament was passed, which is usually known as Bovill's Act, enacting that the advance of money by way of loan to a person engaged, or about to engage, in any trade or undertaking, upon a contract in writing with such person that the lender shall receive a share of the profits arising from carrying on such undertaking, shall not, of itself, constitute the lender a partner. The lender, however, cannot recover his loan, or his share of the profits, or his interest, until the claims of the other creditors are satisfied. The Act also provided that a contract for the remuneration of a servant or agent by a share of the profits shall not of itself constitute a partnership, and it also exempted from partnership a widow or child of a deceased partner receiving, by way of annuity, a portion of the profits.

Partnership Act, 1890. The Partnership Act, 1890, has put the law on a clear basis by enacting that "the sharing of gross returns does not of itself create a partnership, whether the persons sharing such returns have, or have not, a joint or common right or interest in any property from which, or from the use of which, the returns are derived," but "the receipt by a person of the share of the profits of a business is *primâ facie* evidence that he is a partner in the business."

All the circumstances, however, must be regarded,

Lecture VIII. and an inference drawn from them as a whole. In a case where partners borrowed money on the security of freeholds of which they were tenants in common, and expended the money in improving part of the freehold in which the business was carried on, it was held that none of the freehold had become partnership property.

Holding-out.

Whatever may be the private arrangement between persons carrying on an enterprise, anyone who holds himself out as a partner is liable to those he thus represents himself as though he were a partner, although they may know he does not share the profits or losses.

A person may be interested in the share of a member of a partnership; this is called a sub-partnership, and the parties to it are partners *inter se*, but it in no way affects the other members of the principal firm, and a sub-partner cannot be held liable to the creditors of the principal firm because he participates in the profits.

Persons may become partners in one single transaction only, such as for the working of a particular patent, in which case their rights and liabilities are governed by the same principles as those which apply to ordinary partnerships.

Co-Owners not necessarily Partners.

It is quite possible for two or more persons to become co-owners of property without their becoming partners, if such be their intention. There are many differences between co-ownership and partnership; for example, co-ownership is not necessarily the result of agreement, which partnership is. Partnership necessarily involves community of profit or of loss; co-ownership does not. One partner cannot, without the consent of the others, transfer his interest; a co-owner can. Co-ownership does not necessarily exist for the purpose of gain; partnership does.

The case of *Coope v. Eyre.*

If several persons jointly purchase goods for re-sale with the object of dividing the profit they create a partnership, but not so if the object is only to divide the goods among themselves. The leading case on this point is *Coope* v. *Eyre*, where one person purchased oil for the purpose of dividing it amongst himself and others. The purchaser became bankrupt, and the seller tried to make the other parties to the agreement pay for the oil. It was held, however, that the purchaser bought as a principal and not as an agent, and that as there was no community of profit or loss the persons amongst whom the oil was to be divided could not be made liable, either as partners or quasi-partners.

Part-Owners.

Part-owners, who divide what is obtained by the use or employment of the thing owned, are not thereby constituted partners. If two tenants in common of a house let it and divide the rent equally, they are not partners, although they may pay for repairs out of the rent before dividing it.

Agreements to share profits, like all other agreements, require to be founded on some consideration in order to be binding. Any contribution in the shape of capital or labour, or any act which may result in liability to third parties, is a sufficient consideration to support such an agreement.

Vice-Chancellor Wigram stated that if one man had skill, and wanted capital to make that skill available, and another had capital and wanted skill, and the two agreed that one should provide the capital and the other skill, there was good consideration for an agreement on both sides, that it was impossible for the Court to measure the quantum of value, and the parties to the agreement must decide that for themselves.

Premiums.

An incoming partner frequently agrees to pay a premium on being admitted into an established business. Such an agreement is valid; and, if the premium be not duly paid, it may be recovered by an action, provided the plaintiff has been ready and

Lecture VIII. willing to take the defendant into partnership as agreed.

If a person has been deluded into becoming a partner by false and fraudulent representations, and has paid a premium, he may either abide by the contract and claim compensation for the loss occasioned by the fraud, which he may do in taking the partnership accounts; or he may disaffirm the contract, and thereby entitle himself to a return of the whole of the money he has paid.

In the absence of fraud the principles applicable to cases where the return of a premium paid is in question are not well settled.

Who may be Partners.

A valid contract of partnership can be entered into between any persons who are not under the disabilities of minority or unsoundness of mind, except convicts. Married women may be partners under certain circumstances; an alien, not an enemy, may be a partner; an infant may be a partner, but while an infant he incurs no liability, and is not responsible for the debts of the firm.

A person may legally carry on business under a name not his own; and when a firm has an established reputation and one of its members dies, it is not deemed wrong for the survivors to continue the business under the old name, although, perhaps, the reputation of the firm may have been due mainly, if not entirely, to the ability and integrity of the deceased partner.

Illegal Partnerships.

A partnership is illegal if formed for a purpose forbidden by the current notions of morality, religion, or public policy; for example, when two countries are at war it is illegal for persons resident in either to have dealings with persons resident in the other. An agreement for an illegal partnership will not be enforced even if it has been partly performed.

Actions by an illegal partnership cannot be maintained, but the partnership can prosecute a person stealing its property, and it can be sued. The members of an illegal partnership have no remedy against each other for contribution or apportionment in respect of the partnership dealings and transactions, and if the illegality be brought to the notice of the Court it will of its own accord decline to interfere between the parties, although there may be no desire on their part to urge such an objection.

Commercial notion of constitution of a Firm.

There is a distinct difference between the legal and the mercantile notion of a firm. Commercial men regard a firm as a body distinct from the members composing it, and having rights and obligations distinct from those of its members. For example, in keeping partnership accounts, the firm is made debtor to each partner for what he brings into the common stock, and each partner is made debtor to the firm for all that he takes out of that stock. Partners are never indebted to each other in respect of partnership transactions, but are always either debtors to or creditors of the firm. In the case of the death or retirement of a partner, or the introduction of a new one, the firm is considered as continuing the same, and the rights and obligations of the old firm are regarded as continuing in favour of or against the new firm as if no changes had occurred. The liabilities of the firm are regarded as the liabilities of the partners only in case they cannot be met by the firm and discharged out of its assets.

Legal notion.

But this is not the legal notion of a firm. The firm is not recognised by lawyers as distinct from the members composing it. In taking partnership accounts, and in administering partnership assets, Courts have, to some extent, adopted the mercantile view, and actions may now be brought by or against partners in the name of their firms; but, speaking generally, the

Lecture VIII. firm has no legal recognition. The law, ignoring the firm, looks to the partners composing it; any change amongst them destroys the identity of the firm. What is called the property of the firm is the property of its members, and what are called the debts and liabilities of the firm are their debts and their liabilities. In point of law a partner may be the debtor or the creditor of his co-partners, but he cannot be either debtor or creditor of the firm of which he is himself a member.

Name of Firm conventional.

It follows, from the foregoing remarks, that the name under which a firm carries on business is, in point of law, a conventional name applicable only to the persons who, on each particular occasion when the name is used, are members of the firm. When a firm is spoken of by its name or style, evidence is admissible to show who in fact constituted the firm at the time in question, and what is done under the name of the firm is as valid as if real names had been used. Partners may be registered as shareholders in the name of their firm, and bills of exchange are valid when signed by a firm.

The name by which a firm is known is not of itself the property of the firm, and there is nothing at common law to prevent persons from carrying on business in partnership under any name they please; but one firm is not at liberty to mislead the public by so using the name of another firm as to pass off itself or its goods for those of the other.

The name of a firm may, moreover, be registered as a trade mark for particular classes of goods, and, if so registered, it is capable of being assigned in connection with the goodwill of the firm.

Determination of a Partnership.

A contract of partnership is determinable at the will of any one of the persons who have entered into it, provided that it has not been agreed that the contract shall endure for a specified time. In other words, the result of a contract of partnership is a partnership at will, unless some agreement to the contrary can be proved. The mere fact that a firm has incurred debts or taken land on lease for a long term is not proof of an agreement that the partnership shall subsist for the same period. Lecture VI

When a partnership originally entered into for a term of years is continued after its expiration, and there is no evidence as to the additional time for which the partnership was to last, it is treated as having become a partnership at will, and not as having been renewed for another definite period.

Partners are Agents.

Every member of an ordinary partnership is its general agent for the transaction of its business in the ordinary way, and the firm is responsible for whatever is done by any of the partners when acting for the firm within the limits of the authority conferred by the nature of the business it carries on. Whatever as between the partners themselves may be the limits set to each other's authority, every person not acquainted with these limits is entitled to assume that each partner is empowered to do for the firm whatever is necessary for the transaction of its business in the way in which that business is ordinarily carried on by other people.

It follows from the principles of agency, coupled with the doctrine that each partner is the agent of the firm, for the purpose of carrying on its business in the ordinary way, that an ordinary partnership is liable in damages for the negligence of any one of its members in conducting the business.

Tort of one Partner not imputable.

As a rule, however, the wilful tort of one partner is not imputable to the firm. For example, if one partner maliciously prosecutes a person for stealing partnership property, the firm is not answerable, unless all the members are, in fact, privy to the malicious prosecution. But a wilful tort committed by a partner in the course

Lecture VIII. and for the purpose of transacting the business of the firm may make the firm responsible.

An ordinary firm is liable for frauds committed by one of its members whilst acting for the firm and in transacting its business, but in order that a firm may be liable for the misapplication of money by one of its members, some obligation on the part of the firm to take care of the money must be shown.

Fraud by a Partner.

Where one partner, acting within the scope of his authority, as evidenced by the business of the firm, obtains money and misapplies it, the firm is answerable for it, and where a firm in the course of its business receives money belonging to other people, and one of the partners misapplies that money whilst in the custody of the firm, the firm must make it good.

If a partner in the course of some transaction unconnected with the business of the firm, or not within the scope of such business, obtains money and then misapplies it, the firm is not without more liable to make the loss good.

In considering the liability of a firm for the false representation of one of its members, it is necessary to distinguish actions for mere damages from actions to rescind contracts and to recover money or property obtained by the firm by misrepresentation.

Damages for misrepresentation.

An action for damages for misrepresentation cannot as a general rule be maintained unless the misrepresentation is fraudulent, *i.e.*, false, and known so to be to the person making it, or false and made recklessly, without any reasonable ground for believing the statement to be true. But whatever doubt there may be as to the liability of a firm to an action for deceit founded on the fraudulent statement of one of its members, there is no doubt that a firm can be compelled to restore property or refund money obtained by it through the misrepresentation of one of its members. Nor in such a case is it necessary to prove that the misrepresentation was fraudulent as well as false.

Whether accounts rendered by one partner in the name of the firm, and showing that money is in the hands of the firm when in truth he has misapplied it, are to be treated as representations by the firm, is a question which has given rise to much discussion, and upon which the cases are not uniform, but upon the whole it is conceived that, if the accounts relate to matters within the scope of the partnership business, the firm is bound by them.

A firm is not liable for a false and fraudulent representation as to the character or solvency of any person unless such representation is in writing signed by all the partners. The signature of one partner in the name of the firm will not bind anyone but himself.

False representation

If a partner, acting apparently beyond the limits of his authority, untruly represents that he is acting with his co-partners' consent, they are not bound by the representation, nor are they liable for what may be done on the faith of it. For example, where one partner gave partnership bills in payment of his own separate debt, and, on being asked whether his co-partner was acquainted with the transaction, untruly replied that he was, and that he consented to it, it was held that the bills were not provable against the joint estate of the firm, they not being in the hand of a *bonâ fide* holder for value without notice of the circumstances under which they had been given. In this case the partner who gave the bills did that which was clearly not within the scope of his authority, and the person who took them knew it. The latter was, it is true, misled by the false answer to his question, but that answer was not referable to a matter within the scope of the partnership business; and the other partner did nothing to lead to the supposition either that he was a consenting partner

Lecture VIII. or that he had authority as co-partner to say that he was.

False statements to incoming Partner.

If a partner induces a person by fraud to join his firm, such fraud cannot be imputed to the firm, unless the partner in question had express authority to seek for a new partner, or unless the other members of the firm ratify the fraud when made aware of it. If, however, the incoming partner has brought in money to the firm, the retention of the money by the firm, with knowledge of the fraud, would amount to a ratification thereof, and would be equivalent to a fraud by all the partners in the first instance.

Each Partner an Agent.

By law every member of an ordinary partnership is the agent of the firm, so far as is necessary for the transaction of its business in the ordinary way, and to this extent his authority to act for the firm may be assumed by those who know nothing of the real limits of his authority. If his co-partners have restricted his authority to narrower limits still, they will be bound to all persons dealing with him *bonâ fide* without notice of the restriction, so long as he acts within the wider limits set by law. On the other hand, if a person seeks to fasten upon the firm liability in respect of some act of one of the members which does not fall within the limits of his authority as set by law, a more extensive authority must be shown to have been actually conferred upon him by the other partners, and if no sufficient authority can be shown the firm will not be liable, even though the person seeking to charge it had no notice of the real authority possessed by the partner with whom he dealt.

Liability of co-Partners for fraud of one.

If one partner acts in fraud of his co-partners, still they will be bound, if he has not exceeded his apparent authority, and if the person dealing with him had no notice of the fraud. For example, where one partner ordered goods on the credit of the firm, and immediately pawned them for his own benefit, the firm was held liable for the price of the goods. If one member of an ordinary trading partnership draws, accepts, or endorses a bill in the name of the firm, but for some private purpose of his own, and in fraud of his co-partners, they will be liable upon the bill at the suit of any holder for value, without notice of the fraud.

The general proposition that a partnership is bound by those acts of its agents which are within the scope of their authority must be taken with the qualification that the agent whose acts are sought to be imputed to the firm was acting in his character of agent, and not as a principal. If he did not act in his character of agent, if he acted as a private individual on his own account, his acts cannot be imputed to the firm, and he alone is liable for them, even though the firm may have benefited by them.

Liability in respect of Deeds.

A distinction is taken between deeds and other instruments with respect to the person bound by them: if a deed is executed by an agent in his own name, he, and he only, can sue, or be sued thereon, although the deed may disclose the fact that he is acting for another. Therefore, when a partner covenants that anything shall be done, he, and he only, is liable on the covenant, and the firm is not bound thereby to the covenantee. A partner who has to execute a deed as an agent should take care that the deed and the covenants in it are expressed to be made, not by him, but by the person intended to be bound.

Contracts made as Agent.

When a partner enters into a contract not under seal as the agent of another, the name of that other may be either disclosed or not. If it is disclosed the contract is treated as that of the principal, and not as that of the agent; whilst if it is not disclosed, the contract is considered as that of the agent. But in this last case the person dealing with the agent can, when he

Lecture VIII. discovers the undisclosed principal, hold him liable instead of the agent.

If, therefore, one partner only enters into a written contract, the question whether the contract is confined to him, or whether it is confined to him and his co-partners, cannot be determined simply by the terms of the contract; for, supposing a contract be entered into by one partner in his own name only, still, if in fact he was acting as the agent of the firm, his co-partners will be in the position of undisclosed principals, and they may therefore be liable to be sued on the contract, although no allusion is made to them in it. If one partner, therefore, acting in fact for the firm, orders goods, and they are supplied to him, the firm will be liable to pay for them, although no mention was made of his co-partners, and they were unknown to the seller of the goods.

Liability of dormant Partners.

It is clear, therefore, that dormant partners are liable for the debts of the firm, notwithstanding their connection with the firm was unknown to its creditors when the debts were contracted. On the other hand, if one partner only is dealt with, and the circumstances are such as to show that he was acting, and was dealt with, on his own account, *i.e.*, as a principal, and not as the agent of the firm, he alone is responsible.

A bill drawn, endorsed, or accepted in the name of the firm is considered as bearing the names of all the persons who actually or ostensibly compose the firm at the time its name is put to the bill, and, consequently, all these persons, including as well dormant as *quasi*-partners, may be sued upon the bill.

Persons may carry on business in partnership in the name of one of themselves; and if they do they expose themselves to serious liability, for, *primâ facie*, his acceptance will bind them, even although dishonestly given. At the same time, if they can show that he gave the bills as his own, and not as the bills of the firm, they will not be liable, even to a *bonâ fide* owner for value.

Partners must use name of Firm.

In the absence of evidence to the contrary, a partner has no authority to use for partnership purposes any other name than the name of the firm, and if he does, and there is any substantial variation which cannot be shown to be authorised by his co-partners, the firm will not be liable; if, however, there is no substantial variation, the firm will be bound. A bill drawn on a firm in its wrong name and accepted in its right name binds the firm, and a bill drawn on a firm and accepted by one partner in his own name only has been held to bind the firm on the ground that the word "accepted," if written by one of the partners, is sufficient, without any signature, and that his signature, if affixed, may be treated as redundant. A bill drawn on one partner, and accepted by him on behalf of the firm, does not bind the firm, the other partners not being drawees. A bill drawn on a firm and accepted by one partner in the name of the firm, and in his own name, does not bind him separately if the firm is bound by his acceptance; but, if he has no authority to bind the firm, he is himself liable on the bill.

Contracts not binding, even when Firm obtain benefit thereof.

As regards the liabilities of partnerships in respect of contracts not binding on them, but on which they have had the benefit, it is an erroneous but popular notion that if a firm obtain the benefit of a contract made with one of its partners it will be bound by that contract; and the question upon which the liability or non-liability of the firm upon a contract depends is not, Has the firm obtained the benefit of the contract? but, Did the firm, by one of its partners or otherwise, enter into the contract?

An agent who contracts for a known principal is not liable to be himself sued on a contract into which he has avowedly entered only as agent; consequently a

Lecture VIII. partner who enters into a contract on behalf of his firm is not liable on that contract, except as one of the firm. In other words, the contract is not binding on himself separately, but only on him and his co-partners jointly.

Rights of Partners *inter se.*

I now come to the consideration of the rights and obligations of members of partnerships between themselves. The first point to mention is that, in the absence of an express agreement to the contrary, the powers of members of a partnership are equal, even although their shares may be unequal, and there is no right on the part of one or more to exclude the other from an equal management in the concern. Indeed, speaking generally, it may be said that nothing is considered as so strongly calling for the interference of the Court between partners as the improper exclusion of one of them by the others from taking part in the management of the partnership business; if, however, partners have agreed that the management of the partnership affairs shall be entrusted to one or more of their number exclusive of the others, it is not competent for those who have agreed to take no part in the management to transact any part of the business without the consent of all the other partners.

High moral standard required.

The utmost good faith is due from every member of a partnership towards every other member, and if any dispute arises between partners touching any transactions, by which one seeks to benefit himself at the expense of the firm, he would be required to show, not only that he has law on his side, but that his conduct will bear to be tried by the highest standard of honour. If one partner knows more about the state of the partnership accounts than another, and, concealing what he knows, enters into an agreement with his partner relative to some matter as to which a knowledge of the state of accounts is material, such agreement would not be allowed to stand. This obligation extends to persons

Lecture VIII.

negotiating for a partnership, but between whom no partnership yet exists; and also to persons who have dissolved partnership, but who have not completely wound up and settled the partnership affairs; and most especially is good faith required to be observed when one partner is endeavouring to get rid of another or to buy him out. A partner is not allowed to derive profit at the expense of the firm from any dealings between him and the partnership, unless it is clearly agreed that he is to have such profit. A partner cannot retain for himself benefits which he ought to share with his co-partners from the use of the partnership property, or by engaging in transactions in rivalry with the firm.

A partner is not allowed, in transacting the partnership affairs, to carry on for his own sole benefit any separate trade or business which, were it not for his connection with the partnership, he would not have been in a position to carry on.

Differences between Partners.

In the event of a difference arising between partners, it becomes necessary to consider whether there is any method of determining which of them is to give way to the other. It is not uncommonly suggested that the minority of the partners, if they are unequally divided, must submit to the majority; but this is by no means the case, the majority cannot oblige the minority except within certain limits. The first point to determine is whether the partnership articles do or do not contain any express provision applicable to the matter in question; for, if they do, such provision should be obeyed; if they do not, then the nature of the question at issue must be examined; for there is important distinctions between differences which relate to matters incidental to carrying on the legitimate business of a partnership and differences which relate to matters with which it was never intended that the partnership should concern itself. With respect to the first class of

Lecture VIII. differences, regard must be had to the state of things existing; for, as a rule, if the partners are equally divided, those who forbid a change must have their way. Thus, one partner cannot either engage a new servant or dismiss one in the employment of the firm against the will of another partner, or, if the lease of the place of business expires, insist on renewing the lease and continuing the business at the same place.

Can a majority bind a minority?

Every partner has a right to be consulted, to express his own views, and to have those views considered by his co-partners, and in disputes on matters arising in the ordinary course of business, although no clear or distinct authority in support of the proposition is in existence, it is presumed that the majority would bind the minority.

With reference to disputes on matters involving a change in the nature of the business, it has been repeatedly decided that no majority, however large, can lawfully engage the partnership in such matters against the will of even one dissenting partner, nor is it at all material that the new business is extremely profitable.

Partnership Property.

The expressions partnership property, partnership stock, partnership assets, joint stock, and joint estate, are used indiscriminately to denote everything to which the firm, or, in other words, all the partners in it, can be considered as entitled as such. The qualification *as such* is important, for persons may be entitled jointly or in common to property, and the same persons may be partners, and yet that property may not be partnership property. For example, if several persons are partners in trade, and land is devised or a legacy is bequeathed to them jointly or in common, it will not necessarily become partnership property and form part of the common stock in which they are interested as partners.

Separate Property.

It is often a difficult matter to determine what is to be regarded as partnership property and what is to be regarded as the separate property of each partner. The question is a matter not only affecting the partners themselves but also their creditors; for, as most of you probably know, if a firm becomes bankrupt, the property of the firm and the separate property of each partner have to be distinguished from each other, it being a rule to apply the property of the firm in the first place in payment of the creditors of the firm, and to apply the separate properties of the partners in the first place to the payment of their respective separate creditors. **Lecture VIII.**

Examples of both.

Whatever at the commencement of a partnership is thrown into the common stock, and whatever has from time to time during the continuance of the partnership been added thereto, or obtained by means thereof, whether directly by purchase or by employment in trade, belongs to the firm, unless the contrary can be shown. The mere fact that the property in question was purchased by one partner in his own name is immaterial if it was paid for out of the partnership moneys, for in such a case he would be deemed to hold the property in trust for the firm, unless he can show that he holds it for himself alone. For example, if shares in a company are paid for with partnership money they would be partnership property, although they may be standing in the books of the company in the name of one partner only, and although it may be contrary to the company's deed of settlement for more than one person to hold shares in it. It by no means follows that persons who are partners by virtue of their participation in profits are entitled to that which may produce those profits; for example, coach proprietors who horse a coach, and divide the profit, may each make use of horses which belong to himself alone, and not to the firm and proprietors. Again, it by no means follows that the property used by all the partners for partnership purposes is partnership property; for example, the house

Not determined by division of Profits.

Lecture VIII. in which the partnership business is carried on often belongs to one of the partners only, either subject to a lease to the firm or without any lease at all. If, however, a partner brings such property into the common stock as part of his capital, it becomes partnership property, and any increase in its value will belong to the firm.

It does not even necessarily follow that property bought with the money of the firm is the property of the firm, for it sometimes happens that property, although paid for by the firm, has been in effect bought for one partner exclusively, and that he has become debtor to the firm for the purchase money.

Conversion of private into partnership Property and *vice versâ*.

It is competent for partners by agreement between themselves to convert that which was partnership property into the separate property of an individual partner, or *vice versâ*, and the nature of the property may be thus altered by any agreement to that effect; neither a deed nor even a writing is absolutely necessary. So long as the agreement is dependent upon an unperformed condition, so long will the ownership of the property remain unchanged. Where a change occurs in the firm by the retirement of one or more of its members, nothing is more common than the partners to agree that those who continue the business shall take the property of the old firm and pay its debts, or that part of the property of the old firm shall become the property of those by whom its business is to be continued, whilst the rest of the property shall be otherwise dealt with. So, again, when a partnership is first formed, or when a new partner is taken into an existing firm, or when two firms amalgamate into one, some agreement is generally come to by which what was before the property of some one or more only of the members of the firm becomes the joint property of all such members. All such agreements, if *bonâ fide*, and not fraudulent against creditors, are valid, and have the effect of altering the equitable ownership of the property affected by them.

Shares in a Partnership.

I now come to the subject of shares in a partnership, their nature, amount, and how they can be transferred. In the absence of a special agreement to that effect all the members of an ordinary partnership are interested in the whole of the partnership property, and what is meant by a share of a partner is his proportion of the partnership assets after they have been all realised and converted into money, and all the debts of the members have been paid and discharged. This it is, and this only, that on the death of a partner passes to his representatives or to a legatee of his share.

Real Property.

As regards real property and chattels real, the legal estate in them is governed by the ordinary doctrines of real property law, and therefore, if several partners are jointly seized or possessed of land for an estate in fee or for years on the death of anyone, the legal estate therein will devolve on the surviving partners, and they can mortgage it for the partnership debts, and sell it for the purpose of winding up the affairs of the partnership; but the surviving partners are, as regards the interest of the deceased partner, deemed to be trustees thereof for the persons entitled to his estate, and are compellable to account to them accordingly.

The proportions in which the members of a firm are entitled to the property of the firm, or, in other words, the amount of each partner's share in a partnership, depends upon the agreement into which the partners have entered.

Disputes as to amount of Shares.

In the event of a dispute between partners as to the amount of their shares, such dispute, if it does not turn on the construction of written documents, must be decided like any other pure question of fact, and if there is no evidence from which any satisfactory conclusion as

Lecture VIII. to what was agreed can be drawn, the shares of all the partners shall be adjudged equal. In order to discharge himself of the liabilities to which a person may be subject as partner, every partner has a right to have the property of the partnership applied in payment of the debts and liabilities of the firm; and in order to secure a proper division of the surplus assets, he has a right to have whatever may be due to the firm from his co-partners deducted from what would otherwise be payable to them in respect of their shares in the partnership. In other words, each partner may be said to have an equitable lien on the partnership property for the purpose of having it applied in discharge of the debts of the firm, and to have a similar lien on the surplus assets for the purpose of having them applied in payment of what may be due to the partners respectively, after deducting what may be due from them as partners to the firm.

Consent of Partners as to introduction of new Partners.

One of the fundamental principles of partnership law is that no person can be introduced as a partner without the consent of all those who, for the time being, are members of the firm. If, therefore, a partner dies, his executors or devisees have no right to insist on being admitted into partnership with the surviving partners unless some agreement to that effect has been entered into by them. Still less can a partner, by assigning his share, entitle his assignee to take his place in the partnership against the will of the other members. The assignment, however, is by no means inoperative; on the contrary, it involves several important consequences, more especially as regards the dissolution of the firm, and the right of the assignee to an account.

Dissolution of Partnership.

As regards dissolution, there is very little authority to be found. It is generally stated that, if a member of an ordinary partnership transfers his share, he thereby dissolves the partnership; but this proposition requires qualification. The true doctrine, it is submitted, is that if the partnership is at will the assignment dissolves it; and if the partnership is not at will the other members are entitled to treat the assignment as a cause of dissolution. It can hardly be that a partner, who has himself no right to dissolve or to introduce a new partner, can, by assigning his share, confer on the assignee a right to have the accounts of the firm taken, and the affairs thereof wound up, in order that he may obtain the benefit of his assignment.

Assignment Share.

Although a partner cannot, by transferring his share, force a new partner on the other members of the firm without their consent, there is nothing to prevent a partner from assigning or mortgaging his share without consulting his co-partners; and if a partner does assign or mortgage his share he thereby confers upon the assignee or mortgagee a right to payment of what, upon taking the accounts of the partnership, may be due to the assignor or mortgagor. But the assignee or mortgagee acquires no other right than this, and he takes subject to the rights of the other partners.

If partners choose to agree that any of them shall be at liberty to introduce any other person into the partnership, there is no reason why they should not; nor why, having so agreed, they should not be bound by the agreement.

Where a partner has an unconditional right to transfer his share, he may transfer it to a pauper, and thus get rid of all liability as between himself and his co-partners in respect of transactions subsequent to the transfer and notice thereof given to them. But the transfer alone does not render the transferee a member of the partnership, and liable as between himself and the other members to any of the debts of the firm. In order to render him a partner with the other members they must acknowledge him to be a partner, or permit him to act as such.

Lecture VIII.

As an ordinary partnership is not distinguishable from the persons composing it, and as every change amongst those persons creates a new partnership, it follows that every time a partner transfers his share to a non-partner the continuity of the firm is broken.

Partnership Accounts.

I now come to matters connected with the keeping of partnership accounts, not, of course, as regards the method of book-keeping, but the law affecting the same. I have already explained the difference between the mercantile and the legal view of a firm; and, as you are all aware, the books of a partnership are kept according to the mercantile view, the partners being, however, considered as debtors to or creditors of the firm. It was observed, however, by Lord Cottenham that, though these terms of "debtor" and "creditor" are so used, and sufficiently explain what is meant by the use of them, nothing is more inconsistent with the known law of partnership than to consider the situation of either party as in any degree resembling the situation of those whose appellation has been so borrowed. The supposed creditor has no means of obtaining payment of his debt; and the supposed debtor is liable to no proceedings, either at law or in equity—assuming always that no separate security has been taken or given. The supposed creditor's debt is due from the firm of which he is a partner; and the supposed debtor owes the money to himself in common with his partners.

Rights of Partners.

In taking a partnership account, each partner is entitled to be allowed against the other everything he has advanced or brought in as a partnership transaction, and to charge the other in the account with what that other has not brought in, or has taken out more than he ought, and nothing is to be considered as his share but his proportion of the residue on the balance of the account. A partner is, therefore, clearly entitled to charge the firm with whatever he may have been compelled to pay in respect of its debts, or in respect of obligations incurred by him alone at the request of the firm. Lecture VIII

An outlay which may have been very proper, and even necessary for the conduct of the partnership business, cannot be charged to the partnership account, if so to do would be inconsistent with the agreement into which the partners have entered.

Interest in Partnership Accounts.

The principles upon which, in taking partnership accounts, interest is allowed or disallowed, do not appear to be well settled. By the common law, in the absence of a special custom or agreement, a loan does not bear interest; and, notwithstanding many dicta to the contrary, the same rule appears to have prevailed in equity. At the same time, by the custom of merchants, interest has long been payable in cases where by the general law it was not; and mercantile usage and the course of trade dealings are held to authorise a demand for interest in cases where it would not otherwise be payable. As a general rule partners are not entitled to interest on their respective capitals unless there is some agreement to that effect, or unless they have themselves been in the habit of charging such interest in their accounts; and even where one partner has brought in his stipulated capital and the other has not, the former will not be entitled to interest, on the winding-up of the partnership, if it has not been previously charged and allowed for in the accounts of the firm.

Advances by Partners to Firm.

An advance by a partner to a firm is not treated as an increase of his capital, but rather as a loan on which interest ought to be paid; and by usage interest is payable on money *bonâ fide* advanced by one partner for partnership purposes, at least when the advance is made with the knowledge of the other partners. The rate of interest given in such cases is simple interest at five per cent., unless a different rate is payable by the custom of

Lecture VIII. the particular trade, or has been charged and allowed in the books of the particular partnership.

Division of Profits.

The realisation and division of profits is the ultimate object of every partnership, and every partner has a right to a share of the profits made by the firm to which he belongs. The times at which the profits are to be divided, the quantum to be divided at any one time, the sums, if any, which are to be placed to the debit of the firm in favour of any particular partner for salary, interest on capital, &c., before any profits are to be divided, these and all similar matters are usually made the subject of express agreement. In adjusting the accounts of partners, losses ought to be paid first out of assets, excluding capital, next out of capital, and lastly by having recourse to the partners individually, and the assets of the partnership should be applied as follows :—

Application of the Assets on a Dissolution.

(1) In paying the debts and liabilities of the firm to non-partners.

(2) In paying to each partner rateably what is due to him for advances as distinguished from capital.

(3) In paying to each partner rateably what is due from the firm to him in respect of capital.

(4) The ultimate residue, if any, will then be divisible as profit between the partners in equal shares, unless the contrary can be shown.

Insufficiency of Assets.

If the assets are not sufficient to pay the debts and liabilities to non-partners, the partners must treat the difference as a loss and make it up by contributions *inter se.* If the assets are more than sufficient to pay the debts and liabilities of the partnership to non-partners, but are not sufficient to repay the partners their respective advances, the amount of unpaid advances ought, it is conceived, to be treated as a loss, to be met like other losses. In such a case the advances ought to be treated as a debt of the firm, but payable to one of the partners instead of to a stranger. If, after paying all the debts and liabilities of the firm and the advances of the partners, there is still a surplus, but not sufficient to pay each partner his capital, the balances of capitals remaining unpaid must be treated as so many losses, to be met like other losses.

Right of every Partner to have proper Accounts kept

It is one of the clearest rights of every partner to have accurate accounts kept of all money transactions relating to the business of the partnership, and to have free access to all its books and accounts. One partner has no right to keep the partnership books in his own exclusive custody, or to remove them from the place of business of the partnership. In the absence of an express agreement to the contrary, every partner has a right, without the permission of his co-partners, to inspect, examine, and make extracts from all the books of the firm, and no partner can deprive his co-partners of this right by keeping the partnership accounts in a private book of his own, containing other matters with which they have no concern. At the same time, if a person entitled to a share of the profits of a business expressly agrees that he will accept the balance sheets prepared by others as correct, and will not investigate the books or accounts himself, he will be bound by that agreement.

Articles of Partnership.

It is difficult in a lecture dealing with the whole subject of partnership law to decide exactly what to include and what to leave out. The consideration of the clauses usually inserted in articles of partnership are, of course, very important, as are also the actions which can be brought by partners against each other, and the method of conducting the action, but I should extend my lecture to an indefinite length were I to touch upon

Lecture VIII

all these subjects. I propose, in conclusion, to deal with the consequences of the death of a member of a partnership as being of more practical importance to you in your studies and future careers. The consequences may be divided under three headings: firstly, as between the members of the firm themselves; secondly, as regards the creditors of the firm; and, thirdly, as regards the separate creditors and legatees of the deceased partner.

Settlement with Representatives of deceased Partner.

As between themselves the surviving partners have, of course, to come to a settlement with the representatives of their deceased partner; unless there is some agreement to the contrary, the death of any one member of a firm operates as a dissolution. The fact that the partnership was entered into for a definite term of years, which was unexpired when the death occurred, is not sufficient to prevent a dissolution by such death. Unless all the partners have agreed to the contrary, when one of them dies his executors have no right to become partners with the surviving partners, nor to interfere with the partnership business; the executors, however, represent him for all purposes of account.

On the death of a partner the surviving members of the firm are the proper persons to get in and pay its debts.

Valuation of Shares.

In the absence of an express agreement to that effect, the surviving partners have no right to take the share of the deceased partner at a valuation; nor to have it ascertained in any other manner than by a conversion of the partnership assets into money by a sale; nor have they any right of pre-emption. Even the goodwill of the business, if saleable, must be sold for the benefit of the estate of the deceased; although the surviving partners are under no obligation to retire from business themselves, and cannot, it seems, be prevented from recommencing business together in the name of the old firm, unless the goodwill has been sold.

Goodwill

Lecture V.

Surviving Partners to account for Profits.

In ascertaining the share of the deceased, the surviving partners must not only bring into account the assets of the firm which actually existed at the time of his death, but also whatever has been obtained by the employment of those assets up to the time of the closing of the account; for so long as profits are made by the employment of the capital of the deceased partner, so long must such profits be accounted for by the surviving partners. The executors of the deceased have, however, the option of taking interest at five per cent.

Where under a partnership deed the value of a deceased partner's share is to be ascertained by reference to the last annual account signed previously to his death, and such annual accounts are directed to be taken and signed by the partners at the end of each partnership year, or as near thereto as conveniently may be; if a partner dies shortly after the expiration of a partnership year, and before the account for that year has been actually signed or taken, the surviving partners cannot insist on the value of the share of the deceased partner being ascertained by reference to the last signed annual account; but the legal personal representative of the deceased partner is entitled to have the account taken for the partnership year which expired immediately before his death, and to have the value of his share ascertained by reference to such last-mentioned account, and this notwithstanding it has been the practice of the firm not to take and sign the annual account till a period of the year later than that at which the death occurred.

Surviving Partners entitled to allowance their servi

On the other hand, the surviving partners are entitled, if they carry on the business for the benefit of the estate of the deceased partner, to an allowance, unless they are also his executors, in which case they can make no charge for their trouble. The right of the

Lecture VIII. executors as against the surviving partners is simply to have the share of the deceased ascertained and paid, but this frequently cannot be done without a general sale and winding-up of the partnership. A *bonâ fide* sale, however, by the executors to the surviving partners, can generally be made with safety if no surviving partner is an executor.

Executors of a deceased Partner.

The position of the executors of a deceased partner is, in fact, often one of considerable hardship and difficulty. If they insist on an immediate winding-up of the firm they may ruin those whom the deceased may have been most anxious to benefit; whilst if for their advantage the partnership is allowed to go on, the executors may run the risk of being ruined themselves. With a view to obviate this, it is not unusual for one partner to make his co-partner his executor; but the difficulty of the executor's position is thus rather increased than diminished, for his own personal interest as a surviving partner is brought into direct conflict with his duty as an executor.

Joint Creditors.

As regards joint creditors the deceased partner's estate is liable to the creditors of the firm, and not only in respect of debts contracted in his lifetime in the ordinary way of business, but also in respect of debts arising from breaches of trust committed in his lifetime by himself or his co-partners, and imputable to the firm. This liability cannot be got rid of by any arrangement between the executors of the deceased and the surviving partners, and the liabilities of the executors continue until it can be shown that the creditors have abandoned their right to obtain payment from the estate of the deceased, or that their demands have, in fact, been paid or discharged.

Risks of an Executor.

It is, of course, clear that if the executor of a deceased partner carries on the partnership business he becomes personally liable to third parties as if he were a partner in his own right, and whether he is entitled to be indemnified out of the assets of the deceased depends upon whether he has carried on the business pursuant to the will of the deceased or the directions of those beneficially interested in his estate. It may be taken as a general proposition that the estate of a deceased partner is not liable to third parties for what may be done since his decease by the surviving partners.

As regards the right of separate creditors and legatees, they must look for payment for what is due to them out of the assets of a deceased partner to his legal personal representative, and to him alone.

It will be observed that in these few remarks as to the result of the death of one of the partners, I have assumed that the firm and the deceased partner's estates are solvent. The question as to how the estate of a deceased bankrupt has to be distributed belongs to the Bankruptcy Law, which forms a separate part altogether of your professional studies.

LECTURE IX.

ARBITRATIONS.

Read before the Institute of Chartered Accountants at the Hall of the Institute, and before the Local Societies at Liverpool, Manchester, Newcastle-on-Tyne, and Sheffield, in 1895 *and* 1896.

Lecture IX.

Increase in number of Arbitrations.

The practice of referring disputes to arbitration, and thus having them settled without recourse to the Law Courts, is one that has very much increased in the last few years, and as it frequently falls to Chartered Accountants to be appointed to the important office of Arbitrator, and also to the still more important one of Umpire, and as also they are very frequently required to give evidence as qualified or expert witnesses in arbitrations, it is necessary that they should be acquainted to a certain extent with the law, and also with the practice, relating to the subject.

Law Relating to Arbitration.

The law relating to arbitrations embraces a very wide subject, and it would be quite impossible in the scope of a lecture to cover the ground in as thorough a manner as one would wish. I can therefore only attempt to give a general outline of it in this address. It is true that the Arbitration Act, 1889, under which all ordinary commercial arbitrations are settled, tended very much to simplify the law, and although there are other Acts of Parliament under which special arbitrations are now held, still, unless I make any special reference to the contrary, you will understand that my remarks to-night are intended to apply principally to arbitrations held under this Act. As regards practice, the method of conducting arbitrations is in all cases the same. Lecture IX.

Definition of Arbitration.

Arbitration is defined to be the submitting of a matter in dispute to the judgment of one, two, or more persons called Arbitrators, and there are four requisites in order that the arbitration shall be a properly constituted and valid one:—

1. There must be parties to the dispute.
2. There must be an agreement to refer the dispute to the decision of a third person, called the Arbitrator.
3. There must be the appointment of such third person as Arbitrator.
4. There must be an acceptance of the office by the Arbitrator thus appointed.

The Submission.

The agreement to refer the dispute to the decision of a third person is called a "submission," which, according to the Arbitration Act of 1889, means, unless the contrary intention appears, a written agreement to submit present or future differences to arbitration, whether an Arbitrator is named therein or not.

Reference under Order of Court.

There are other forms of submission to arbitration in addition to the one indicated, which is practically a voluntary agreement between two or more parties. Very frequently, when there is a cause depending, an order of Court, or a Judge's or Master's order, will by common law be drawn up on consent of the parties referring the cause to arbitration, or the Court may order a reference whether the parties assent or not. I do not, however, propose to enumerate the various ways in which an arbitration can arise when an action at law has commenced, for, as a rule, when arbitration takes place under an order of the Court, the matter is usually

Lecture IX.

referred to one of the official referees of the High Court. Occasionally, however, where questions of account, or matters requiring scientific investigation, are concerned, a special referee—as a private person, nominated by the Court or selected by the parties, is styled—may be appointed by the Court.

A Valuation not an Arbitration.

The object of an arbitration is the settlement of matters in dispute between the parties, and consequently a valuation or an appraisement is not an arbitration. On a sale of landed property it is one of the usual conditions of sale that the purchaser shall pay for the timber on the land at a valuation, and he and the vendor then each appoint a valuer; the valuers usually appoint an umpire, who makes the valuation in the event of the valuers not being able to agree on the price to be paid for the timber. Such a valuation is not in the nature of an award or an arbitration, and an application to the Court to set aside a valuation of this nature has been refused on that ground.

Nomination of Arbitrators.

It is frequently the custom, after it has been decided by two disputants to refer the matter at issue between them to arbitration, for each of them to name an Arbitrator; this, to my mind, is open to many objections, as, in the first place, there is a natural inclination on the part of each Arbitrator to lean towards the party nominating him, and to regard him as his client; in which case it is always necessary for them to agree upon an umpire, as he is called, who will give the final decision in the event of the Arbitrators being unable to give an award. This is an exceedingly wrong practice, and contrary to all notions of an Arbitrator's duty; and one of the principal objections to it is that it greatly adds to the expense, as it requires three professional men where one is really sufficient. Although you will, doubtless, consider this may be to the interest of the profession, yet I think you will agree that for two members of any profession, who have accepted the appointment of Arbitrators, to contend for some advantage on behalf of the parties nominating them, which they would not attempt to put forward were they left to act as sole Arbitrator, is not calculated to add to the dignity of that profession; and I am glad that it is, perhaps, less likely to happen to us than to any other class of arbitrators, as, where accounts are concerned, there is not much left to imagination, we having to deal principally with facts. Lecture IX.

Arbitration Act, 1889.

The late Lord Justice Erle, in the case of *Oswald* v. *Grey*, commented strongly on the notion that an Arbitrator should consider himself appointed to take care of the interests of the party nominating him; and stated that it was his duty to take as much care of the interests of the other party.

In submissions under the Arbitration Act, 1889, the reference is to a single Arbitrator, where no other mode of reference is provided; but should two Arbitrators be appointed, they then have power to appoint an umpire at any time within the period during which they have power to make an award. As a matter of practice, however, it is the custom for the Arbitrators, unless they feel there is a strong probability of their being able to agree, to appoint an umpire before they enter upon their duties, and for the umpire to sit with them; and he may be appointed before entering on the reference, although the submission may give the Arbitrators power only to appoint an umpire in case of disagreement. It also occasionally happens that the two parties will, in order to save expense, request the Arbitrators to withdraw and leave the umpire to sit alone; first of all, of course, agreeing to abide by his sole award.

Appointment of Umpire.

The appointment of the umpire should be in writing, and should be signed by both the Arbitrators together; as, should one sign the appointment alone, and send it

Lecture IX.

for signature to the other Arbitrator, the appointment of the umpire is invalid, and his award, consequently, a nullity. Should, however, the two Arbitrators have met, and agreed on the umpire, then it is not necessary they should sign the appointment together, as the signing is the mere record of their previous judicial decision. The umpire should accept his office in a formal manner, and after his acceptance the appointment cannot be revoked. Should he not accept the office another may be appointed in his place.

Failure to appoint Umpire

Where the parties, or two Arbitrators, are at liberty to appoint an umpire or third Arbitrator, and do not appoint him, or when the umpire or third Arbitrator refuses to act, or is incapable of acting, or dies, and the submission does not show that it was intended that the vacancy should not be supplied, and the parties or Arbitrators do not supply the vacancy, any party may serve the other parties or the Arbitrators, as the case may be, with a written notice to appoint an Arbitrator, umpire, or third Arbitrator; and, if the appointment be not made within seven days, the Court may make the necessary appointment.

An agreement to refer to arbitration will not be specifically enforced, but should an action be brought after such an agreement has been entered into, the Court has power to stay the proceedings in the action, which has, practically, the effect of specifically enforcing the agreement.

Power of Court to stay Legal Proceedings.

The Court, on being satisfied that there is no sufficient reason why a matter agreed to be referred should not be referred in accordance with the submission, has power to stay any legal proceedings commenced after the execution of the submission, provided the applicant was, at the time when the proceedings were commenced, and still remains, ready and willing to do everything necessary for the proper conduct of the arbitration.

Lecture IX.

Failure of one Party to appoint his Arbitrator.

Where a submission provides that the reference shall be to two Arbitrators, one to be appointed by each party, then, unless the submission expresses a contrary intention, either party has the right to appoint a new Arbitrator in the place of his nominee, should the latter refuse to act, or is incapable of acting, or dies. Should one party fail to appoint an Arbitrator, either originally, or by way of substitution, for seven clear days after the other party, having appointed his Arbitrator, has served the party making default with notice to make the appointment, the party who has appointed an Arbitrator may appoint him to act as sole Arbitrator, and his award is as binding on both parties as if he had been appointed by consent. The Court, however, has power to set aside any appointment thus made.

Parties to a Reference.

Nearly every person who can enter into a contract may be a party to a "reference," as an arbitration is usually called in professional circles, as can everyone capable of making a disposition or release of his right. If a partner, however, submit for himself and his partners matters in difference between the partnership and another, he alone is bound by the award, the other partners being considered strangers to the award. Infants, who cannot make a binding contract, except for necessaries, cannot, as a rule, be parties to a submission. Should an infant be a party, he is not bound by the award of the Arbitrator, and it is open to him on his coming of age either to accept it or not as he may please, but the father or a guardian of an infant may bind himself so that an infant, son, or ward shall perform an award so far as it lays upon the infant some obligation that he can perform while he is still a minor.

Infants.

Corporations.

A corporation aggregate may be a party to a reference, but the reference must be an act of the corporate body.

Agents.

If one person authorise another on his behalf to

Lecture IX. refer a dispute between himself and a third party, an award consequent on such submission is binding on the principal alone, and it is no objection that the agent had not any interest in the subject of the dispute. If, however, the agent expressly bind himself for the performance of the principal, they are both bound by the award.

Married Women.

The law relating to married women having been considerably altered within the last few years, they can, in certain cases, be a party to a reference; for example, a married woman having a trade in the City of London can submit all matters in connection with her business to arbitration. If a married woman is judicially separated from her husband, or has obtained a separation order, she can, under certain conditions, be a party to a reference in accordance with the Married Woman's Property Act, 1882.

Trustees in Bankruptcy.

Chartered Accountants, when acting as trustees in bankruptcy, can, as trustees, be parties to a submission, as the Bankruptcy Act, 1883, Section 57, Sub-section 6, gives a trustee power, with the consent of the committee of inspection, to refer any dispute respecting the debts, claims, and liabilities of the bankrupt to arbitration. The Conveyancing and Law of Property Act, 1881, gives an executor, or two or more trustees acting together, or a sole acting trustee where, by the instrument (if any) creating the trust, a sole trustee is authorised to execute the trust and powers thereof, power to submit to arbitration.

An indorsement on the brief of the counsel for each party in an action in the following terms: "Claims to be referred to arbitration as quickly as possible," has been decided to be a submission. Deeds of partnership, policies of insurance, and other instruments, frequently contain a covenant or agreement providing that if any disputes shall arise they are to be referred to arbitration.

The Arbitrators are usually appointed by the parties or some third person when any dispute arises; occasionally they are designated in the original agreement.

It is not usual to name the Arbitrator in these agreements, as it is very possible that when his assistance is required he may not be alive; or from age, infirmity, or absence, be unable to act; even if procurable, he may be unwilling to take upon himself the office. When, however, he is named, the agreement seems to differ little, if at all, from an ordinary submission; but when he is not so named, the agreement can hardly be considered a complete submission, for, until the Arbitrator is determined, there is no one who has the binding authority to decide the questions submitted. The Arbitration Act, 1889, provides, however, for the appointment of an Arbitrator in such a case, but the Court has no power to compel a party to appoint an Arbitrator.

The arbitration clause in a deed of partnership does not deprive the Court of jurisdiction over the matters referred in accordance with such a clause, and the addition of a covenant not to sue in respect of such matters does not prevent either party from bringing them into Court.

The matters which may become the subject of a reference may be said to be almost innumerable, but they must be legal, and there must be no fraud on the part of any of the parties to the reference.

Matters referred to Chartered Accountants.

The most likely matters to be referred to Chartered Accountants for arbitration are disputes involving accounts, such as those arising from a partnership dispute either during the life of the partners or on the death of one partner. In such cases the Arbitrator may have to determine the value of the share of the goodwill of a deceased partner, or the amount to be paid by the surviving partner to the representatives of

Lecture IX. a deceased partner. In the reconstruction of a company the amount to be paid for the shares of those members dissenting from the scheme under Section 162 of the Companies Act, 1862, is frequently referred to members of the Institute, as are also disputes relating to accounts generally.

In addition, however, to acting as Arbitrator where accounts are in dispute, a Chartered Accountant is the best Arbitrator to be chosen in any mercantile reference, as, while merchants, brokers, &c., have very little acquaintance with business matters outside their particular markets, Chartered Accountants acquire, in pursuing their ordinary avocation, a general knowledge and those broader views which are essential qualities of a good Arbitrator, and any special technical knowledge they may be deficient in may be supplied by witnesses called before them.

What Matters may be referred.

It therefore becomes desirable to state generally what are the subjects on which an Arbitrator may be called upon to award, omitting those of a criminal nature, and only including, therefore, matters affecting the civil interests of the parties. All matters in dispute concerning any personal chattel or personal wrong may be referred. For example, breaches of contract generally, breaches of promise of marriage, trespass, assaults, charges of slander, differences respecting partnership transactions, or the purchase price of property, and questions relating to tolls or the right to tithes may all be the subjects of a reference.

Questions of Law.

Pure questions of law, such as the liability of a party on a promissory note, the construction of an Act of Parliament, or the construction of the effect of a will, may be referred to an Arbitrator's decision. The future conduct of parties with respect to the enjoyment of property, in matters beyond the power of any Court to prescribe, is often submitted to the regulation of an

Arbitrator; and parties may also agree to refer any future differences between them, though none at the time exist.

In any cause before the Courts, if a prolonged examination of documents, or a scientific or local investigation is necessary, or if the question in dispute consists wholly or in part of matters of account, the Court may order the reference of the whole cause or matter, or any question or issue of fact arising therein.

Compensation for compulsory taking of Land.

When lands are authorised by any Act of Parliament to be taken for undertakings of a public nature, the party interested in the lands may, when the compensation claimed or offered exceeds fifty pounds, require to have the amount determined by arbitrators.

Private persons are frequently unable to deal with their interests in lands in the manner they may wish for several reasons, such as the fact of there being a public right which affects the property and does not allow of any alteration, or because some other persons interested in the land are unable to enter into a contract. Under these circumstances an Act of Parliament is frequently applied for, which enacts that the interests of all concerned shall be submitted to arbitration, and in this way have been settled the amounts to be paid for the commutation of tithe, compensation for rights of common, also the enclosing of common, the definition of boundaries, and the allotment of lands.

Within the last fifty years many statutes have been passed containing clauses which specially enact that the amounts to be paid for compensation in various forms shall be determined by arbitration. In this way, therefore, are settled the prices to be paid for lands taken under the authority of an Act for undertakings of a public nature, for railways, harbours, waterworks, town improvements, and cemeteries, also the amount of compensation under the Public Health Act, or Housing

Lecture IX.

of the Working Classes Act, for injuries to mines caused by railways, and in many other cases.

Wide range of Arbitrator's practice.

I cannot, of course, attempt to enumerate in detail every possible subject-matter of a reference, but it will be seen from the foregoing examples over what a wide field the practice of an Arbitrator can range. Many of the cases referred to are not, under any circumstances, likely to be submitted to Chartered Accountants, as it is evident they would be better dealt with by other experts, such as lawyers, engineers, or surveyors; but I venture to submit that a lawyer should only be chosen as an Arbitrator where a question of law has alone to be decided, or an engineer or surveyor where a question of engineering alone, or of surveying alone, has to be settled, and to again assert that where it is considered advisable to obtain an Arbitrator of general experience, he is most likely to be found in the list of members of the Institute of Chartered Accountants.

Modes of Submission.

The submission to arbitration may be by parol, but is usually either an ordinary agreement, or by deed, or by bond. Should the reference involve differences relative to an Act to be perfected by deed, then the submission must be under seal. Whichever of the three documents be preferred, it is usually prepared by the solicitor to one of the parties to the matter in dispute, and settled by him with the solicitor to the other party, and the document must be signed or executed by both parties. In order to provide against any difficulty arising as to the manner in which the award is to be carried out in the event of one of the parties refusing to abide by it, there formerly used to be a clause inserted that the award should be made a rule of Court, so that the award could be enforced in the same way as a judgment; but Section 1 of the Arbitration Act, 1889, which enacted that a submission should, unless a contrary intention be expressed therein, have the same effect in all respects as if it had been made an order of Court, has rendered the insertion of this clause in submissions altogether unnecessary.

Lecture IX.

Submissions are Irrevocable.

By this Act, under which now nearly all arbitrations are conducted, submissions are, unless a contrary intention is expressed therein, irrevocable, except by leave of the Court or a Judge, and they are very much simpler in form than before the Act came into force, as, unless a contrary intention is expressed, every submission is deemed to include the provisions set out in the first schedule of the Act, so far as they are applicable to the reference under the submission.

Submission by Bond.

When the submission is by bond, each party executes a bond to the other in a certain penalty, subject to the condition of his abiding by and performing the award of the Arbitrator. The amount the Arbitrator may award is not in any way limited by the amount of the penalty named in the bond, but should the award exceed that limit, and either party have to bring an action on the bond, no larger sum than the penalty can be recovered.

Objections to Parol Submissions.

Parol submissions are generally valid, but they very rarely occur in practice, as there are very many disadvantages attending them. Like all verbal contracts they are open to dispute respecting the exact terms used; and since a parol submission and a written award made thereon form but one parol contract, if, on a parol submission, a written award were made respecting real property, and the provisions of the award were such that, if they had been verbally agreed to by the parties themselves, they would have been void by the Statute of Frauds, the award cannot be enforced.

A submission which provides that under no circumstances shall the Court have anything to do with disputes arising under the contract is bad. So long, however, as the submission is limited to an agreement

Lecture IX. that arbitration shall be a condition precedent to the maintenance of an action, it is good. An agreement that neither party will try to set aside the award for fraud does not invalidate a submission.

The particular words of the submission decide as to over what subject matters the Arbitrator is to exercise his powers; and, in order to avoid any doubt, they usually include "all matters in difference between the parties." When, however, the reference is to settle a pending action, and is to be limited to that, the submission is usually "of all matters in difference in the cause." The Arbitrator would then merely decide on the question raised by the pleadings which are necessary for the determination of the cause.

Jurisdiction of the Court.

The Court has jurisdiction to interfere by injunction, on equitable grounds, to restrain a defendant from proceeding to arbitration where an action has been brought impeaching the instrument containing the agreement for reference. It also has jurisdiction to restrain proceeding to arbitration when the instrument containing the agreement for reference is impeached by proceedings in the High Court.

The Court is bound on application to appoint an Arbitrator where one of the parties to an agreement to submit differences to a single Arbitrator refuses to concur in an appointment, even after being served with a written notice "to concur in the appointment of a sole Arbitrator in the matter."

When Submission Revocable.

A submission may contain a clause making it revocable at the will of the parties; in which case, should either of the parties wish to withdraw, he can do so, up to the time allowed by this clause, and on the terms (if any) contained therein. Should, however, there be no such clause, then, as already stated, a submission is irrevocable except by leave of the Court. The application for leave to revoke the submission must be made before the award is made, and sufficient ground must be shown to obtain leave; the power to revoke is a matter of discretion, the exercise of which must depend upon the circumstances of each case.

Lecture IX.

The refusal of an Arbitrator to act, corruption in the Arbitrator, the bankruptcy of one of the parties, where all his interest in the matter in dispute is vested in the trustee of his estate, have been considered sufficient ground for the Court to give leave to revoke a submission.

In order to make the revocation complete, notice must be given to the arbitrator, or his authority will not be determined; but no notice is necessary when the revocation is by marriage or death.

Who may be an Arbitrator.

I now come to the duties of an Arbitrator, which, naturally, raises the question, Who may be an Arbitrator? It appears to me, in answer, that any person may accept the office, and that there is no reason why a lunatic, an infant, or a married woman should not act, if the parties to the submission are so foolish as to appoint any such to the office. The Arbitrator, however, should be a person who is also independent of either of the parties to the submission. He should not, of course, have any interest in the subject matter in dispute; but if he has an interest, and does not conceal this fact from the parties, his award is good, if they, with the knowledge of this interest of the Arbitrator, allow him to continue the reference.

When Arbitrator may not Act.

The Court has power to restrain an Arbitrator from proceeding if it has reason to believe he is not a fit person, and that owing to certain circumstances it is improbable that he will faithfully perform and honestly discharge his duties. In order, however, for him to be so disqualified, the interest must be of such a nature as to bias or influence his mind, and in a case where an Arbitrator had advanced money to the defendant before

Lecture IX. his appointment, and it was objected that that fact gave him such an interest in the case as would prejudice his award, the Court held that it was not sufficient interest to call for its interference.

Should one of the parties object to the Arbitrator, he should insist in his objection, and either apply for leave to revoke the submission or for an injunction to restrain the Arbitrator from acting. Should any party proceed in the arbitration with knowledge of any objection to the Arbitrator, he will be deemed to waive his objection.

The rule that a judge ought not to hear cases in which he might be suspected of bias does not apply to an Arbitrator named by the parties in a contract under which all disputes are to be referred to him. To disqualify such an Arbitrator, at least a probability of bias must be shown.

Acceptance of Office.

Before the appointment of the Arbitrator is valid, his formal acceptance of the office must be intimated to the parties; and his authority commences, not from the date of his appointment, but from the actual commencement of his duties as Arbitrator.

The Arbitrator having been appointed, and he having accepted the office, it is desirable that he should enter upon his duties as soon as possible, so that he will be able to make his award within the specified time.

The time and place of meeting are entirely in his discretion, but it is a matter of practice for him to consult the convenience of the parties, more especially in those cases where counsel are engaged.

Course of Procedure.

The usual course of procedure is for the submission to be left with the Arbitrator, and, either at that time or after he has had time to peruse the submission, to obtain an appointment from him for the first sitting, and notice of this appointment, and also of every subsequent appointment, must be served on all the parties to the reference.

The Arbitrator should not appoint too early a day, but should allow the parties time to prepare proofs of themselves and witnesses; at the same time, when either party is anxious to press on the case, he should not on light grounds appoint a distant day, for delay in the decision often causes serious inconvenience to the party entitled to recover, and may amount even to partial injustice. The Arbitrator may, of course, revoke any appointment he has given should he think fit.

If from any cause either party find that he will not be able, or that it will be very inconvenient for him to attend at the specified time, he should give timely notice of it both to his opponent and to the Arbitrator; and the latter will, in his discretion, either insist on his attendance or put off the meeting and appoint another day.

Where Submission not clear.

As a rule, the submission clearly defines the matters in dispute upon which the Arbitrator is to adjudicate, but should this not in his opinion be clear, he should then require each party to state in writing the particular matters for his decision, and, should they not do so, he should then put into writing himself the points upon which he considers he is asked to adjudicate.

It is, of course, essential that the Arbitrator should make himself fully acquainted with the contents of the submission before the first sitting, as it is therefrom he will learn the intention of the parties, and, to a certain extent, his powers and duties. He is, as a rule, the final judge of law and fact, and is frequently armed with powers beyond those of any Court of Justice to control the future conduct of parties, and to regulate their enjoyment of their property.

An Arbitrator, like any other judge, is bound by the principles of law, and it is beyond his authority to award anything contrary to law, for the ordinary presumption

Lecture IX.

is that the parties intend to submit to him only the legal consequences of their transactions and engagements.

Arbitrator should be acquainted with Law.

It is exceedingly desirable, in order to conduct the arbitration in as proper a manner as possible, that the Arbitrator should be acquainted with the ordinary rules of evidence, as he will, of course, have to decide whether to admit, or not, any evidence submitted by one of the parties which is objected to by the other. After any dispute of this nature has arisen between the parties, the Arbitrator should reflect before he gives his decision, but having once given it he should adhere to it, and allow no further argument on the subject. This, however, is practically the only decision that an Arbitrator should give during the hearing of the case, as his award is liable to be set aside on the application of either party should he give his decision during the hearing on any point actually submitted to him.

Arbitrator may not Delegate his Authority.

An Arbitrator is not allowed to delegate his authority; he is appointed by those who repose in him confidence and trust, which cannot be assigned to a stranger of whose ability and integrity he, for whom the act is to be done, can form no opinion. He must, therefore, perform his duties in person, and may neither delegate them to another, nor elect others to act with him, unless the submission expressly authorise such a course. He may, however, delegate to another the performance of acts of a ministerial character only; but it is not always easy to ascertain what acts are included under the head of ministerial acts. The measurement of the number of acres in a field, or the surface of a lake, has been considered ministerial, as would, probably, the functions of a professional Accountant, who is employed merely to make up the accounts of a firm.

He may, however, consult Experts.

An Arbitrator may, however, consult others, such as men of science, valuers, &c., on any material question, and may adopt their opinion as his own. On the other hand, should he be appointed on account of his special qualifications, a legal Arbitrator having been objected to, he may not, if either party object, call in a solicitor to sit with and advise him; and if he be authorised to call in a professional Accountant, not objected to by either party, he must give the parties an opportunity of objecting.

An Arbitrator may inspect premises, or may refuse to do so, at his discretion.

Is bound by practice prevailing in Courts as to Evidence.

As regards the evidence tendered, an Arbitrator is bound by the same rules as prevail in the Courts; but should he make a mistake in his view of the law on a point of evidence, this will not invalidate his award. Either of the parties can, however, pending the reference, make an application to the Court for leave to revoke the submission on the ground that the Arbitrator is mistaken as to the law of evidence.

An instrument chargeable with stamp duty is not admissible in evidence unless properly stamped, but if it be one which may be stamped after execution, the party producing it may use it in evidence upon paying to the Arbitrator the amount of duty, and the amount of penalty, and £1.

Materiality of Evidence.

The Arbitrator is not a judge as to whether evidence is or is not material, neither has he any discretion as to the amount of evidence to be submitted to him. He may reject evidence which, in his opinion, is foreign to the subject to the reference, but he must use great caution in his rejection of evidence. Declining to hear evidence on any matter is a delicate step to take, for the refusal to receive proof, where proof is necessary, is fatal to the award.

There is, however, a distinction in principle between refusing to hear evidence on any particular matter and rejecting a piece of evidence deemed by the Arbitrator inadmissible, as the exercise of his judgment

Lecture IX. in receiving or rejecting evidence, according to his opinion as to its admissibility, is not open to review. Should one of the parties consider a witness essential to his case, and the Arbitrator refuse to hear him, the party, in order to impeach the award, must distinctly tender the witness to the Arbitrator. It is not enough to put an abstract proposition to an Arbitrator, and upon his answer to decline to give evidence or prefer a claim; the party should tender a specific case and specific evidence.

Method of Procedure.

The method in which the arbitration is to proceed is also in the discretion of the Arbitrator, as he is not bound by any rules of practice which prevail in the Courts, and he can refuse to hear counsel or solicitors, and he may exclude witnesses. When one party determines to employ counsel he must give due notice to the other side of his intention; otherwise when they appear before the Arbitrator he would properly adjourn the case if the party unrepresented by counsel were to ask for an adjournment, on the ground that he was taken by surprise, and wished also to employ counsel.

It is the practice in all arbitrations for either parties, or any witnesses giving evidence on their behalf, to do so on oath, and for that purpose the Arbitrator has power to administer the oath. A Mahomedan or Quaker may make an affirmation instead of taking an oath. The usual practice is then for the counsel or the solicitor for the plaintiff to open his case and then to call him and his witnesses and examine them, the Arbitrator entering in a book such part of the evidence as he may think desirable, so as to enable him to make his award. The defendant, or his counsel, or solicitor, can cross-examine the plaintiff and each of his witnesses, who can then be re-examined for the plaintiff. When the plaintiff's case is finished that of the defendant is taken in the same way, and

Opening the Case.

should he not call any witnesses then either he or his professional adviser is entitled to last address the Arbitrator. Lecture IX

Production o Documents.

The parties are required to produce before the Arbitrator all books, deeds, papers, accounts, writings, and documents, within their possession or power respectively, which may be required or called for, and do all other things which, during the proceedings on the reference, the Arbitrator may require. If, for example, on a general reference, the Arbitrator were to call for certain books of account, it is no answer for the party who is ordered to produce them to say that they relate to accounts long since settled, and not now matters in dispute, as it is for the Arbitrator to determine what are the matters in dispute.

As Chartered Accountants are frequently called upon to give evidence as witnesses before Arbitrators, I think you will consider it comes within the scope of the title of this address if I make some comments upon their duties as witnesses. Chartered Accountants are, of course, only likely to be called as witnesses when matters of account are in dispute.

Facts deposed to must be within knowledge of Witness.

In the first place, it is absolutely necessary that every fact to be deposed to by a witness before an Arbitrator must be within the actual knowledge of the witness the same as in a case before the High Court, and therefore a Chartered Accountant who is going to give evidence as to facts ascertained in the investigation of books of account or other documents must either examine the books or documents himself and take out every figure that he intends to give evidence upon, or else, if it be a lengthy matter and it is desirable that the work should be done in the first instance by clerks, he must, before he is called as a witness, go through all these figures himself with the original books, otherwise he will not be able to answer a question put to him in

Lecture IX. cross-examination, if he has done the work himself? Should he not be able to answer this in the affirmative, his evidence will be ridiculed, and he will do more harm to his client than if he had never been called. Where it is impossible for the principal to go through a great deal of detail in this respect, either for the reason that he may not have the necessary time, or that it would be too costly to his client, it is very frequently the practice for one of his managing clerks who is a Chartered Accountant to be called as the witness to give the evidence as to the details, leaving it to the employer to deal with the questions of principle which may arise.

Notices to Witnesses.

Witnesses must be served with a notice that their attendance will be required at the time and place fixed upon by the Arbitrator, and the notice must be prepared by the solicitors to the parties, or the parties themselves if unrepresented, and must be signed by the Arbitrator. Should any witness refuse to come, either of the parties may sue out a writ of *subpœna ad testificandum*, or a writ of *subpœna duces tecum*, and the Court or a judge may order that either of these writs shall issue to compel the attendance before the Arbitrator of any witness who may be within the United Kingdom. Any person compelled under either of these writs to attend is not obliged to produce any document which he could not be compelled to produce on the trial of an action. Witnesses are entitled to conduct money and payment of expenses, and also compensation for loss of time.

Parties must have opportunity of submitting Evidence.

The Arbitrator must give both parties a reasonable opportunity of submitting all their evidence to him, and should one of the parties cause any delay in the proceedings the Arbitrator must not on that account close the case and make his award, as each party has a right to bring his evidence before the Arbitrator, and he must have reasonable allowance as to time for that purpose. If one party, however, after due notice has been given, and full opportunity has been afforded to him, does not appear, the Arbitrator may, in his absence, proceed with the reference, unless the absent party has submitted to him reasonable and satisfactory excuse for his absence.

Stating of a "Special Case."

A question of law may very possibly arise in the course of an arbitration, in which case the Arbitrator, should he feel unable to decide it himself, is allowed—at any stage of the proceedings, that is, before they have come to an end by a completed award—to state it in the form of a special case for the opinion of the Court. The drawing up of a special case, and filing it for hearing, would, of course, have to be entrusted to a solicitor; and, on obtaining the opinion of the Court, the Arbitrator would resume the hearing. I use the word "opinion" and not "decision," as the jurisdiction of the High Court, in dealing with a special case, is consultative only. The opinion expressed is not an order, and therefore there is no appeal against it. Sometimes the terms of the submission are compulsory that the Arbitrator shall state a case at the request of the parties; it is then his duty to set forth fully in his award all such facts as will raise all the questions of law on which the opinion of the Court is desired, and should he fail to do so the award will probably be bad. In order to prevent any mistake, it is advisable for him to call upon the parties to furnish him with a written statement of the question of law they require to be raised.

Arbitrator no always bound to state a "Special Case."

Should, however, the terms of the order of reference merely give the Arbitrator liberty to raise any point for the opinion of the Court at the request of either of the parties, then he is not bound to state a case unless he think fit.

When the Arbitrator is at liberty, if he shall think fit, to report specially to the Court, he does not duly

Lecture IX.

exercise his power if he set out in his award a long statement of the evidence, leaving the Court to draw the inference of fact, as it is part of his duty to draw the necessary inference from the facts.

An alternative Award.

An Arbitrator sometimes decides the various matters submitted to him subject to the opinion of the Court, and then, after setting out all the facts, states particular questions on which he requires the decision of the Court, and concludes with awarding that if the Court shall decide a particular question one way, then he awards in one way; if in another, then he awards in another way.

It is very desirable that an Arbitrator, although he determine the matter himself, should make a provision in the event of the Court differing from him in opinion, for should he find for the plaintiff in an action referred, and then state facts for the opinion of the Court which show that the plaintiff ought to have been non-suited, the Court cannot direct a non-suit to be entered, but can only set the award aside, and thus all the litigation becomes useless; whereas, if he direct that, in case the Court differ from him, the verdict shall be entered for the defendant, the decision of the Court in favour of the latter will probably entitle him to have the verdict entered for him.

When the case is closed it is in the discretion of the Arbitrator whether he will reopen it and receive further evidence. He must be careful not to mislead the parties with a supposition that the case is still open, and then unexpectedly make his award, or this may be sufficient for it to be set aside. Even though there has been some useless delay, the Arbitrator must give the party who has caused it proper opportunity to complete his case, and not make the award too hastily, without giving the party due notice of his intention to do so, or it may be set aside.

The Arbitrator's Award.

After the evidence has been closed, the Arbitrator has then to draw his award. Previous to doing this he should, of course, go carefully through the notes taken by him during the reference, and all the exhibits which have been put in, and which he should retain either at the time they are put in, or if any of them have been subsequently required during the reference, he should have them placed in his possession at the conclusion of the last sitting. He should then make himself fully acquainted with their contents, for he must remember that as his award will bind the parties, except under certain circumstances, it is clearly his duty to thoroughly understand the evidence before he settles his award. The Arbitrator must also be careful that, if there is any time named in the submission for making the award, he makes it within that time; and where a month is mentioned it refers to a lunar month, except under a statute, when a calendar month is meant.

Time within which Award must be made

When no time for making the award is stated in the submission, it must be made within three months after entering on the reference, or after the Arbitrator has been called in to act by notice in writing from any party to the submission. But the time for making the award may from time to time be enlarged by order of the Court or a judge, whether the time for making the award has expired or not.

Enlargement of time.

It frequently happens that circumstances prevent the award being made in time, so, in order to prevent the expense and trouble incurred being lost, it is very desirable that submissions should not exclude the terms contained in the schedule to the Arbitration Act, 1889, which gives the Arbitrators power themselves to enlarge the time for making their award. I may mention here a distinct blot in this Act, and that is the absence of clauses as to whether the powers given to two or more Arbitrators apply where there is only one, but the

Lecture IX. general opinion appears to prevail that such is the case. Assuming this, an Arbitrator who desires to use this power should be careful to make the enlargement during the time primarily fixed for making his award, as the general opinion is that an enlargement by the Arbitrator made after his original time has expired is inoperative.

Where a third Arbitrator.

When a case has been referred to two Arbitrators, with power to them to appoint a third, the award to be made by a day named, or such other day as they or any two of them shall appoint, the first two named cannot make a valid enlargement of the time until the third is appointed, as enlarging the time is an act of judgment, and the parties have a right to have all three in a situation to exercise a judgment on the point.

If the submission direct the manner in which the enlargement is to be made, that direction should be followed, otherwise it should be in writing signed by the Arbitrator. The Arbitrator, unless restricted by the submission, is not limited to a single enlargement, but may enlarge the time as often as he finds necessary.

Should the power to enlarge the time have been omitted to be exercised, and the award has not been made, the authority of the Arbitrator may be revived, and further time granted by the consent of the parties. This, if in writing, requires a stamp, as it is practically a new submission. If an Arbitrator has made his award after the time has elapsed, the Court may, notwithstanding, after that enlarge the time.

Arbitrator may employ Solicitor or Counsel.

A Chartered Accountant, or any other Arbitrator not a lawyer, is, unless he is barred by the submission, entitled to employ a solicitor or counsel in drawing his award; but it is not necessary that technical language shall be employed if the award shows clearly that it is the final decision of the Arbitrator upon all the matters submitted to him. Should the Arbitrator make any mistake of a clerical nature, or an error arising from any accidental slip or omission, in his award, he has power to correct it, unless the terms of the submission expressly prohibit this, and any formalities required by the submission must be observed.

Lecture IX.

Should the submission direct that the award be in a particular form, the Arbitrator must adopt this form. A direction that the award shall be made under hand and seal would not be satisfied by one in the form of an unsealed document.

Execution of the Award.

The award must be signed by the Arbitrator, and if there is more than one Arbitrator it must be signed by all at the same time and place, and in the presence of each other, as otherwise it is not the joint judgment of the two or more Arbitrators as stipulated for by the parties. The award is considered to have been published immediately on its execution, even although no notice may have been given to the parties, but the time for setting an award aside runs from the day from which it is published to the parties, which is the day notice of it has been given to them.

A map, and words of explanation thereon, an indenture, or other writing, may be incorporated with the award by reference.

Arbitrator should not exceed his powers.

The Arbitrator must be careful not to exceed, in his award, any power given him by the submission, otherwise his award will be bad, and he must also be careful that his decision on all matters referred shall be included in the award, as, should he omit to decide upon any one of the matters referred to him, the whole award is bad. Should he find a sum of money to be due, he must, in his award, direct payment of it; he may also appoint a time and place of payment, and even direct in what manner the payment is to be made, as for example at a future date. He may also, when the circumstances require it, direct an indemnity, and may award an aggregate sum for distinct claims.

Lecture IX.

Arbitrator may order Security, &c.

The Arbitrator, under a general submission by partners of all matters in difference between them, may order one partner to pay or give security for the payment of a certain sum to another, may apportion the amounts between them, may order conveyance to be executed, may direct one partner to sue in the name of himself and others, and give them a bond of indemnity; may restrain one partner from carrying on business without certain limits, and may direct mutual releases. He cannot, however, appoint a receiver to collect partnership assets, nor direct that a sum of money be paid to himself to apply in payment of certain specified debts, nor decide as to whether any part of a premium shall be refunded.

The award should be stamped, as otherwise it cannot be enforced; the necessary stamp duty is settled by the Stamp Act, 1891.

Legal result of Award.

An award is both in law and in equity a final judgment as between the parties on all the matters referred to the Arbitrator by the submission, unless it has been expressly provided that it shall have a temporary effect only. No action will lie for any matter in difference between the parties within the scope of the submission which was not, in fact, brought before the Arbitrator.

Termination of Office.

As soon as the Arbitrator has made his award his authority, having once been completely exercised according to the terms of the reference, is at an end. He may not alter the award in any particular, and if, in fact, he does so, the alteration will be merely nugatory, and the award, as originally written, will stand good. He may, however, in submissions made out of Court, correct any clerical mistake or error arising from any accidental slip or omission. Should his award be set aside as void, his authority is not renewed so as to enable him to make a fresh award.

Lecture IX.

Every submission contains some words which express or imply that the parties agree to abide by the award of the Arbitrator, and perform what may be enjoined upon them by the award. It is as much a breach of the agreement to prevent the award being made as it is not to perform it when made, and should the submission be by bond a forfeiture of the penalty will occur. In other cases the punishment is by attachment.

Referring back an Award.

The award of an Arbitrator may, under certain circumstances, be referred back to him for his reconsideration, and the Court or a judge has power from time to time to remit matters referred. The power is usually exercised on a motion being made to set the award aside, and, on a defect being pointed out, in opposition to the party objecting to the award.

An award will be sent back when it is bad on its face, such as not being sufficiently final or certain, or where, though good on its face, it is invalid; as, for instance, for not having been executed by all the Arbitrators together, as already referred to.

The submission frequently contains a clause giving power to remit the award to the same or a fresh Arbitrator. Unless, however, the Court is of opinion the Arbitrator can no longer be trusted, it will remit the award to him.

It appears to be doubtful as to how far the discovery of new and material evidence will justify the setting aside of an award, but the discovery may be good ground for referring it back to the Arbitrator.

When the matters submitted, or any of them, are referred back by the Court to the Arbitrator, all his original powers so far as they are not affected by the order referring the award back are revived, except that the award must be made within three months after the date of the order. The parties, however, have probably the

Lecture IX. power to extend the time by consent, and the order may direct the time within which the award must be made.

Additional Evidence.

The Arbitrator must, of course, hear any additional evidence on the points remitted to him for his consideration, and if all matters be sent back he must hear evidence, if tendered, on all, and not merely on the point on which the award is deficient.

It is desirable the second award shall embrace every matter originally referred, either by confirming the first award in terms as to matters not referred back, but the more usual practice is for the portion of the first award which stands good to be re-copied with the second award.

An application to the Court to refer back an award must be made within a reasonable time, although there is no limit as to time; but the Court has power to refer back, even after the time limited for setting the award aside. The application must be made by motion, stating in general terms the grounds of the application. Two clear days' notice must be given; and a copy of the affidavit in support must be served with the notice of motion.

Any ground sufficient to set aside an award will generally be sufficient to refer it back to the Arbitrator.

Irregular Procedure of Arbitrator.

Though the Arbitrator may have been guilty of some irregularity in the course of the reference, it will not vitiate the award, if the conduct of the parties be such as shows that they waive any objection on account of it; but the waiver must be clearly made out, and the party must be shown to have full knowledge of the defect which he is said to waive.

Application to Court to set the Award aside.

Should any of the parties be of opinion that an Arbitrator or umpire has misconducted himself, or that the arbitration or the award has been improperly procured, he may apply to the Court to set the award aside, which must be done by motion before the end of the sittings next following the publication of the award; it is sufficient if notice of motion be given before the last day of such sittings. Lecture I:

The application to set aside the award is made by giving two clear days' notice of motion to the parties, but not to the Arbitrator. The notice must state in general terms the ground of the application, and a copy of any affidavit to be used in support must be served with the notice. The Superior Courts cannot set aside an award on a reference by a County Court order; this must be done by the County Court Judge, on application made to him at the first Court held more than a week after the entry of the award as the judgment.

Legal Misconduct.

There may be misconduct in a legal sense which will induce the Court to set aside an award, even where there is not any ground for imputing the slightest improper motive to the Arbitrator. Should an Arbitrator receive affidavits instead of *vivâ voce* evidence when he is directed to examine the witness on oath, or should he make the award without having heard all the evidence, or he examine a witness or a party privately or in the absence of his opponent, these would be good grounds for having the award set aside.

On a voluntary submission, an award, good on its face, cannot be set aside for an erroneous judgment of the Arbitrator on a question of law; nor will the Court review his decision as to the facts, or allow the merits of the case to be gone into.

An award made after the time for making it has expired will be set aside, unless the conduct of the parties have amounted to an enlargement of the period.

Should the Arbitrator without special power make two awards, each deciding part of the matters referred, and not one entire award on all together, both may be set aside, for there is no one final award on all the subjects.

Lecture IX.

Costs.

A very important point for the Arbitrator to consider, in framing his award, is as to who are to bear the costs of the proceedings. Should there be any directions in the submission as to the costs, the Arbitrator will, of course, be guided by his instructions; but if there be no clause, then the costs of the reference and the award are in the discretion of the Arbitrators or the umpire, who may direct to and by whom and in what manner these costs or any part thereof shall be paid, and may tax or settle the amount of costs to be so paid, or any part of them, and he may award costs to be paid as between solicitor and client.

Now, there is a distinction between costs of the cause, costs of the reference, and costs of the award.

Costs of the Cause.

As regards costs of the cause, when an award but not merely a certificate is to be made, the costs of the cause comprise those incurred in the cause up to the time of the submission; the costs of the order of reference, and of making out, if necessary, a rule of Court, and costs of ulterior proceedings, if any, after the award; they also include the cost of witnesses present at the trial ready to be examined.

Costs of the Reference.

The costs of the reference include the expense incurred by the parties of the whole inquiry before the Arbitrator, whether relative to the matters in the cause or those out of it. These are taxed usually as between party and party. It has been settled that should a professional accountant be employed by the Arbitrator, with the consent of the parties, to examine the defendant's books, his fee, and also the attendance of the plaintiff's solicitor with the accountant, may be costs of the reference.

Costs of the Award.

The costs of the award is the amount of the charges of the Arbitrator or Arbitrators. There is no scale for these charges or those of an umpire except the fees fixed for those who have agreed to act under the rules of the London Chamber of Commerce as arbitrators and umpires, and perhaps also of those who have agreed to act in a similar way in any particular trade or representative body. Occasionally the fee is arranged previous to the commencement of an arbitration, but this is not usually the case, as it is generally impossible to calculate the number of sittings required.

Arbitrator's Fees.

As a rule the Arbitrator fixes his own fee, and this he is at liberty to do, but the amount should not be stated in his award unless authorised by the submission. The usual practice is for the Arbitrator to inform the parties of the amount of his fees when he notifies to them that his award is ready, and the award is then handed to the party who takes it up in exchange for the fees. Although the Arbitrator is allowed to fix his own fees, he is not at liberty to fix an exorbitant sum, and although he can refuse to deliver up his award or communicate its contents until his fees have been paid, still, should he do so and fix an exorbitant fee, the party paying the fee in order to obtain the award may recover the excess beyond what is a reasonable fee in an action against him for money had and received.

When the submission provides that the costs "shall abide the event," then the Arbitrator has no control over them, and his award should be silent respecting them.

His lien until paid.

If the parties have agreed to pay the Arbitrator a certain sum, then, in the event of their not fulfilling the agreement, the Arbitrator may sue them for this sum, but not otherwise. The security to the Arbitrator for his fees is his right of lien on the submission and award. His notes also are his own, and he cannot even be compelled to show them; but he has no lien upon documents which have been produced as evidence before him.

When the award is made by an umpire, he may

Lecture IX.

make the fees of the Arbitrators part of the costs of the umpirage, and if he do not do so the party who has paid such fees will, nevertheless, be entitled to the amount as part of the costs of the reference.

Legal knowledge required by Arbitrators.

It will, I think, be evident from my remarks that those who hold themselves out as willing to act as Arbitrators in general matters must possess, not only a large and varied experience, but must also be acquainted with the law of evidence, in addition to the law and practice relating to arbitrations and awards. With the law of evidence I have not attempted to deal, but those who may be inclined to give it attention will find it not devoid of interest. As regards the law of arbitration, the time at my disposal has only permitted me to give you a general outline. To no subject does the saying, "A little knowledge is a dangerous thing," apply more strongly than to the law. This branch of the law is no exception; and I can only express a hope that what I have said has been of sufficient interest to induce you to devote some attention to it.

WORKS BY THE SAME AUTHOR.

AUDITORS:

THEIR DUTIES AND RESPONSIBILITIES UNDER THE COMPANIES ACTS AND OTHER ACTS OF PARLIAMENT.

SEVENTH EDITION.

PRICE 21s. NET CASH PRICE 16s. 9d.

THE

SHAREHOLDER'S HANDBOOK.

SECOND EDITION.

PRICE TWO SHILLINGS AND SIXPENCE.

THE

DIRECTOR'S HANDBOOK.

Revised to date of Directors' Liability Act, 1890.

SECOND EDITION.

PRICE TWO SHILLINGS AND SIXPENCE.

www.ingramcontent.com/pod-product-compliance
Lightning Source LLC
Chambersburg PA
CBHW030342270326
41926CB00009B/925